KEY WEST SKETCHES

KEY WEST SKETCHES

Writers at Mile Zero

Edited by Carey Winfrey

BLAIR

Printed in South Korea

Blair is an imprint of Carolina Wren Press.

*The mission of Blair / Carolina Wren Press is to seek out, nurture,
and promote literary work by new and underrepresented writers.*

We gratefully acknowledge the ongoing support of general operations
by the Durham Arts Council's United Arts Fund and
the North Carolina Arts Council.

Library of Congress Control Number: 2023935715

For our grandchildren
(in order of appearance)
Millar, William, and Georgette
and their parents

Contents

"To write about Key West, I also needed some local characters . . . who belong to the place and even typify it," Alison Lurie writes in "The Last Resort."

Absent Friends

Might his changed prose "have something to do with [Hemingway, left] getting out of those tight, damp streets of Europe?" Paul Hendrickson asks in "Farther Out."

Preface

CAREY WINFREY

EVER SINCE John Dos Passos persuaded Ernest Hemingway—looking to resettle in the United States after six years in Paris—to try Key West, "the island of bones" has been attracting writers of all stripes and interests. The poets Wallace Stevens, Robert Frost, Elizabeth Bishop, James Merrill, and Richard Wilbur followed Hemingway, to be joined in time by Tennessee Williams, Thomas McGuane, John Hersey, Alison Lurie, Robert Stone, Judy Blume, and countless others. Today the number of writers who live or winter in Key West is exceeded only by the island's feral chickens.

Having retired as editor of *Smithsonian* magazine in 2011, I was looking for a project to keep my mind from turning to mush. I settled on making a documentary about the island as a magnet for writers. Our first full Key West winter, my wife Jane and I began filming the first of what would turn out to be interviews with nearly forty scribes.

One of our subjects was William Wright, a three-decade Key West resident who had written best-selling biographies of Lillian Hellman, Marjorie Merriweather Post, and Christina Onassis, among other books. Bill had also been the editor of *Chicago* magazine.

I think it was our common magazine experience that led us to follow up that first brief encounter with a lunch, during which we shared stories of editorial compromises we had been asked to make for the bottom line and the consequences of our disinclination (and sometime refusal) to do so.

At a second lunch Bill arrived with a large envelope under his arm. He had been writing, he told me, some Key West "sketches" I might enjoy reading. One was a profile, included here, of his friend the real estate developer David Wolkowsky, who, Bill said, had done more to lure writers to Key West than anyone since Hemingway himself.

William "Bill" Wright, a three-decade-long resident of Key West, wrote best-selling biographies of Lillian Hellman, Marjorie Merriweather Post, and Christina Onassis.

Bill said he had wanted to write a follow-up to John Hersey's *Key West Tales*, a collection of stories published in 1994, the year after Hersey's death.

"But I ran out of gas," Bill confided. (Wright's foreword to his abandoned book follows.) He handed me the folder, which I read with pleasure and filed away.

Then, in 2019, the Key West Literary Seminar purchased the "eyebrow" house at 624 White Street, where the poet Elizabeth Bishop lived from 1938 to 1946. When the Seminar announced a capital campaign to raise money for the house's long-overdue restoration. I dug out Bill's "sketches."

Rereading them, it occurred to me that by soliciting essays, reminiscences, and poems from Key West's current crop of writers, I might produce a collection that would honor Bill, who died in 2016, as well as support the Bishop house. The response, in the book you hold in your hands, has been gratifying beyond my wildest hopes.

Foreword

WILLIAM WRIGHT

A FRIEND OF MINE, who had never been to Key West but knew I lived there half the year, startled me by saying he could think of no American city that had so caught the American imagination. I was stunned by the remark's breadth but, remembering how Key West's image had once caught my own imagination, decided my friend might be on to something.

After my sophomore year in college, I wheedled a summer job as a "wiper" on a tanker that hauled crude oil from Galveston, Texas, to a port on the Delaware River just below my Philadelphia hometown. In tanker hierarchy, wipers are the lowest of the low—eight hours a day in 130-degree heat, slapping a kerosene-soaked rag at the engine room's hot bulwarks to wash off the oil film.

Knocking off at 4:00 p.m., soaked with sweat and kerosene, I would shower, then climb to the highest, breeziest deck to read and write in the four hours of remaining sunlight. One afternoon, I spotted a misty string of mirage-like islands just visible on the horizon. Pointing, I called down to a deckhand. "What are those specks of land?"

"The Florida Keys," came the reply.

Now, having spent thirty winters in those keys, it is hard to summon the surge of adolescent emotion I felt seeing them for the first time. To me, they conjured up daring, unfettered pleasures, waived inhibitions, release from the shackles of mainland propriety. In those hazy apparitions I could see a world beyond family, school, fears for a solid future. In short, I saw in them possibilities for a life I'd never thought existed—or whose relevance to me I was too self-deluding to recognize.

It would be another twenty years before I got to Key West and found no Shangri-la, but a seedy tropical island, three by seven miles, the Atlantic Ocean on one side, the Gulf of Mexico on the other, a

Chickens are everywhere in Key West, more roosters than hens, Wright noted, "even table-hopping in the town's more tolerant restaurants."

town of once-handsome wooden houses, modest yet dignified, almost all needing paint — tangled-jungle front yards, dogs sleeping mid-street on hot afternoons, chickens wandering everywhere (even table-hopping in the town's more tolerant restaurants) — and a few sorry beaches. On the plus side were abundant palm trees, lush tropical growth, ubiquitous vistas of open water — and more young people than old. I knew I had arrived at my destination.

Now, a half century later, when from the beach near my house I watch a freighter glide across the horizon, I still feel stirrings of romance.

But while my friend's view of Key West's claim on the American imagination had worked on me, his assertion still seemed too sweeping. Didn't many towns have exotic locations? Quaint houses? Interesting histories? Bohemian reputations? Then it came to me: what made Key West unique was the special breed of humans drawn to it.

Since its beginnings in 1822, Key West has been a magnet for waves of eccentrics, mavericks, weirdoes, crooks (it was founded on a land scam), fugitives, supersized personalities, and, of course, men and women enticed by the live-and-let-live ethos—gays, artists, writers, painters—restless spirits warmed and comforted by proximity to people more peculiar than themselves.

Another friend of mine, the late writer John Knowles, once told me his theory of bad guys and geography. "All the scoundrels," he said, "slide to the southern extremities of the country—southern California, south Florida, and especially, Key West."

It's a concept I would amend to say not only scoundrels but anyone who wants more from life than a tidy house, rosy-cheeked family, backyard barbeques, little league games, and jaunts to the supermarket. Among the many who rightly consider such lives ideal are a few who scan the horizon for passing freighters and yearn for

Key West has long been a magnet, Wright observed, for "restless spirits warmed and comforted by proximity to people more peculiar than themselves."

something beyond. From the mayor to the humblest hourly laborer, Key West is made up of such people and, I've come to believe, always has been.

Of course, the island has also attracted a goodly number of kooks and loonies. The town's catalogue of bizarre characters runs from a German count who kept the corpse of a young Cuban girl in his bed for twenty years, to a homeless vagrant who rides his bicycle around town, stopping to bloviate in Harvard-accented English to stunned tourists on his plans to buy Sony Pictures. And then there is the art gallery owner who, stark naked and wielding a kitchen knife, chased her husband up Duval Street. Happily, most of the eccentrics are less intemperate.

In thinking about a book I might write about my much-loved island, I pondered how to capture Key West's variegated facets—its skewed characters, off-shore isolation, tropical setting, and tenuous relation with the United States—without writing a plodding history or worse, a six-hundred-page tome. I finally hit on the idea of a series of "sketches" that would produce an evocative picture, impressionistic to be sure, but dead-on accurate.

The hope was to create a lively book that captures a lively place, some of its history, and its most memorable characters. With luck, it would pin down the elements that have come together to make America's quirky island outpost one of kind—one of a precious and vanishing kind.

Island Fever

Vroom Vroom Vroom

FRANK DEFORD

IT'S VERY POSSIBLE to dismiss Key West, as the British say, as just too much by half. I mean, you arrive at the airport and it says WELCOME TO THE CONCH REPUBLIC—and everybody is quick to let you know that Key West really isn't Florida—which is to say: it's too good for Florida or, for that matter, too good for any mere state of the union. The taxis are pink, the houses are cutesy-poo, and the residents act like only Key West, in all the world, has a sunset. Whatta nerve. Yet, for all this snobbery, the main drag, Duval Street, may be the tackiest thoroughfare in all of touristland. How can any place that is so smug explain away a t-shirt economy and schlocky saloons that look like Disney would have designed them if only Disney designed saloons? And yet, the day I arrived about fifteen years ago to do a story for *National Geographic* magazine, I wasn't moseying around Key West for more than a couple of hours before I found a pay phone and called my wife and said, "You're gonna love this place."

As contradictory as that sounds, I suppose that's the point. It is the very contradictions of Key West that make it unique. I mean, this is a subtropical resort by the sea that had to truck in sand to build a beach. You have to go out of town to find a golf course. No golf course! In Florida! You might as well have a resort where chickens and deformed cats wander around like they own the place. Oh, yeah, that's Key West, too. Not only that, but gay people basically saved the town when it was in economic distress. In a country that has become so homogenized, so franchisable, so one-size-fits-all, Key West—all right: The Conch—by God!—Republic—is not only unique, but proud to be different. And I like that.

I'm a romantic enough to believe that you can't order up ambiance, that the current edition of Key West is founded on its bizarre layers of history. It's been a place of extremes, gone through boom and bust since it opened for business as a cheeky outpost that got

Key West has always welcomed "scoundrels and oddballs," but the town is "naughty more than dangerous and whimsical more than cynical."

rich on the misfortunes of others—or, specifically, the ships that would, conveniently, crash onto the nearby reefs. (It wasn't just fish that the natives hauled in.) At other times, cigars, booze, and pot have fueled the local economy. So Key West has always been a place where freebooters and scoundrels and oddballs were welcome. The sense of that is in the air. But Key West is naughty more than dangerous and whimsical more than cynical. So it was, back all those years ago, that a few weeks later, when I returned to Key West, as I'd promised my wife, I brought her along with me from our home in Connecticut. Our first night in town together, there was a Christmas parade down Duval Street, and in the middle, right after your all-American high school marching band, here comes a phalanx of motorcycles, all going *vroom vroom vroom*—driven by forty fat, gay Santa Clauses. I turned to my wife. "I told you you'd love this place." She was enthralled.

Vroom vroom vroom. We've been back every year since.

Finding Mañana

MIRTA OJITO

Adapted from a talk given by Mirta Ojito at the 2018 Key West Literary Seminar

THE FIRST TIME I saw Key West, which was almost forty years ago, I was disappointed. There were chickens running around everywhere. Small wooden houses dotted the view. Men and women in green military fatigues milled around. People were yelling, others were waving flags. It was chaotic and, well, not exactly pretty. Where others may have seen charm, I saw decay, even poverty.

I was coming from an island where scenes like these were common, but I'd imagined that the United States—the *entire* United States—looked like New York City, the city some members of my family had moved to. Though I had never been there, I had seen plenty of pictures. Where were the tall buildings? The muted light of winter? And where, oh where, was the snow? Not here.

Now of course I see Key West in a completely different light. It is, indeed, charming and poetic and dreamy—everything that was written about this place before and after I arrived. It is possible that Key West has changed in these past four decades, but I think what happened was that once again, and not for the first time, I was falling victim to my own ignorance, a consequence of geography and ideology. You see, I grew up in Cuba in the 1960s and the 1970s. The '70s, in particular, were very harsh for Cubans. It was really the only time—probably from 1972 to the end of 1978—when Cuba was truly an island. No one was getting in, and no one was getting out. There was no information, and everything was forbidden, including God and the Beatles.

I grew up in a family whose main goal was to get out of Cuba, to go north to the United States. My parents met in 1959 and married three years later, during the Cuban missile crisis. During their honeymoon they could see tanks rolling in Havana's streets. From the

In 1975, "Communist Pioneer" Mirta Ojito (with her Havana elementary school principal, left, and one of her teachers, right) graduated from the sixth grade.

time I understood what my parents were saying I knew that one day we would leave Cuba. We just had to wait longer than many of their friends and relatives. Frustrated, they watched as neighbors—and siblings in my dad's case—left Cuba while they stayed behind. And so I grew up with an embittered father and a lonely mother.

And yet, my parents were intent on providing so-called normal lives for my sister and me, which meant we needed to participate in the revolutionary process. We even became "Communist Pioneers," so that we wouldn't be too different, so that we could thrive and study and be good revolutionaries. That was the only path to success.

Therefore, I lived on a fence — I went to church every weekend, and I also had family members who lived in the U.S. and with whom we communicated. But I was also a Communist Pioneer and a student leader.

Every morning in school I promised to grow up to be like Che Guevera. In the evenings, I did volunteer work on my neighborhood watch committee. I knocked on doors to convince people to participate in a variety of activities, some of which I believed in (like vaccinating kids or planting trees); others I did not. I joined highly politicized school plays. I went camping with other Pioneers. We built fires and sat around them singing songs praising the revolution. I don't think we knew what we were saying, but we sang anyway.

But it wasn't enough, because at that time when the revolution was consolidating itself, it demanded not just our obedience but something else. It wanted our souls, which was far more pernicious and far more dangerous. Therein lies the tragedy of the Cuban revolution: the appropriation of children's souls.

Then something extraordinary happened.

In the late '70s, Cuban exiles returned to the island. Having been told that they could never, *ever* return to Cuba, they were, in fact, eventually allowed to go back. And the Cubans who, like us, had remained behind, realized that life in the U.S. wasn't as bad as we had been told and that the relatives who left maybe five, ten years before had many of the things we wanted but couldn't have. Things like toilet paper, ham and cheese, orange juice, gum, school pencils with erasers, and, of course, freedom.

Despair settled on the island.

People who wanted to leave but had no other recourse began crashing into Latin American embassies seeking asylum. Literally crashing. One was an unemployed bus driver who rammed a bus carrying six people, including a teenager, into the Peruvian Embassy. Immediately, the Cuban government asked for the gate-crashers to be turned over. But the acting ambassador from Peru refused to do so.

Enraged, the Cuban government withdrew protection of the embassy. Within forty-eight hours more than ten thousand people had crowded into the embassy, its manicured grounds, and the home of the ambassador.

Suddenly, there was a crisis. There were thousands of people — workers, intellectuals, young, old, Black, white, women, men, children — clamoring for freedom inside an embassy. Cuba no longer seemed a "workers' paradise." And the entire world was watching.

A solution needed to be found. And it came from Napoleón Vilaboa, a used-car salesman from Miami who met privately with Castro in Cuba and told him, "What you need to do here is engage the Cuban community in Miami. They will come for their relatives, if you allow it, and they'll also take these other people from the embassy off your hands."

Castro agreed to the plan and personally decided that the departure port would be west of Havana, from a town called Mariel. Vilaboa returned to Miami and went to a struggling radio station. The manager was looking for a way to boost its ratings, and he thought that a well-orchestrated campaign to bring Cubans from the island might be just what was needed. And it *worked*.

Between April and September 1980, as many as 2,000 boats brought more than 125,000 Cubans from Mariel, 25 miles west of Havana, to the United States.

Seemingly overnight hundreds of Miami Cubans sought out boats to take their relatives off the island. My father's older brother, my uncle, who was an accountant for General Electric in Miami and didn't even know how to swim, was among them.

I found out we were leaving Cuba in late April 1980, two months after I turned sixteen. I woke up when I heard the sobs of my mother and her sister, my aunt, at the foot of my bed. They told me that we were leaving that very day. As it turned out, that wasn't the case. We waited for about two more weeks. The wait was tense because Cuba was never closer to a civil war than during the days of Mariel. Neighbors turned against neighbors in so-called acts of repudiation. People in the streets threw eggs at those who wanted to leave the country. Some people died, some people were killed, some people killed themselves. We'll probably never know for sure just how many were victims of those barbaric acts.

In my family we were very lucky that we were not subjected to attacks or insults by our neighbors. Nevertheless, my parents warned my sister and me not to stray too far from the house, to go about our business as if everything was normal, and not to tell anyone we were leaving. Eventually, on May 7, the police knocked on our front door. It was time to go.

At the port of Mariel we found my uncle, who had been waiting there for sixteen days. He had insisted he wasn't returning to Miami without us, all of us. This was crucial, because many families were divided during the boatlift, but he had decided that he was taking the four of us—my mother, my father, my younger sister, and me— or none of us at all.

When we got to the boat, the *Valley Chief*, there were more than thirty people whose relatives had come from the U.S. to take them away. But while we waited to board, so many others were added to the boat that when the order to depart was finally given, the *Valley Chief* stalled. Eventually we transferred to a different boat, the *Mañana*.

In all, between April and September 1980, about 2,000 boats brought more than 125,000 people to the United States. Some twenty-five people died, mostly from drowning—a low number considering the circumstances and the capricious currents of the Florida Straits.

When we arrived in Key West, we were quickly picked up by two aunts who had come all the way from Miami for us. We were wet, dirty, nauseated, and disoriented. We had nothing—no money, birth certificates, visas, or any documents except a piece of paper with an alien number on it. But apparently that was enough for the U.S. government to simply let us get in the car and go.

SO, YOU SEE, Key West—charming, crazy, chaotic, beautiful Key West—will always be dear to me as the place where my new life began and my ideas about personal freedom in the United States were confirmed.

Key West was also where—in a way I didn't know back then—I began to think about *Finding Mañana*, my memoir about the boatlift, published in 2005. I remember consciously making a point to remember everything about that period.

Years later, reporting the book, I discovered that history is not always made by those in power. Sometimes history wells up from below, made by men and women who one day decide to change their circumstances. In the late '70s and most specifically in 1980, Cuban men and women determined they had had enough and made the only choice they could: they voted with their feet. And in so doing they shattered the decades-long myth that the Cuban revolution had been waged and won for the benefit of the working class.

If at the beginning of the revolution many of the people who came to the United States from Cuba were middle class—even upper class—those who came in the Mariel Boatlift were not. They—we—were working class: bus drivers, secretaries, factory workers, teachers, students, artists, and writers.

After two decades of oppression, the boatlift people had decided to take their fate into their own hands. And to me that is the most important narrative of Mariel: we had the courage to wrestle our lives from the hands of the state and decide, finally, how we wanted to conduct our lives, even if it was far from everything we knew and had once held dear.

Welcome Home

―――

MEG CABOT

LIKE SO MANY PEOPLE who've ended up moving to Key West, my husband, Benjamin, and I first came here on vacation. We enjoyed the island's laid-back, Bohemian atmosphere, especially in comparison to the sometimes-stuffy Upper East Side of Manhattan, where we lived. Key West felt more like the small town where we'd both gone to college—Bloomington, Indiana, where on summer evenings the place was so quiet and empty you could safely ride bikes down the middle of the street.

It was only after 9/11—which Benjamin experienced firsthand since he worked across the street from the World Trade Center— that we decided to give living in Key West full-time a try. The southernmost city in the U.S. felt like home. But was it?

It took us until 2004 to find our "maybe" southernmost home. Move-in day was crazy, and we were exhausted and hungry after long hours of unpacking and deciding where to place the few belongings we'd brought from our (comparatively) tiny Manhattan apartment to our (comparatively) spacious new house.

That's when Benjamin had the idea to go to Meteor Smokehouse, the (sadly, no longer existing) barbecue place next door to the Green Parrot. What could be better after a long, hot day of unpacking than a few cold beers, smoked ribs, and some live music?

So we jumped on our bikes and rode to Meteor, where the perfect table was waiting for us. We were seated and quickly served our beers before we noticed a few young white men sitting at the bar in the center of the open-air restaurant. One of these guys had a dog tied by her leash to the leg of his barstool.

Judging by the number of empty beer bottles in front of him and from the way his dog, a pretty black-and-white border collie mix, would occasionally look up and whine, anxious to leave, this guy had been at the bar for some time.

He wasn't ready to leave though. Every time the dog made a sound, the guy would give her a quick kick in the side and say, "Shut up!"

The bartender, his gaze on the ball game playing on the TV screen in the corner, continued to polish glasses, while everyone else in the restaurant went on drinking.

I was shocked! This kind of behavior seemed absolutely antithetical to the Key West we'd come to know. The locals we'd met so far were kind to animals, feeding (and spaying) stray cats, rescuing pelicans in distress, and going far out of their way to avoid hitting sea turtles and manatees while boating. One neighbor had even named all of the chickens that roamed our street. "Christopher" the rooster came running whenever he heard his name.

"Shut up!" we heard the dog's owner say again. Kick. Yelp of pain.

This was terrible! Had we made the wrong decision moving to this place? I wondered. This was not the gentler pace I'd envisioned when moving away from Manhattan. Should I call 911? In New York City, animal cruelty wasn't considered an emergency. Would Key West police even respond to —

That's when it happened.

"It's a third-degree felony in the state of Florida to intentionally inflict pain or suffering on an animal, punishable by up to $10,000 in fines."

"If you kick that dog one more time," a long-haired, mustached stranger at the end of bar startled me by saying coolly to the dog owner, "I will lay you out."

Whoa.

Surely, I thought to myself, this would be the end of it. The stranger at the end of the bar was quite a bit older—but also bigger—than the scrawny dog owner, whom I'd later learn to recognize as a type of resort town resident committed to the rejection of societal norms such as gainful employment and hygiene. Known in some circles as "beach bums" or "dirtbags," these individuals were not to be confused with homeless persons, whose lifestyle was not a choice.

The dog owner, however, seemed unaware of the danger he was in. He simply laughed.

It couldn't have been more than a few minutes later when I heard his dog yelp in pain again.

"That's it." The mustached stranger slapped his fist on the bar. Then he got up, walked over to the dog owner, and punched him in the face. Bam!

The dog owner flew backward from his barstool. He lay on the floor of the Meteor, clutching his nose.

"He *hit* me!" he cried in surprise. "Oh, my God! He *hit* me!"

As surprised as the dog owner was, I don't think he was nearly as surprised as either Benjamin or me. Especially when the tall, mustached stranger returned to his seat, lifted his beer, and continued calmly to watch the ball game, as did everyone else in the bar . . . with the exception of the dog owner.

"You all saw it! He *hit* me!" The dog owner had leapt to his feet and, still clutching his nose, pointed at the stranger. "I have witnesses. He *hit* me!"

It was true that the dog owner had witnesses—a lot of them.

But no one seemed very interested. Everyone had turned back to their meals and drinks as if nothing had happened. All except for Benjamin and me, who were watching the drama unfold with disbelief—and, I have to admit, a little bit of delight.

The dog owner—perhaps because he'd failed to find sympathy from any of his fellow customers at Meteor—stormed out, leaving his dog behind. No one remarked upon this, though by now I was

In Key West's Old Town district, houses must conform to regulations set down by the Historic Architectural Review Committee (HARC).

wild with curiosity. Where had he gone? Who was going to take care of his dog—and his bar bill? What was going to happen next?

What happened next was that the bartender, looking irritated by the interruption of his ball game, ducked out from behind his work-station to unleash the dog and refill her water bowl—which he'd clearly supplied for her earlier—as well as feed her from a bag of dog food he kept behind the bar. The dog ate and drank, looking much happier now that she was free from the barstool . . . and maybe because she was free from her owner, too.

By this time Benjamin and I had finished our meal. There was no reason to stay. Except that we had to stay and support this amazing business. This was the Key West we'd come to know and love.

If only we'd known what was to come next.

Our server had just delivered our third round of beers when the dog owner reappeared . . . with two Key West policemen in tow.

My heart dropped. No!

"There he is, officers!" the dog owner cried, pointing at the tall stranger. "That's the man who hit me! He hit me so hard, I fell off my barstool!"

Everyone in the restaurant froze, including the guy with the mustache. The more senior police officer asked the bartender gravely, "Is this true?"

My pulse hammered. This couldn't possibly be happening.

The bartender slowly shook his head. "I don't know anything about that, officer," he said. "But I did see that fellow kick that dog over there." He pointed at the black-and-white dog, who was sitting by her bowls, serenely licking a paw. "I saw him kick her more than once."

The police officers looked startled. They glanced around at the rest of us. "Is this true?" they asked.

I held my breath. What was going to happen?

What happened was that every single customer sitting in the restaurant nodded in agreement.

"Oh, yes, he was kicking that poor dog all night," said a woman in a pink tube top. "It was terrible."

"I saw him kick that dog more than once. About five times, I think," a man in leather motorcycle chaps agreed with a nod.

"It was horrible," his boyfriend added.

"The dog was crying," two Cuban men who'd been playing dominoes chimed in. "She couldn't get away because he had her all tied up. You should arrest him for cruelty to an animal."

And to our astonishment—and joy—that's exactly what the Key West police did. They ordered the dog owner to put his hands behind his back and then slipped handcuffs on him.

"But my *face*," the dog owner wailed. "He *hit* me! In the face!"

One of the police officers said they would happily take the man to the ER on his way to jail if he wanted, but this didn't seem to be the answer he'd been hoping for. The other officer glanced questioningly at the dog, then at the bartender. "You got this?" he asked.

The bartender, who'd gone back to polishing glasses, nodded. "I'll take her."

And with that, the police removed the still-protesting offender.

Then, without another word, everyone in the place went back to doing what they'd been doing before the interruption as if nothing out of the ordinary had happened.

But something had.

It's a third-degree felony in the state of Florida to intentionally

Says author Meg Cabot (home at last in Key West), "All we knew then was that we'd just witnessed something we'd never forget—something amazing!"

inflict pain or suffering on an animal, punishable by up to $10,000 in fines. It's an even greater moral crime in the city of Key West, where more than forty cats freely roam the Hemingway Home and Museum and where the county jail keeps a "farm" tended by inmates of more than 150 animals that have been abandoned or abused (open to the public every second and fourth Sunday of the month).

My husband and I didn't know any of this that night, of course. All we knew then was that we'd just witnessed something we'd never forget—something amazing! Nothing like that ever would have happened in Bloomington, Indiana, let alone the Upper East Side of Manhattan. Only in Key West would so many people have instinctively banded together to lie to the cops to punish a man who'd been mean to his dog.

As we rode our bikes back to our new house through the empty streets of the southernmost city that night, we were anything but quiet. We were whooping with joy, because we knew we'd made the right decision: we were *home*!

Poetry Workshop Held in a Former Cigar Factory in Key West

BILLY COLLINS

Until the 1930s, readers known as "lectors" would read newspapers and novels aloud to cigar rollers (in Key West, above) to alleviate the work's monotony.

After our final class, when we disbanded
as the cigar rollers here had disbanded decades ago,
getting up from their benches for the last time
as the man who read to them during their shift
closed his book without marking the page where he left off,
I complimented myself on my restraint.

For never in that sunny white building
did I draw an analogy between cigar-making and poetry.
Not even after I had studied the display case
containing the bladed *chaveta*, the ring gauge,
and the hand guillotine with its measuring rule
did I suggest that the cigar might be a model for the poem.

Nor did I ever cite the exemplary industry
of those anonymous rollers and cutters —
the best producing 300 cigars in a day
compared to 3 flawless poems in a lifetime if you're lucky —
who worked the broad leaves of tobacco
into cylinders ready to be held lightly in the hand.

Not once did I imply that an intuition, tightly rolled
into a perfectly shaped, handmade thing,
might encourage a reader to remove the brightly colored
encircling band, slip it over her ring finger,
and take the poet as her spouse in a sudden puff of smoke.
No, I kept all of that to myself, until now.

Standoff at Sea

MARY KAY ZURAVLEFF

A LIGHT RAIN was falling in Key West as people were deciding whether to board the good ship *Hindu* for a sunset cruise. Billy Collins was a big attraction, as was the beautiful 1920s schooner awaiting us with its gaff-rigged, four-cornered sails billowing in the wind. Also, Fin-the-dog is a member of the crew, and the crew had laid in a goodly supply of wine, cheese, and nibbles. What rain?

Yet as Billy and I were walking toward the gangway, others held back. "My shoes." "My hair!" I heard a couple of women say. But Billy's hair is waning, and my flat, straight tresses are unaffected by foul weather. With no lightning in the sky, the worst we'd get was wet. And that wine wasn't going to drink itself.

A mere dozen of us were aboard the nearly eighty-footer as Fin-the-dog brought in the lines and another crew member filled our glasses before we shoved off, toasting those alongside and those we left behind. Soon, we too were toasted, and the first mischief Billy put me up to was feeding me embarrassing questions to ask the crew. With a straight face, I asked the captain, "How many sunset cruises do you run a night?"

Stories ricocheted around our tight group, laughter, too. And then Billy said to me, "I'm throwing down the gauntlet. Poetry versus prose!" So much for braving a light rain—going up against the former poet laureate of these United States, it was all I could do not to jump ship.

I'm passionate about prose; my family still ribs me about our trip to Copenhagen, where a Viking exhibit was promoted on banners all over town, asking, "Who needs fiction?" These offended me so much that I threatened to shimmy up to the banners and add an "r" with spray paint so they'd read, "Who needs *friction*?"

I took a deep breath, threw my shoulders back, and lifted a glass. "In the beginning was the Word," I said.

"People were deciding whether to board the good ship Hindu *for a sunset cruise. . . . The crew had laid in a goodly supply of wine, cheese, and nibbles. What rain?"*

I have no memory of Billy Collins's rejoinders, though I'm sure they were deft and smart. He may have said, "Sing in me, Muse," or "I celebrate myself, and sing myself." He may have aptly quoted himself.

My turn. "Once upon a time." I said, "Tell me a bedtime story." I said, "We tell ourselves stories in order to live."

There was cheering after each of our parries. And then Billy said, "We should do this onstage!"

"Absolutely!" I said, knowing that the only reasons I had taken the bait were the sunset, the *Hindu*, and the wine.

The Geographical Cure

LEE SMITH

MY SWEET DADDY, Ernest Smith of Grundy, Virginia, was "kindly nervous," as he put it, his own euphemistic term for bipolar illness, or "manic depression" as it was then called. But the manic phase was no fun for him—no elation, no wild sprees—instead, he just worked harder than ever running his dime store until weeks of intense activity led inevitably to a downward spiral. He'd talk less and less, stay in bed more and more, finally "going off" someplace to get treatment—the Highland Hospital in Asheville, North Carolina, or Silver Hill in New Canaan, Connecticut, where he had been hospitalized for about six months in 1958.

My beautiful mother, Virginia Marshall Smith, "kindly nervous" herself, was simultaneously being treated for anxiety and depression at the University of Virginia hospital in Charlottesville.

Upon my father's discharge from Silver Hill, his physician prescribed not only lithium for him but also a "Geographical Cure" for their marriage, now apparently "troubled" in some way that nobody would explain to me. The Geographical Cure was the good doctor's way of saying a *big long trip*! As our destination Daddy chose Key West, because he had been stationed there in the navy and loved it.

But as my father drove our big white fishtail Buick endlessly down the eastern seaboard that January of 1959, the Geographical Cure did not seem to be working. Mama and Daddy were barely speaking, except for things like Mama saying, "Lee, will you please tell your daddy to stop for more cigarettes?" which I would dutifully repeat even though he was sitting right there. Or me screaming "Can't we go to Weeki Wachee Springs? Please please please!" as the billboard flashed past, for I planned to be a professional mermaid when I grew up. Nothing doing. We pressed on in the smoke-filled car. I felt like the marriage was a fourth passenger, sitting glumly next to me in the back seat.

The author's mother and father were both treated for depression. Her father's physician prescribed a "geographical cure" for their troubled marriage.

Each night in the series of little tourist cottages was grim, with Mama and me in one bed and Daddy in the other, and several times I awakened to see his bent shadow pacing back and forth outside the window. What if he had another breakdown? What if the marriage couldn't be cured?

But I loved that final part of the drive, with the luminous sea and sky surrounding us and the Florida Keys with their wonderful names: Key Largo, Cudjoe, Sugarloaf, Saddlebunch, Raccoon.

"We're almost there," Daddy said.

Mama reapplied her lipstick, Revlon Fire and Ice.

And finally we were in Key West—the scruffiest, wildest place I had ever seen, a bright buzz of noise and color. We turned left off Truman Avenue onto Duval Street, and now I could glimpse a shining patch of ocean. Daddy pulled into a motel named the Blue Marlin with a huge fish on its sign. Mama and I waited in the car while he headed for the office. The motel was made of blue concrete, two stories in a U-shape around a good-size pool with a diving board and a slide. Perfect for a mermaid.

Finally Daddy got back in the car with a funny look on his face. "Girls, you're not going to believe this," he said slowly.

"What? What is it? Is it bad news from home?" Mama's pretty face was an instant mask of alarm.

"Oh no, nothing like that." Daddy really smiled for the first time on the trip. "It appears that this entire motel has been taken over by the cast and crew of a movie that they are shooting on location right now in Key West, over at the Navy Yard. There are only four rooms that they're not occupying, and now we've got two of them. They asked me a lot of questions. I had to swear that we weren't journalists or photographers in order to stay here. And Lee," he added in a no-nonsense voice, "I promised that you would not bother the stars. Do you hear me? Or the crew, or anybody else."

"Which stars?" Mama hardly breathed. She was already in heaven.

"Well, there's Dina Merrill," Daddy said, "and Tony Curtis."

"*Tony Curtis!*" Mama and I squealed together. At home, we pored over the *National Enquirer*, the *Midnight Star*, and countless other movie magazines that we read cover to cover. Every week when the movie changed at the Lynwood Theater downtown, we were right there in our favorite seats, tenth-row aisle, clutching our Baby Ruths.

"And that's not all," Daddy said.

"Who?" we shrieked.

"Cary Grant."

"*Cary Grant!*" We couldn't believe it. The most gorgeous, the most elegant, the biggest star in Hollywood. "The man at the desk says he's a real gentleman," Daddy said. I wasn't so sure, thinking of his recent love affair with Sophia Loren. Mama and I knew everything.

Thus it began, and so immediately my mother stopped being mad and started wearing high-heeled shoes and wearing a hibiscus—a pink hibiscus—in her hair. And she and Daddy went out dancing. And Daddy went deep-sea fishing with a guy named Captain Tony and played poker with the film crew.

Every night at 7:00 p.m., Mama and I seated ourselves on a rattan loveseat in the lobby of the Blue Marlin pretending to read newspapers while we eavesdropped on Tony Curtis's daily call from the

The Blue Marlin motel "was made of blue concrete," Smith remembers, "two stories in a U-shape around a good-size pool with a diving board and a slide."

public telephone to his wife, Janet Leigh, back in Hollywood, which always ended with Tony's words, "God bless you, my darling!" We rattled our newspapers emotionally.

One day at the pool, Tony Curtis offered me a package of cheese nabs; I would save it for decades. Near the end of the second week, one of the directors asked our family if we would like to be in the movie. "You bet!" I cried out. "Oh, brother," Daddy said. But there we were, and there we still are to this day in the giant crowd on the Key West dock when the pink submarine comes into port at the end of the movie, cheering and waving hello.

As for the movie itself, *Operation Petticoat* featured a real pink submarine, anchored out in the ocean off Key West. Its flimsy plot involves a navy lieutenant commander (Cary Grant) and his con man executive officer (Tony Curtis) who must take the fictional damaged sub USS *Sea Tiger* into a seedy dockyard for repair during World War II, rescuing a crew of stranded army nurses on the way. The only available paint for repair is red and white (hence the sub's pink color), and the only available bunks for the nurses are down in the submarine's tight quarters (wink, wink).

The film takes place during the Battle of the Philippines in the opening days of the United States' involvement in World War II. Some elements of the screenplay were taken from actual incidents that happened with some of the Pacific Fleet's submarines during the war, though points of histori-cal accuracy are few. Most film-ing was done in and around Naval Station Key West, now known as the Truman Annex of Naval Air Station Key West.

Operation Petticoat was a huge box-office hit, the number three moneymaker of 1960, earning $6,800,000 — just behind number one *Psycho* and number two *Ben-Hur*. The review in *Variety* was typical: "*Operation Petticoat* has no more weight than a sackful of feathers, but it has a lot of laughs. Cary Grant and Tony Curtis are excellent, and the film is directed by Blake Edwards with a slam-bang pace." Cary Grant's residu-als topped $3 million, making it his most profitable film to date. The film was the basis for a TV series in 1977.

The Geographical Cure worked. My parents made up and Mama and Daddy would go home refreshed and stay married for the rest of their lives, and Daddy would run his dime store in Grundy, Vir-ginia, for thirty-three more years.

So it was a hugely successful trip. And I've been coming back to Key West every year, ever since.

Our First Time

GEORGE COOPER

HOW CAN WE FORGET our first moments in Key West? In pursuit of my wife Judy Blume's desire for "more summers," we rented, unseen, what looked to be a handsome house in Old Town. We're city people and wanted nothing of the automobile-dependent life for our two-month stay.

Arriving at the house, located in the Truman Annex (later dubbed by a friend as "The Truman Show," after the Jim Carrey movie), we were met by the owner, David Wolkowsky, and his good friend Bill Wright. Little did we know that we had stumbled into the heart of Key West's literary scene.

Wolkowsky was charming in his greeting, but not Wright, who exclaimed, "You're not Judy Blume. I know Judy Blume, and you're not her." Wolkowsky took a step back. Had he been scammed by our references?

We hesitated. Would a driver's license suffice? Probably not; maybe we could prove she was *a* Judy Blume but not *the* Judy Blume. Thank goodness for book jacket photos. Digging one out of our luggage, we quickly established our bona fides.

The house was perfect. Furnished to Wolkowsky's eclectic taste, it was full of collectible art painted by his favorite forger. It was also, on occasion, full of Wolkowsky, as we discovered the first time we returned home after an evening out to find our landlord seated in the living room in want of a nightcap conversation.

And Bill Wright could not have become a better friend. His mistake, derived from having been seated at a dinner party next to Francine Pascal of *Sweet Valley High* fame, put him forever in our debt. (When you've been seated next to one children's book author, you've sat next to them all, apparently.)

Sometimes there's no better way to start off than on the wrong foot.

A Susurration of Palms

THOMAS SWICK

FOR MANY PEOPLE, a visit to Key West is a trip to the fringe, a louche dead end filled with exotic slackers. "If there was any place on the map of the United States where the elevated ideology of being an American finally unraveled," Jonathan Raban wrote in *Hunting Mister Heartbreak*, "it was on the Keys." Yet if you live elsewhere in Florida and happen to have grown up in another state, Key West provides a nostalgic return to normalcy.

The first time I drove into town, in 1991, from my new home in Fort Lauderdale, I was struck not by the alien but by the once-familiar: porches, alleys, chickens, white picket fences, people on bicycles. I had left the world of condos and gated communities and seemed to be on a childhood trip to my grandmother's house, a house that in a bewildering but beguiling twist had been uprooted from central Pennsylvania and set down in a tropical garden.

Turning onto Duval, I headed down the Conch version of Main Street, U.S.A. As at Disney World, the buildings were pretty and seemed to have been built on a slightly smaller scale than usual. There were numerous places to buy ice cream. Mixed in with them, of course, were loudmouth bars and shops with t-shirts carrying X-rated aphorisms that often constituted one of the lower forms of authorship.

Key West has long been a writers' town. The purpose of that first trip was to report on the annual Key West Literary Seminar, which that year was devoted to travel writing. The keynote speaker, John Malcolm Brinnin, was also a resident, and he validated my impressions of the place by noting that he and his septuagenarian friends lived very much as they had as children: they wore short pants, they rode around on bikes, they took afternoon naps. This constituted more of a regression than an unraveling.

My room was at the Pier House, and my chambermaid was Polish, which seemed serendipitous—I had lived in Warsaw in the early

"The delightful porches full of palms on which you take your meals are just as good as they ever were," poet Wallace Stevens wrote to his wife in 1935.

'80s—until I discovered that the town was sprinkled with Poles. They made beds, bused tables, washed dishes, poured drinks, scooped ice cream. I found myself, remarkably, in an evocative old-fashioned town covering a conference of writers I admired while in my spare time brushing up on my Polish. Adding to my satisfaction with the world was the fact that it was January and I didn't need a coat. Subsequent trips to Key West happily reinforced for me this unlikely triumvirate—for a wayward, subtropical isle—of the bygone, the literary, and the Polish.

The literary seminar didn't tackle travel writing again until 2006, a gap that might conceivably be attributed to the fact that the town has inspired so much bad travel writing. This time I stayed, more appropriately, in a three-story Victorian with a porch and a balcony. Every morning I'd come downstairs and find Dervla Murphy eating breakfast in the garden. I drank tea with Pico Iyer and went barhopping with a group that included former poet laureate Billy Collins.

When not attending panels, I researched a story about the Eastern European workforce. I was the travel editor of the newspaper in Fort Lauderdale at the time, and while I'd read hundreds of articles on Key West, I'd never come across anything about the heavily accented and sometimes highly educated help. They were service people, invisible to anyone not transported by the accent.

As I made my rounds, I discovered that over the years the Poles had been joined by others from the old neighborhood: Hungarians, Ukrainians, Moldovans, Belarusians, Lithuanians, Latvians, and Czechs, who, it was said, now outnumbered the Poles. Most people I talked to spoke very highly of their Czech carpenter or their Latvian salesgirls. I met a Belarusian waitress, a recent English major whose favorite American writer was O. Henry. A young Polish woman working in a sunglasses shop wrote poems in her free time that she described as "hermetic."

Not long ago I returned to Key West to write an article about Casa Marina, the hotel that first began hiring Poles in the early '90s. I had missed it on my first visit, since it's not in the center of town but tucked away—if a grand hotel can ever be "tucked"—in a quiet neighborhood bordering the Atlantic. Envisioned by Henry Flagler and opened in 1920, it seems less a part of Key West than of the Florida tradition of great outpost hotels. Because tourists were, at least in the southern half of the state, the real pioneers, hotels are our most historic and iconic structures. They are to Florida what castles are to Europe.

When I mentioned to a friend that I would be writing about the hotel, he promptly informed me that the bar had been the setting for a fistfight between Ernest Hemingway and Wallace Stevens. This was not true, I discovered after doing a little research; the fight took place on a street in town. But the hotel was where Stevens would stay when he'd come seeking refuge from Connecticut winters. Most of the letters in the last chapter of *The Contemplated Spouse: The Letters of Wallace Stevens to Elsie* were written on Casa Marina stationery. One informed the left-behind partner: "Robert Frost was on the beach this morning and is coming to dinner this evening. We are having what is called conk [*sic*] chowder, a thing in which he is interested."

Stevens was more impressed with the hotel than he was with the town. "The delightful porches full of palms on which you take your meals are just as good as they ever were," he wrote to his wife in 1935, one year after proclaiming, "Key West is extremely old-fashioned and primitive. The movie theatres are little bits of things."

Built in 1897, the Southernmost House has been a residence, speakeasy, nightclub, and, currently, a hotel. Thomas Edison himself installed the electricity.

The city inspired his poem "The Idea of Order at Key West," if not also "The Emperor of Ice-Cream." Alfresco dining at Casa Marina has moved from the porches to a small beach, where every evening, weather permitting, white-clothed tables are set up in the sand. Inside the hotel, the bar in which the famous fight never happened is hung with enlarged, black-and-white photographs: Henry Flagler on the day his train first pulled into town; a shirtless Harry Truman proudly holding up a fish; John F. Kennedy sitting in the back seat of a convertible and getting an earful from a local in swim trunks. There is a picture of Tennessee Williams having drinks with Truman Capote but, sadly, none of Wallace Stevens sipping soup with Robert Frost.

Leaving the hotel and taking a stroll, I was reminded that the town's homey otherness is heightened at night. The humid air is perfumed with flowers and salt. Softly lit rooms endowed with antiques appear through cracks in front-yard jungles. Porch lights produce primeval shadows. The susurrations of palms—or are they Poles?—caress the ear.

Lucky Ducking

ARLO HASKELL

The shadows are long, the moon's
not yet set, and the cactus
flowers are puckered open
still like lips which beckon
and expect to taste and feel.

The bigger birds
are singing. Summer's
trying to roll me
and this island.
It's doing the leer,
the weave-and-wobble,
we're doing the flat-
footed-drunk-ducking-punches,
and the aggressors on the
dance floor are the seas
that would surmount us.

Until the rest of these days go by,
there's fear. That's fine. This
day has the usual objects
traversing the regular sky and so—
we can almost count on it—
will the next.

Duck, Boogie

MARK HEDDEN

I HAVEN'T BEEN over to Grinnell Street for a while. Or maybe I have. You live in Key West long enough and you go through these long stretches where you move around on autopilot, inured to it all — the place nothing but wallpaper with an excess of gingerbread and palm trees. Other times, memories attach themselves to you like burrs.

I've done that thing where I pass by our old house and, after I'm a block away think, hey, we used to live there, that used to be the center of our world. And I wonder how often I've passed by without even noticing that much.

Our old house stopped looking like our old house long ago. It's been renovated a couple times, dandified, turned into one of those showplaces that gets used six weeks out of the year, tops. But the neighborhood still boasts a little grit. Honestly, the only thing I'm sentimental about are two words that may or may not still be written in the concrete in surprisingly neat block letters: Duck Boogie.

Boogie was a dog. Big, thick, coal black, Lab-ish — not unfriendly but not all that friendly either. About as close to a nondescript dog as you can get.

Duck was Charlie Duck, a.k.a. Charlie Russell, Duck being his street name, one of those Conch nicknames no one ever explains. Maybe he had one of those duck's ass haircuts back in the day. Maybe things ran off him. Maybe he was just always an odd one.

We lived next door to Charlie for thirteen years. The first time we met him he was slumped in a plastic chair, drinking Budweiser at a junk-covered plywood-on-sawhorses table in the front yard. Lynn Kaufelt had just shown us the house next door, an alternative to the house we had called her about but could not afford. We said a tentative hello as we passed him by, and he gave us a ten-minute monologue in this gravely smoker's voice. He told us he was a Conch but wasn't born here (birth here being the definition of Conchdom). He told us he got fucked up by Vietnam but never went there. Then he went on a tirade about what a rip-off the house was, what fools we would be to buy it, how he had seven better houses he could sell us.

We backed away—slowly.

After we moved in, sitting at the junk-covered table drinking Budweiser—never anything else—was what Charlie did most of the time. You'd hear the clink of the first bottle going into the trash before you were out of bed in the morning.

It was rough at the beginning, before any of us knew how to handle each other. He was strangely turfish about things. I'd be cutting two-by-fours with a circular saw in the backyard and he'd yell over the fence that he had a better circular saw. I'd fire up the chainsaw and he'd yell over that he had three chain saws and I should use one of his.

The day I brought home a big, new window-unit air conditioner, he demanded to know why we didn't buy one of the half dozen ancient ones he had arrayed around his yard, then paced back and forth in front of our house, grumbling at me while I installed the thing.

Later, when we were a little skint in the middle of another long hot summer, we bought one of the ancient units he had in the yard. I still regret it.

He played the radio a lot, a light jazz station. I wondered if Kenny G really recorded that much music or if light jazz was nothing but indistinguishable musicians noodling infinitely on alto saxes. It was like the soundtrack to a never-ending elevator ride, hold music you could not escape.

He would blast the light jazz, and I'd occasionally go over and politely ask him to turn it down. He would. Or he would wait until I left and double the volume for thirty seconds to show me who was boss. Or he would turn it down, turn it back up, then leave it on and disappear for a couple hours.

I tried to accept the fact that every movie we watched would have light jazz underscoring it, that if I played my own music I'd have to listen to it and light jazz at the same time, that if I put in earplugs the light jazz would somehow insidiously work its way through them. But my new-neighbor civility began to fray.

I reached the end of my tether in January, two or three years after we moved in. I turned our stereo speakers around, put them in the windows that faced his yard, and blasted Hüsker Dü's "I'll Never Forget You" on auto-repeat for two hours. (Google it if you don't know it. It's a toe tapper.)

The light jazz issue diminished.

I CALL IT Charlie's yard, but it wasn't his. Ed owned it; Ed lived in the dilapidated, pink, one-bedroom, shotgun house with asbestos siding. Charlie rented a shed somewhere back behind the falling-down arbor, though we never went back to see the actual shed and never knew for sure if he paid any rent.

Occasionally Ed would sit at the plywood table, rarely at the same time as Charlie.

Ed was not young. He talked about being in the Pacific in the navy during World War II, though someone said he was in the Coast Guard and never left the country, and someone else said he was too crazy to have been in either. I found a photo of him as a senior in the 1946 Key West High yearbook, which was a year after the war ended, though I suppose he could have gone back to high school after serving. He had a gold minivan he used to drive vets up to the VA in Miami. He had a flattop and always wore a white v-neck t-shirt tucked into khakis.

Ed glowered. He would read the *Citizen* and foment, muttering to himself. If he didn't like the look of somebody walking by, he would unleash a stammering pinwheel of slurs, touching all the bases—Blacks, Jews, gays, women, hippies, and several other offending demographics.

It was a busy neighborhood. The Conch Train passed by thirty times a day, the guides announcing the same point of interest over the loudspeaker every time—a snippet about the home of Antonio Diaz y Carrasco, the first Cuban Consul to the United States, and the ship's wheel gingerbread in the balcony railings.

Our block was sort of a domestic dispute zone. Couples who'd been drinking all evening would fight on the way back to their guest house. Things would be said. Stands would be taken. Yelling and hitting and, occasionally, ring throwing would take place. Once, after Fantasy Fest, when I was dressed as Yanni, the New Age musician, wearing a pink silk shirt and a cheesy fake mustache, I went over to stop a guy roughly dragging a stumbling woman down the sidewalk by her arm, and my wife Nan started referring to me as Yanni the Vigilante.

Nan was pretty sure Ed came into the *Miami Herald* bureau when she worked there to complain about the Conch Train driving past his house, saying it made him feel like a monkey in a cage, demanding she do something about it.

Generally we tried to say polite, neighborly things to him and get in the house before he could rope us into his hate-spiel.

But you can't keep your guard up all the time. I sat on the front steps one morning waiting for a friend, and Ed wandered through the gate with a hose to water the giant pink bougainvillea that was rooted in his yard and covered the wall of *our* house.

"I got twenty-seven dogs buried in the yard," he said. "Someday they're going to dig the place up and think I was a serial killer."

We'd hear him a couple times a day standing at his front door, yelling "Queenah!" for his dog Queenie. He had two other dogs, but he never yelled for them.

Sometimes Loggerhead would be there in the yard, sometimes with a walker, sometimes with a wheelchair. According to Charlie, Loggerhead had been a shrimper until he got hit in the head by a boom. Now he lived most of the time in the state hospital. (A disconcerting amount of his skull was missing in the back.) He didn't talk, but when I walked by one day and said hi, he looked up and broke into an achingly beautiful version of "Ave Maria" that haunts me to this day.

I'm not sure what tumbler clicked in the rusty hate-vault of Ed's head, but when I was leaving the house one afternoon and gave a friendly wave, he screamed, "Fuck you, you tub of shit."

I said, "What?" And he stood up, threw his chair back, and came at the chain-link fence the way his dogs did, screaming, arms waving, spittle flying everywhere. Which kind of changed the tone of things. Someone told me later he decided he didn't like my ponytail.

I walked away then, and most times afterward I crossed the street and avoided the sidewalk in front of his place—you don't want to add fuel to the dumpster fire that lives next door. But occasionally I'd forget.

Two out of three times, nothing would happen. But that third time he'd go off.

"Boogie was a dog. Big, thick, coal black, Lab-ish — not unfriendly but not all that friendly either. About as close to a nondescript dog as you can get."

During one of his tirades, I told him he was evil and had a black heart whilst flipping him off with both middle fingers, but usually I just walked away.

IT WAS NOT HARD to see Charlie Duck coming. He was tall and skinny with a long, loping shamble. (Walter Brennan in *To Have and Have Not* had a perfect version of the walk twenty years before Charlie was born.) He talked to himself a lot. Boogie's collar would jangle. A couple times a day the duo made the circuit between the yard and the convenience store at the end of Elgin Lane for cigarettes and a six-pack. Sometimes Charlie would drink for a while in front of the store, then wander off and leave most of a six-pack behind. The convenience store owners would put a couple fresh bottles in the empty holes, put it back in the fridge, and sell it to him again later, which sounded like a dirty trick until you balance it with how much business he probably scared away.

You hardly ever saw Charlie eat, though he would get stale loaves of Cuban bread from the Blossom's trash and throw it around the yard and onto Ed's roof for the doves.

There was a gregarious Cuban family in the small concrete block house across the street. They too lived mostly in their yard, playing music, dancing, sitting in lawn chairs, kids running around the yard in diapers, someone washing a car. We were never sure how many bedrooms there were, how many people lived there, who was family, who was just stopping by. Two of the brothers at one point got arrested for hauling drugs up and down the Keys in a garbage truck, but they were one of the most wholesome, happy-to-be-in-each-other's-company families I'd ever seen. If anyone looked out for Charlie, they did. Maybe they didn't treat him like family, but they always let him sit on the edge of their hubbub, gave him a plate, tried to get him to dance.

IF CHARLIE had a profession, it was as a kind of low-level fence, hauling stuff in and out of the yard at all hours. Bikes, tools, fans, cases of glassware, plants, magazines, kitchen appliances, televisions—things that shouldn't get rained on but did.

In hurricane season we started referring to the place as Projectile Land. I envisioned rusty garden shears and old jelly jars coming at the house in ninety-mile-per-hour winds.

Men would show up and scream "Charlie Duck!" over the fence, and he'd appear under the falling-down arbor, grab a shirt, and disappear for an afternoon or a couple days. We were never sure what the deal was, though he told us once that a local realtor sometimes hired him to throw old fish under the homes of people he didn't like.

When Ed got older, Charlie took a broom and a bucket of blue paint and framed out the borders of a handicapped parking spot that convinced no one. When people continued parking there, he came back with a handicapped parking sign he'd sawed down somewhere, broke a hole in the cement, and planted it next to the parking spot, the sign tilting a bit and about two feet shorter than it should have been, which scared off most people, if only with its strangeness.

After a few years, Charlie started leaving us gifts of a sort on our porch. Semifunctional blenders, handfuls of unmatched forks, handsaws without handles, ten-year-old computer manuals. He gave a full-on wedding dress to our dog sitter, Alison, something she made use of during multiple Fantasy Fests. One night he tossed me a marijuana bud wrapped in a scratched-off lottery ticket,

For thirteen years, the author and his wife lived just across the fence from Charlie Duck's rental (above). It was torn down more than a decade ago.

another time a marijuana bud wrapped in a page from the Bible. (I smoked neither, though I might still have them around somewhere.) The best thing he ever left was a swordfish bill with an orange-and-red sunset scene painted on it by Monkey Tom, the locally famed Stock Island folk artist. (At least we *think* Monkey Tom painted it.)

Usually, a couple hours after he left a gift there would be a knock on the door and he'd ask to borrow money. This progressed to him asking to borrow money without leaving gifts. We considered it the Charlie tax, the cost of peaceful living. Nan kept a running total of how much we loaned him and how much he paid back, until she got too discouraged.

He knocked one night when I was feeling a financial pinch, and I said, "Dude, you have to stop asking me for money."

He was taken aback for a second, then said, "Is Nancy home?"

From then on, if I answered the door, he asked for her.

If friends came by looking for us when we were out, Charlie would tell them which direction we went off in and how long ago we left. We'd come home later and he'd describe whoever it was who stopped by, a sort of Neighborhood Drunk Watch.

I heard a noise in the kitchen one night and came downstairs to find Nan's wallet on the floor. I had the sense someone had been there a few seconds before.

Our dog went out and sniffed at the low fence between our yards, the only one that was easily climbable.

The next day, I asked Charlie if he'd seen anybody, and he said he saw a couple of untrustworthy-looking Black dudes eyeing our place, which I'm quite certain he did not.

ONE NIGHT I was up late, reading in the living room, when Charlie yelled in through the open window, "Hey Mark, you got a tire iron I can borrow?"

I said no, I did not, then posted something snarky on Facebook about the neighbor yelling in the window about a tire iron at 2:00 a.m. I got a like from Andy Thurber, the painter laureate of the Key West cuzzy bubba world, who knew Charlie a bit. The next time I went into my studio, there was a small acrylic-on-wood piece leaning against the door, Andy having painted the scene for me.

When artist Andy Thurber learned that Charlie Duck had asked to borrow a tire iron from the author at 2:00 in the morning, he envisioned the scene.

ED DIED on the Fourth of July. Nan and I came home from the fireworks at the Casa Marina to find the street filled with cop cars and an ambulance, red and blue lights chasing each other around the neighborhood.

We'd lived next door to him for close to a decade.

He'd had a heart attack loading laundry into the washer in one of the sheds, fell facedown in the dirt. At least that's how Charlie described it.

He told us this while we stood on the sidewalk, Boogie on a leash, the uniformed forces of official death flowing around us. We asked Charlie if he needed anything. He said he was good, and he and Boogie headed down the lane to the convenience store.

After they took Ed's body away, Charlie knocked on the door and handed me a well-worn paper bag, the kind you'd bring your lunch in in middle school.

"Hold this for me," he said, and left.

Warily, I looked in the bag and was unsurprised to see a .38 snub-nose pistol and a handful of loose bullets.

I told Nan about it and put it in a drawer, making sure not to get fingerprints on anything.

With Ed gone, I think Charlie was expecting to get kicked off the property right away, but it didn't happen. Ed died without a will. There was no money, but there was a double lot in Old Town Key West, which was worth a great deal, with a house so dilapidated that even the Historic Architecture Review Committee would not argue against tearing it down.

Things were complicated. Lawyers got involved. The place fell into limbo; no one really worried about whether Charlie was there or not.

After a couple weeks he knocked on the door, asked for the paper bag back, and disappeared into the night with a wave and a gun.

THE CUBAN FAMILY across the street eventually moved away, sold the concrete block house for a tidy sum, and bought something three times the size in Ocala. A local contractor came in, tore down the house—it was not considered historic—and built an oversized faux Conch house on the lot, pushing up against the lot lines and the height restrictions, installing such tiny windows the place looked like it was squinting.

Bert, the circumspect taxi driver on the other side of us, who we saw only at 2:00 in the morning when he hosed off his pink cab under the streetlight, died also. His brother Lee inherited Bert's house and started to visit every couple weeks, ostensibly to work on the place but instead went on a series of benders. He got drunk one night and blasted the Beach Boys "Be True to Your School" for a couple hours solid. I banged on the door and the wall to no avail. When I brought it up with him the next day he said nope, sorry, wasn't him.

Lee sold the house to a pharmacist and her husband, relentless spiffer-uppers who kept asking what we were going to do about the peeling paint on our place.

Suddenly we were the old guard in the neighborhood, the ones not living up to the newcomers' standards. Us and Charlie.

WE CAME BACK one day to find a lobster boat parked in Charlie's yard, a mountain of white fiberglass on an oversized trailer. A small crew spent a couple months sanding and painting the hull and rebuilding the engine. The cabin was eye level with our upstairs bedroom window, so we kept the blinds down.

When they were done, they backed a truck up to the trailer hitch, blocking the street. Charlie sat on top of the wheelhouse, straddling the new masthead light, looking not unlike Slim Pickens in *Dr. Strangelove*. A Conch Train turned onto the block and stopped head-to-head with the truck.

"Sir, please reverse your vehicle. You are blocking the road," the driver of the Conch Train said over his loudspeaker.

"Fuck you! You back up!" Charlie yelled from atop the wheelhouse.

"Sir, this vehicle cannot back up," said the voice on the loudspeaker.

"Fuuuck yooouu!" Charlie yelled. "Fuck you! Back up!"

He yelled it over and over again until they did back up.

I felt strangely affectionate towards him for a while after that.

CHARLIE ASKED US for money less often after he moved into the pink house and rented out his old shed to a series of sub-squatters. It's hard to remember all of them, but the first notables were two guys we called the Heroin Brothers—a duo of user-dealers who took over the yard, parking beater cars in Ed's old faux handicap spot, treating Charlie like he was a guest at their place. A stream of people stopped by for five-minute visits throughout the day and night.

The Heroin Brothers eyeballed people as they went by, but differently from Ed—more a juvenile dare than a hope for confrontation. After them came the murderer. He'd worked as crew on a Stock Island commercial fishing boat until he bludgeoned the captain to death, wrapped him in an anchor chain, and threw the body overboard into the two-thousand-foot-deep trench of the Florida Straits. He eluded arrest and lammed it to Georgia, where he hid out until he drove his car into a ditch one day and someone recognized him from his mug shot on *America's Most Wanted*.

We knew all the details because Nancy recognized him. She'd covered his murder trial when she first moved here in the early nineties. And now he was out, living next door, saying hello to her by name whenever he saw her.

I told Charlie we were not happy about a convicted murderer living next door.

"He's alright," he said, "that captain had it coming."

The murderer stayed about a year. One night we heard him yelling, "You think I can't do the time? You think I won't do it?" just before the cops came and took him off in cuffs. Apparently he'd threatened his girlfriend with a pair of scissors over a stolen bicycle, which violated his parole.

I HEARD the tires squeal, then the thump, then the sound of a truck speeding off, followed by an angry howl from Charlie.

I ran out the door.

"It was a black truck. They just kept going," Charlie yelled.

Boogie lay in the street, trying to get up, his legs not working, his head lolling. Blood came out of his mouth. He couldn't get traction.

Charlie stomped back and forth, yelling, unable to look at the one creature on the planet who depended on him, ranting about getting a gun and finding the people in the truck.

I knelt down, tried to pet Boogie from behind, wary of getting bit by a scared and wounded animal. Cars stopped, then the Conch Train. Someone on a scooter went around us.

"Charlie," I said, but he couldn't look. He kept ranting, making violent threats to the driver of the long-gone truck, swearing vengeance, rage being his only bulwark to the reality of it.

The Conch Train driver got out, then a few of the passengers.

"Look at him," one of them said, gesturing toward Charlie. "He doesn't even care about his dog."

Others took pictures.

The driver looked at the dog, looked at Charlie, came over to me.

"Do you know how long this is going to take?" he asked.

I can't remember if I told them all to back up and fuck off individually or as a group.

I found some plywood in the yard, got Charlie to help me slide Boogie onto it, and loaded it into the back of our Saturn wagon. The Conch Train went by before we had the tailgate closed, the driver starting in about Antonio Diaz y Carrasco and the ship's wheel gingerbread.

We headed towards the vet on Flagler. Charlie sat in the front with me. Boogie thrashed in the back, no comfort to be found for anyone.

The vet and his techs came out to the parking lot with a small gurney, told me that they would do everything they could, but that I needed to get Charlie out of there because he was so agitated and overwrought.

I asked Charlie where he wanted to go, and he gave me barely audible directions to a place off Northside Drive. I'm not sure who it belonged to — a friend, a relative, someone he did some work for — but he disappeared up the walkway of a surprisingly trim house.

I went home and spent two hours trying to clean all the blood out of the car.

THE VET put Boogie down. It was the only real option. For days after, Charlie groused angrily, made some empty threats, and began to drink more.

A few weeks later he had a new dog — big, thick, coal black, Lab-ish.

"What his name?" I asked.

"Boogie."

WE NEVER PUT the house on the market. A realtor tracked Nan down at work and made an offer at the behest of two gentlemen from Atlanta.

We loved our house, but it leaked in a dozen places when it rained, and we were looking at $100,000 that we didn't have to make the place waterproof and nice. And we were getting a little tired of the hubbub and the Conch Trains and the domestic disputes.

I asked the realtor if the Atlantans were trying to combine our property with Ed's.

"What? Not that I know of," she said.

We researched listings on the MLS, gave Lynn Kaufelt a list of six places we wanted to see, and scheduled a morning with her.

"I'll show you these," she said, "but you're going to buy the seventh place I'll show you at the end."

The seventh place was on the edge of Old Town, on a street far away from bars, guest houses, and Conch Trains. It was in pretty good shape and had the Key West high-living trifecta: a pool, central air, a driveway.

We hired a moving crew for the first time in our lives.

I DON'T THINK we ever said goodbye to Charlie. It was Key West. You could not *not* run into someone. We knew we'd see him and Boogie II—or whatever number Boogie he was—again.

It turned out the realtor representing the buyer was wrong or, more likely, had lied to us. The two gentlemen from Atlanta combined our property with Ed's. A few years later the combined lots would be featured in the *New York Times* with a three-million-dollar price tag and a glowing description of its "original Dade County Pine floors"— they were not—and its "'informal' cocktail pool." No mention of buried bones or serial killers.

To get Charlie off the property the buyers rented him a trailer somewhere and paid the rent for six months. Nan and I both wondered what would happen after that but didn't know who or how to ask. Charlie's connections had always been murky.

Soon after, we heard Charlie had been diagnosed with throat cancer and was told he had two months to live; he lived three weeks.

We never learned what happened to Boogie II.

AT THE END of that year Nan was writing a piece on the annual communal funeral service for the homeless at the Key West Cemetery. The mayor read off the list of names, slowly and solemnly, until he got to Charlie Russell, then choked up slightly, saying he knew Charlie in high school, didn't know he was homeless (he wasn't, quite), didn't know he had died.

Now, a few years later, those two words written in neat block letters in the Grinnell Street sidewalk in front of our old house might be the last thing left of Charlie, or of either of the Boogies. That, and Andy Thurber's acrylic-on-wood painting. And maybe this.

Otherwhere

———

HAL CROWTHER

IT'S A LITTLE after seven when I walk out on the balcony for my morning survey of the Gulf of Mexico. There are scattered clouds, a steady wind out of the Northeast, and on the beach below me two street urchins, teenagers, doing what they so endearingly call "the wild thing" on our Smith and Hawken deck chair. On the striped cushions under the coconut palm they're fully dressed but fully engaged, managing nicely. Since they had climbed over an eight-foot fence or crawled through the surf under security wires to reach this love nest, it was no insignificant passion that brought them to our beach.

If it had been my front yard in North Carolina, I might have dialed 911 or at least yelled something sarcastic and discouraging ("May I bring you some coffee?") at these callow fornicators. But that's not the Key West way. A certain permissiveness, a hesitation to judge or censor your fellow sinners is part of making yourself comfortable here where the South ends and the United States of America never really found a foothold.

Flexibility is the only viable moral option in Key West, where some of the nicest people you'll meet smuggle marijuana. I overheard two grandfathers doing a domestic drug deal at a cocktail party. Each October, to mark the island's improbable survival through yet another hurricane season, islanders celebrate Fantasy Fest—think Halloween, Mardi Gras, and a touch of the *Rocky Horror Picture Show*—ten days of parades and excess when the boldest revelers stalk Duval Street wearing nothing but body paint. On New Year's Eve, Duval challenges Times Square with its own tradition, a drag queen named Sushi descending from Crabby Dick's balcony in a giant pink slipper. On every moonlit night Cuban boat people stumble up on the beaches, gambling that these islands with too few rules will suit them better than an island with too many.

"The middle-aged traveler [to Key West] feels a little younger, a little thinner and wilder just for walking by and listening."

The most I can manage at the sight of the coupling campers is a heartfelt "Damn." But it's louder than I intend and they disengage, in no particular panic, and the boy helps his girlfriend scramble over the wall. It gives us something to talk about at breakfast. Sex is the least of Key West's favorite mysteries; there's the sense here that unspeakable things are developing behind every garden fence. The middle-aged traveler feels a little younger, a little thinner and wilder just for walking by and listening.

ALISON LURIE titled her Key West novel *The Last Resort*. Though the town makes few demands on its residents or its visitors, there are caveats if Key West is a destination you're considering. If you like your egg the same way every morning, if you praise Holiday Inns because every room's identical, if your world is a geography of golf courses, stay away. If you're a homophobe or a cat-hater, if sloth and scruffiness and ambiguities disturb you, this is not the island of your dreams.

If you ask me why I repeatedly spend part of the winter in Key West, I don't have an easy answer. Does something much deeper than habit draw a reclusive, law-abiding, culturally conservative old gentleman to an island that's his opposite in every way? There are a couple of relevant lines by W. H. Auden:

> Out of a Gothic north, the pallid children
> Of a potato, beer-or-whisky
> Guilt culture, we behave like our fathers and come
> Southward into a sunburnt otherwise . . .

Otherwise is the wonderful word.

I'D NEVER ARGUE that Key West has the best beaches, the best food, or the most remarkable tourist attractions. It may, however, have the best sunsets. Sunset is an elaborate ritual for Key Westers, celebrated every evening with an eccentric beggars' carnival — trained cats, the escape artist, the sword-swallower — on the wharf at Mallory Square. But the sky itself usually steals the show. The journals of John James Audubon, a visitor here in the 1830s, describe the pleasure of spectacular sunsets shared with friends. This year I witnessed a classic, a rare ring of bright clouds like the burly arms of Poseidon reaching toward the ocean, the sun a huge burning ruby cradled in his hands.

The island's elegance ends with its sunsets and the cream of its architecture. Like any winter resort, Key West includes the walled compounds and cool, tiled hotels of the very rich. But they don't set the tone or even noticeably alter it. Words like *raffish, jaded, louche,* even *unwholesome* come to mind when I think of this place.

The drugged and mad and muddled are prominent, sleeping on the sand, moaning in leafy corners. A stone's throw down the beach from our tasteful quarters is the notorious gay entertainment pier locals call "the Dick Dock," where the music is deafening and strobe lights reveal dirty dancing till long after midnight. Duval Street is a wasteland of predatory retailers, selling everything from sex — "The Scrub Club" massage parlor, the drag shows — to rubberized Key Lime pies.

Key West is a warped, elusive aesthetic, a siren song not every traveler can hear. A winter resident, a painter, helped me define it when he asked me if I ever planned to buy a house here, as he had.

"Words like raffish, jaded, louche . . . come to mind. . . . The drugged and mad and muddled are prominent, sleeping on the sand, moaning."

I didn't say so, but for me buying a house in Key West would be like building a hut at Machu Pichu—I love the view, but I could never imagine being part of it. My attachment to the island begins with the fact that it's incurably exotic. It doesn't remind me of anything. You could call it home, it seems to me, only if home was a difficult concept for you, an issue. Except for the handful of Conchs—born in the Keys—everyone here is a visitor.

In my rented house I found Shirley Hazzard's memoir (*Greene on Capri*) of the quintessential traveler, novelist Graham Greene, one of the last of the haunted race of English nomads who fled, in the words of John Updike, "their wet, gray climate, their restrictive class system, their Victorian inhibitions, their Protestant work ethic with its grim Industrial Revolution."

"Even in a chosen setting, he retained the quality of wanderer," Hazzard says of Greene, and quotes Malcolm Muggeridge: "Whatever his circumstances, [Greene] had this facility for seeming always to be in lodgings, and living from hand to mouth. Spiritually, and even physically, he is one of nature's displaced persons."

Nature's displaced persons come in different shapes and colorations. I'm not immune to the charm of family holidays, dogs by the fire, the myth of the rose-covered cottage where the wanderer comes to rest. On the other hand, I noticed early on that most people have one place they write and talk and reminisce about, while I always had many.

I never acknowledged—or needed or missed—one home place where I belonged entirely. I judge each place on its merits, and strangeness is a quality I prize. There are only a few places that seem to recognize the spiritually homeless and make them welcome. Key West is surely one of them. If we're displaced, then this must be a "dis-place," a non-place—a permanent outpost of the Other-where. Nature's DPs, her chronic travelers, are only at peace with the unfamiliar.

Authentic travelers gather here like migratory birds. A young American filmmaker, raised in Rome, confessed that to the best of his knowledge his parents own no furniture. Winter birds of Key West, they rent and make do from season to season, and always have.

Another itinerant Englishman, Cyril Connolly, wrote of "the brisker trajectory of the travel addict, trying not to find but to lose himself in the intoxication of motion." To understand him we need to distinguish between the traveler and his opposite, the tourist, who moves through exotic landscapes collecting snapshots and souvenirs, preferably in a herd of his own kind and loaded down with every-thing familiar he can carry, including his family.

Tourist money saved Key West after the hurricane of 1935 washed away its railroad and the Great Depression put 85 percent of its residents on welfare. (In its nineteenth-century wreck-salvag-ing heyday, Key West was Florida's largest city and the wealthiest community per capita in the United States.)

Bus tourists and cruise-ship lemmings throng Duval all winter. Nowhere in America is there a more existential interface—alien worlds touching briefly—than that Duval Street encounter between a blistered clueless tourist and a salt-cured, sun-dried old wino shrimper with the accusing eye of the Ancient Mariner, who looks as if nothing this side of hell could take him by surprise. But a block or two from Duval, it's as if tourists never existed.

Writers also come to the Keys; never Graham Greene, as far as I can figure, but Hemingway (of course), Tennessee Williams, Wal-

Sunset is an "elaborate ritual" celebrated at Mallory Square with trained cats, escape artists, unicyclists. "But the sky itself usually steals the show."

lace Stevens, James Merrill, scores of others. They're more prized here than in the rest of America, but they overestimate their own impact on the ecology of this strange, slow place. I'm convinced that colonies of writers are on the whole a poor idea.

Don't come to Key West to meet writers. I come here to celebrate diversity, after my own fashion. I climb up to the observation deck on our rooftop just before sunset and survey a Scottish wedding on the hotel pier next door, a bagpiper playing "Amazing Grace." I can see the first lights on the shrimp fleet and on the Dick Dock and a ravaged derelict sleeping something off on the Dog Beach next to Louie's restaurant.

An in-line skater glides up Waddell Street singing softly in Spanish, scattering feral cats. Around the hotel pool, rich Europeans and Latinos air their tans and their sneers. In their midst, oblivious, a teenage boy with Down's Syndrome repeats a yoga routine I seem to recognize as "Greeting the Rising Sun." The local paper reports two albino turkey vultures circling off Big Pine Key. I'm as far from home as I can go without a passport.

Floating Island

KATHRYN KILGORE

They picked up its bones
And built a ship
Practically all ears
Took years to wreck it right

Spit and polish thin they wrenched it
Loose to cruise. Christened it
Key West. Come stay
Afloat Cuban sugarcane
And rum, Stock Island
Cows milk, fighting cocks
Hen's eggs, Saltpond salt juice
Of Key Lime trees, Bahamas cool Spanish
Treasure, cheap square groupers sharks
Stir in slowly
Beat in gradually
Whip until stiff
Scald.
It's so beautiful, or so close to it
Its domicile the blue-green Gulf Stream
Home port coral fossil spindly end
Of an old spine. Stay here.
Live aboard move in go on fly off drive to the end
Capacity to love leaked at the seams 'til it got sick, and
Pirates stole it. Road the Key up the Coast
Shredding shrimpers drifters settlers folks
With songs and tales lost souls great hearts
The usual, painted art bare wood homes, cisterns, fruit trees, trust.
Came back Package Deals. Added to its Rep:
A ride of mangled conch-train rants on cholera and Christ

Whores, wars typhoid salvaged slaves and yellow fever drug
Runners, soaring prices jet ski flu, malaria cheap
Flights, shop here. You told me
I told you Eyebrow house I was Gingerbread sick
By now of cabbages and Covid tourists by the maskless pound.
Stir in slowly:
The night sky
It is beautiful. Or so close to it.
Beat in gradually.
Scald.

Many tourists and cruise ship day-trippers experience the town primarily by strolling up and down Duval Street or riding the Conch Train. Or both.

Squall

JEFFREY CARDENAS

BOOMING cumulonimbus clouds, some as high as sixty-five thousand feet, form over the Everglades and sweep across the Florida Keys with spectral beauty. Below the clouds, tides pulsate in celestial transition, a connection to something extraordinary.

Pilots refer to flying into these clouds as entering IMC—instrument meteorological conditions—the moment when land, sky, and horizon disappear into a blank nothingness. In these conditions, a person's body and mind send contradictory messages to the central nervous system. Weather takes control of even the most basic human instincts: up is down, right is left. Disoriented pilots sometimes fly directly into the sea.

On the water, situational awareness in a whiteout is no less severe. The horizon is shrouded in gauze, a reminder that we can never fully trust what our eyes tell us.

In an open skiff there is no place to hide from the wrath of a tropical squall. Weather commands the moment. Electrical discharge illuminates cloud cocoons, and the convulsion of thunder is visceral. The intense power of the squall actually rips air molecules apart and rearranges them, leaving a hint of sulfur and an acute sense of vulnerability for those caught without cover.

But because this is the tropics, the intensity of the weather can be as ephemeral as a cloud itself. One moment it is blind hell; in the next shafts of light penetrate the gloom and the world slowly reappears, like a photograph developing in a darkroom. What was foreign to the senses becomes familiar. Breathing slows and pulse rates moderate. The squall passes.

There is a crisp quality to the light after a tropical downpour. Nature's brilliant optics are enhanced by sunlight passing through individual drops of water. In a super-saturated atmosphere there is a new dimension to the distant clouds. Shadow and light define the

In the tropics, "the intensity of the weather can be as ephemeral as a cloud itself. One moment it is blind hell; in the next, shafts of light penetrate the gloom."

texture of the water. Few other natural environments change their landscapes so dramatically. Nowhere is the quality of water more sublime than in the calm surface of an ocean tidal flat after the passing of a tropical squall. And, in as little as eighteen inches of fluctuation, this tropical flat produces a life-and-death drama for predators and prey.

As the water rises, bonefish and other shallow water predators press up against the edges of the flat. The first to gain access will have the best seat at a banquet laden with crab and shrimp. Knowing this, bonefish feed on the incoming water with eagerness and enthusiasm; dorsal fins flare, tails quiver. The fish light up with pigments in their cell structure, and they radiate with each discovery of food.

The predatory chain lengthens as the water depth increases. The first arrivals are now prey themselves. The same cell structure that moments before reflected enthusiasm now camouflage the bonefish from sharks and barracuda. Their scales scramble the polarization that many predators—including man—employ to isolate prey.

Even to those of us who live under tropical skies, this urgency of change in weather and tide can seem startling. As the incoming water approaches its peak, an ocean flat can become unrecognizable from what it was mere hours earlier. The fish deviate from the sea bottom's established low-tide trails and disperse. The sheen of high water becomes a quilted patchwork with softer edges. Turtle grass is olive green, a pallet of blues identifies deeper channels, and light patches of sand and marl remain almost translucent. At the flood apex all movement seems to stop, as if the environment takes a breath before beginning the process anew.

More than three hundred years ago, Isaac Newton likened himself to "a boy playing on the seashore . . . whilst the great ocean of truth lay all undiscovered before me." The truths he would ultimately discover included the paths of planets, the ebb and flow of tides, the dissimilarities in rays of light and the properties of their colors. He also defined gravity, this thing that holds us to the earth. We are now the children playing on the seashore.

"Even to those of us who live under tropical skies, this urgency of change in weather can seem startling. . . . At the flood apex all movement seems to stop."

Turtle Eggs

BRIAN ANTONI

I remember watching a turtle lay eggs in the full moon on a sliver of silvery shore as tears dripped from her eyes leaving a trail flowing; notes flowed into the air as I followed the jazz funeral to the graveyard on this bone island trying to avoid the skeletal arms that tried to yank me down.

I was a kid, and I said to my mom, "She's in pain." My mom replied. "A parent will go through endless pain for her child." I tasted them once as a kid: turtle eggs. They were gritty and hard to pierce, like a Ping-Pong ball. I scooped the dripping yellow yoke with a spoon.

Like the little golden spoon that seemed to drip from his shell-like ear. Later he would remove this spoon from his pierced ear and dip it into white powder and hold it up to my nose like a blessed host.

Bridget-the-Turtle has lived through many a resident of a house in Old Town, where she shares a small pond with a school of minnows.

And it was on this trip, on this little speck of hueso, that I discovered there was a place for me in this world.

I was sixteen, running away from boarding school in Ft. Lauderdale; I had found my tribe of misfits and perverts and sodomites and saints, and I knew it would get better. I found myself in Key Weird, found my huevos.

And wounded again by the death of my grandfather, many a life later, I was introduced to a little old man who was bigger than life, at a pretentious South Beach party where everyone was sucking up to whoever was richer or prettier.

Laughing eyes. "I read your novel. I liked it." We talked for hours. "If you ever want to come to Key West, you can stay in my guest apartment above Fastbuck Freddie's on Duval." I knew nothing about him. Before Google. The street I parked on was named after him. I found my new grandfather — Mr. Key West.

The cock crowed as the sun was rising, and the sensual smell of subtropical as I sang a verse from my favorite calypso, "Conch ain't got no bone." I was still pretty in Key West as I smiled to myself after another night of festive-fantasy-fucking.

In South Beach I was old and used. It was a model's world for those who were or wanted to buy them as garnish. Dr. David nursed me back to health with Hershey bars named Barbara and Fridays with Nancy and Writings with Bill and key lime pie and sunset claps and cheap hotdogs and tuna tartare and tales of Tennessee and Truman and "theatre types" which translated to gay-gay in old camp-speak, wink-wink, which led to naughty guffaws with Gary on beloved Ballast Key.

Once again Cayo Hueso seduced me until I threw anchor and bought Herlihy's haunted house. I Midnight-Cowboyed around until the skeletal arms started to yank my OGs down, one by one. Wasted Away by Margaritaville. I held the conch shell against my ear and listened for the answer to the question: "Why do we have to die?"

"The cock crowed as the sun was rising," the poet writes, "as I sang a verse from my favorite calypso, 'Conch ain't got no bone.'"

Now they are all bones on bone island, and tears are dripping down my face as I write this. I am wearing a t-shirt that has a picture of a dinosaur on it that says, "All my friends are dead." And I wish I could jump into my car and just go. Blare Belafonte—Back to Back, Belly to Belly, I don't give a damn, I done dead already, and head south to mile zero, all the way on A1A, to the beginning of the end, and bury myself in that bleached blanket of bones and cry, like that turtle on the beach, and just get the pain out, extrude it like those eggs.

Would you still be able to cure me, my Key West, my one faithful lover? But I am floating on an endless sargasso stuffed sickened sea of death. Stuck. Quarantined. Fighting to keep my parents alive. I've been to three zoomerals this week. Corona. No Lime. Just death! Mayday! Mayday! I am the turtle now, and my mom and dad are the eggs. "This child will go through endless pain for his parents."

The Last Resort

ALISON LURIE

KEY WEST is the last and largest of the Florida Keys, a linked chain of islands running southwest from below Miami. It is sometimes referred to as "the last resort," not only because of its geographical position, but because for people who have not prospered elsewhere it can be the end of the line, a final chance. Mostly, it is a famous tourist destination, known for its warm climate, exotic flora and fauna, and laid-back, permissive ambiance; for many years my husband and I have escaped northern winters here. But it took me a long time to dare to write about it. I had never been there before January 1 or after April 15, and I knew that much of the life of the island was probably hidden from me.

For a documentary film in 2012 Alison Lurie read from The Last Resort, *the only novel she set in Key West. In 1984 she won a Pulitzer Prize for* Foreign Affairs.

I decided that I could get away with setting a novel in Key West, however, if my main characters were also what are called on the island, sometimes a little scornfully, "winter people." They would not know much about the place, so its impact on them could be more surprising and dramatic. They would be relatively inexperienced travelers, but they need not, indeed must not, be fools, because then the book would be boring. They would also have led a relatively sheltered life, and for maximum effect, they would not be a good fit with the place.

I therefore made my hero, Wilkie Walker, a lifelong New Englander, and a professor at Converse College, the smaller and more isolated of the two imaginary educational institutions I had invented for earlier novels. He is a scientist and also a rather con-

"For many years my husband and I . . . escaped northern winters [in Key West]. But it took me a long time to dare to write about it."

ventional person, someone whom the arty reputation of Key West will repel rather than attract. His wife, Jenny, is intelligent but less well educated than Wilkie. She is also somewhat shy and unworldly and does not really consider herself a feminist. She is considerably younger than her husband and has devoted her life to him and his work.

Wilkie and Jenny have never up to now been winter people. They have spent most of their lives in New England and are not drawn to the tropics, nor to any crowded, colorful, laid-back location. Wilkie assumes that when strong, active, serious people like him take a winter vacation, they will go north to cold steep places—ski resorts, for instance. Weak, lazy, frivolous people will go south, to warm flat places. Key West is a good example of the kind of resort Wilkie Walker would avoid under normal circumstances. But at the start of my book his circumstances are not normal. He believes that he is suffering from terminal cancer and has selected Key West as a good place to commit suicide by drowning and make it look like an acci-dent. It is his hope that in this way he can avoid a painful and pro-tracted death and spare his beloved wife the pain of witnessing it.

If I was going to write about Key West, I also needed some local characters who live and work there year-round, people who belong to the place and even typify it. I invented two principal ones: Perry Jackson, known as Jacko, a lovable young gay gardener, and Lee Weiss, the tough, warmhearted owner of a women-only guesthouse. Though they have been residents and citizens for years, neither Jacko nor Lee are native Key Westers, but this in fact is typical. Jacko grew up in Oklahoma, where, except for his mother, his family is political and reactionary and ashamed of him. Lee is a former therapist from Brooklyn who eventually decided that nothing she could do for her clients could counteract the malevolent influence on them of urban life.

I also reused at least five characters from my earlier novels. When I can, I always try to do this, because it saves time and gives them depth and interest. I don't always know what has become of people after the end of their books, however, and when I do, it sometimes bothers me. Barbie Mumpson, the unhappy, awkward daughter of the hero of *Foreign Affairs*, was someone I felt particularly guilty about. When that novel ended, Barbie's father, an admirable and affectionate person, was dead, and since then she has continued to be oppressed and exploited by her ambitious mother, Myra, who has married her off to a narcissistic, adulterous right-wing politician. I decided to bring Barbie to Key West, where she could possibly grow up and find a happy future. Of course, Myra had to come too, and so, it turned out, did Dorrie Jackson, Myra's much nicer sister, who is the mother of Perry Jackson and very much resembles him. When these people got to Key West, things would happen to all of them. Key West would also change Wilkie Walker's life and the life of his wife, Jenny, as it has in the past changed many other lives, including mine.

Right now, though, in the spring of 2020, it is Key West that seems changed. Because of the worldwide virus epidemic, a lively, noisy, crowded resort town has become a silent, almost deserted stage set, through which a few solitary ghosts in white masks, some of them on bicycles, move through empty streets. Sometimes a pool service truck or a police car passes; otherwise the only sound is the crowing of many roosters and the roar of an occasional unmarked plane.

Normally, my husband and I would be long gone by now, but this year we may spend much more than a few months in Key West, especially if we become ill. Even if all goes well, the island I wrote about years ago will never be the same, and neither will any novel anyone else writes about it. I wish them all good luck.

Grinnell Street Rag

ROSALIND BRACKENBURY

Last night we sat on broken chairs
to hear the guitar man across the street
play us the old songs.
Two tiny girls danced in their skirts,
people paused on their bicycles.
We sipped our wine from jars
and no cars passed.
This is how it used to be, we said,
back in the day. When the island
was still and we could play and sing
and hear each other speak
and sit out on the street.
It's like finding an old love, we said,
or someone we used to love but no longer can.
Here it is, our old love —
the island they call paradise,
stripped of all pretension,
traffic, tourists, planes, and massive ships —
death ships we call them now —
free of its blight,
calm, as the sun sets, lovely,
ours again tonight.

Homesick

PEYTON EVANS

I'M ON THE PORCH of a white Victorian cottage on Shelter Island, a picturesque four-by-five-mile enclave between the north and south forks of eastern Long Island. I've rented it for the month of August. The porch overlooks an expanse of rolling green—a tiny park—that drops down to a quiet harbor. The water is still. I can see a dock, a yacht or two. A couple of dinghies are lassoed to some pilings. There is no one about. An hour ago, I saw a man paddle by in a canoe; occasionally a few people in tennis whites pass by on their way to the courts, and oh, there goes a guy on a bike. This seems to be a very quiet island.

This porch is nice, just like the pictures I saw on the rental website: a wicker loveseat, soft nautical-striped pillows. Potted geraniums. A metal dining table and four chairs under an umbrella. When my guests come, we can sit, have lunch, and look down at the harbor—if this heat relents by then. There's air-conditioning inside, thank God, comfy beds, a shabby-chic living room—white curtains, white cotton slipcovers—this is the way I like it. There's a country kitchen and a sun-drenched breakfast table by the window. This is a good house.

Across the street there's an old inn. It has a wide porch set up for dining, a view of the harbor, and next to the inn there's an old-fashioned pharmacy with a soda fountain. I sat at the counter there yesterday for lunch and ordered a burger. A thin gray patty came on a cold bun with a slice of partly melted American cheese, pickle on the side. I chomped it down, thinking about Azur's cheeseburger on ciabatta bread with that incredible sauce and a heap of featherlight shoestring fries scattered round. I wouldn't mind having the plump burger at Sarabeth's either, sitting on a bed of arugula with a side of jicama slaw.

This morning I went to stock up on groceries at the IGA. There were local summer tomatoes, corn, farm-fresh eggs, juicy peaches. I piled some of all that into my cart. The IGA seemed fine, but Jimmy Weekley wasn't behind the meat counter, and there was no one I knew in the aisles. I found no wine for sale in this grocery, and there were no *Key West Citizens* stacked by the door, no copies of *Conch Color* either. There were notices on the bulletin board for yard sales to be held at houses of strangers and an announcement of a bake sale at the firehouse. As I drove back to the rental, I passed a church. Clapboard and steepled, it was set back against a shadowy woods. I'm thinking of the white steeple of St. Paul's and how when you look up at it from the corner of Eaton and Duval Streets it shines crisply against the deep blue Key West sky.

The houses scattered over this island are dollhouse size and out of a storybook. Peaked roofs with gothic windows, a turret here and there, front porches, swings, dappled sunlight spread over wide lawns. There's much fretwork of course and gingerbread—a lot of ginger-bread. But I'm thinking of the yellow house with the wraparound porch on Southard Street, the one that was built by a baker a hundred and fifty years ago, where the gingerbread is jigsawed into long rows of wooden gingerbread men. And there's the musician's house with vi-olins as gingerbread—is that on Elizabeth Street? Or is it Frances?

I guess I could rent a bike. But there are a lot of hills here, steep ones. I'd like to go to a movie, but there's no theater on the island. I'd have to take a ferry to one of the busy little towns across the bay, and that seems a lot of effort. I wonder what's playing at the Tropic?

"I'd like to go to a movie, but there's no theater on the island," the author remembers thinking. "I wonder what's playing at the Tropic?"

Varadero Dreaming

ALEJANDRO F. PASCUAL

I FEEL BLESSED to have been born and raised in the charming, historic city of Cardenas, Cuba. Two hours east of Havana by car and smack under the Tropic of Cancer, it boasts a port where most of Cuba's fishing fleet was built and from which refined sugar in white bags and brown sugar in brown bags was exported to the far corners of the world. As kids, my friends and I would follow the sugar trucks on our bicycles to watch the stevedores load the sweet cargo into awaiting vessels.

Historically the city is known as the place where in 1850 the Cuban flag was first raised, as troops under the command of Narciso Lopez, a Venezuelan-born Spanish army general, tried and failed to liberate Cuba from Spain. (Lopez had designed the flag for his troops to carry.) Grateful to the local citizenry for not joining the invaders, the Queen of Spain gave Cardenas a statue of Christopher Columbus that adorns the city's Central Colonial Plaza to this day.

Cardenas's Varadero Beach is considered one of the world's most beautiful, with more than twenty kilometers of powdered white sand shaded by casuarina trees, protecting it from erosion. I loved it passionately. Varadero's tip is Cuba's northernmost point, a mere 89.7 miles due south of Key West.

The Cuba I knew growing up in the 1950s was ruled by a corrupt dictator, Fulgencio Batista, but if you did not challenge his authority—and we did not—things were mostly ok, at least for us kids. Besides, we had Freedom Fighters in the mountains battling Batista's forces and promising to deliver what Cubans most wanted: an honest government attuned to the needs of its people. Little did we know what was to come.

We were extraordinarily proud of our country; the "Cuban soul" possessed us. (My wife, Gloria, who was also born in Cuba, calls it the "Cuban *ego*.") We knew we lived on an island of only nine million

Growing up in Cardenas, Cuba, the author loved Varadero Beach "passionately"—twenty kilometers of powdery white sand shaded by casuarina trees.

people, but we felt it an enchanted land. Our sugar sweetened the world's tea and coffee. Our cigars were prized the world over; our rum was without equal. (We boys were also in love with Cuban girls, who we were certain were unrivaled in beauty, grace, and sweetness. Gloria agrees.)

We also loved our Spanish ancestors' seafood and paellas, as well as our own black beans, rice, and fried plantains—with mouthwatering desserts of guava, mangoes, and tamarind followed by strong black coffee. Our capital, Havana, had become the playground of the rich and famous. The international crowds who filled the city's nightclubs swayed to the rhythms of the rhumba, mambo, son cubano, and cha cha cha.

We had other reasons to be proud. The University of Havana attracted students from all over the Caribbean and beyond. In 1921, Cuba's Jose Raul Capablanca had become the first world chess champion from a non-European country. When Ernest Hemingway's marriage to second wife Pauline Pfeiffer ended, he moved with his third wife, Martha Gelhorn, to a finca outside Havana, where he lived for the next two decades. After 1954, the year he won a Nobel Prize for his novel about a Cuban fisherman, *The Old Man and the Sea*, it was not unusual to see a copy of *El Viejo y el Mar* on display in many a Cuban household. (John Dos Passos had first lured Hemingway to Key West in 1940 with, among other promised attractions, authentic Cuban cuisine.)

Many of us would carry our pride with us into exile—through survival, setbacks, and successes—in my case for almost sixty years. I think we will always be nurtured by the Cuba our grandparents and parents built with love and tenacity. But the advent of Fidel Castro would destroy much of this feeling, even as it fills our hearts to this day.

Fidel Castro came to power on January 1, 1959. Within two years, he had embraced Communism for himself and his government. He decreed that all schools emphasize the evils of past governments, U.S. aggression, and the injustices of capitalism. We were also to be taught the virtues of the Revolution; progress, happiness, and fulfillment would soon be ours.

Along with a few schoolmates, I began to speak out in class against what today might be called a disinformation curriculum. Despite teacher reprimands to keep quiet, three of us refused to do so. Police soon picked us up at school and took us to a police station, where our parents were summoned to come and get us.

As kids, the author (above) and his friends followed the sugar trucks on bicycles to watch stevedores load their cargo onto waiting vessels.

When my father—a clothing merchant whose business had been confiscated the year before—arrived, the police captain told him I had been spouting imperialistic propaganda. And since I was a minor (I was then twelve years old), my father would be held responsible for any future disobedience on my part. When we got home, he told me I had done nothing wrong, but I had to please stop speaking out in class. For a time I held my tongue, but one day I just couldn't take it anymore. When I got home from school, I told my father I wanted to punch the teacher.

That did it! My father told me he was taking me out of school; he said he would find a way for me to follow my older sister, Marta, out of Cuba. I began taking private English and math classes. The government announced that boys like me—active in a church—would be sent to a re-education camp to be molded into proper revolutionaries. In response, my church, the Presbyterian church of Cardenas, concocted a plan to obtain visas for three boys to attend a nonexistent youth meeting in Mexico City. I was one of the lucky three.

On November 23, 1964, I flew to Mexico City and was met at the airport by an American missionary, who had found a family to house me in a Mexico City suburb. With the help of the missionary and the International Red Cross I was able to contact Marta in New Jersey; she sent me an affidavit attesting to our relationship and guaranteeing my financial security. That made it possible for me to go to the U.S. as a permanent resident. On January 25, I flew from Mexico to New York. It would be three long years before my parents could join us in New Jersey.

Five years earlier, my sister Marta and her then boyfriend Juan Jose had become Presbyterian missionaries in Cardenas. But because the revolutionary government frowned on religion, Juan Jose was falsely accused of antirevolutionary activities and sent to jail. Repeatedly. In 1961 he and my sister got married and decided to leave Cuba, which, after clearing a few hurdles, was still possible to do. In the United States Juan Jose was offered a job as a pastor in a largely Hispanic Presbyterian church in Vineland, New Jersey.

I moved in with Marta and Juan Jose and enrolled in Vineland High. Adjusting to my new surroundings was not easy, but "Cuban soul" and memories of Varadero helped keep a smile on my face. To escape New Jersey's harsh winters after high school, I enrolled in Eckerd College in St. Petersburg, Florida, where I studied international affairs.

After graduating from Eckerd in 1973, I bought a car and pointed it south. Even as a child I knew of Key West, which was reachable from Cuba, by airplane or ferry, and I wanted to see it for myself. The farther I drove, the more the aromas and scenery reminded me of my childhood. And when I reached Key Largo and saw a sign that read "Crocodile Crossing," I knew I would feel at home in the Florida Keys with that bright sky and sunshine reflecting off clear blue waters. (And with mangroves, coco plums, palm trees, bougainvilleas, casuarinas, and crotons in profusion.) The stacked lobster traps in Islamorada brought tears to my eyes; I almost felt I was back in Cuba.

When I reached Key West, a rooster chasing an iguana caught my eye. *This is it!* I remember thinking. If I cannot return to Cuba, I will someday make Cayo Hueso (Bone Island) — as Ponce de Leon called it for the Indian remains he found there — my home. On Duval Street, Key West's main drag, I drove by an abandoned school known as the San Carlos Institute, not then knowing what it would come to mean for me decades later.

Returned to New Jersey I landed a job with the state's Department of Education as a consultant to Hispanic migrant parents and their children. Before long I was able to buy a condominium, the sale of which five years later at a handsome profit — after casinos had come to Atlantic City — financed my wanderlust. I bought a Volkswagen camper and for the next two years drove it through Mexico and Central and South America, exploring pre-Columbian sites, for which I'd developed a passion, and searching for Varaderos. More importantly I was meeting people in many countries, which would serve me well in the months and years ahead.

The "Crazy Trip," as my family called it, led to a job as a marketing director for Latin America and the Caribbean for Newsweek International, where I met Gloria. For the next two decades, I visited advertising, subscription, and distribution managers in forty-two countries all over the hemisphere. (Some days I would have breakfast in one country, lunch in another, and dinner in a third.)

By 1994, Gloria and I had three children, two boys and a girl. On vacation each summer for a decade, we would all pile into a car filled with bicycles and gear and drive to Key West. Once there, Fort Zachary Scott's rocky cove became our favorite hangout place. Increasingly, I relished visiting the San Carlos Institute, where Rafael Peñalver, a Miami lawyer born in Cuba, was leading the effort to bring the Institute back to life as a bastion of Cuban history.

BY 1868, Cuba and Puerto Rico were Spain's last remaining colonies in the Americas; of course, both sought independence. Carlos Manuel de Cespedes, a wealthy Cuban landowner, launched an insurrection from his farm in the town of Yara. On October 10, 1868, he freed his slaves, enlisted them in the revolt, and, joined by other landowners and their slaves, led guerrilla attacks against the Spanish army in what would become known as the "Ten Year War."

Spain responded by jailing suspected and potential insurrection-
ists. Cubans, eventually in the thousands, fled, most to Key West.
Among them, in 1869, were two journalist activists — José Dolores
Poyo and Juan Maria Reyes. Each would play outsized roles in the
exile community and, with José Martí, the Cuban writer and nationalist, in the Cuban independence movement. (Martí made several
visits to Key West where he united the exile community and helped
plan the efforts that led to the Spanish-American War and, in 1902,
to a free Cuba.) Poyo would start a newspaper (*The Yara*), which
would become the main source of news for Cuban exiles in the
United States of the late nineteenth century. Along with Reyes, Poyo
also founded the San Carlos Institute, which became the town's
center of Cuban social, cultural, and political life.

Key West was growing rapidly. Two years before Poyo's arrival,
a German entrepreneur named Samuel Seidenberg had opened a
cigar factory, where his workers, mostly from Spain, rolled tobacco
leaves imported from Cuba (allowing him to evade the large taxes
levied on Cuban cigars). Two of Cuba's other cigar makers — Vicente
Martinez Ibor and Eduardo Hidalgo Gato — soon followed. Within
a few years no fewer than 119 factories were flourishing in Key West.

By 1878, Carlos Manuel de Cespedes, son of the same wealthy
landowner who launched the Ten Year War a decade earlier, was
elected the first Cuban mayor of Key West. Within another two
years, Cubans had become the largest ethnic group in the city, esti-
mated at ten thousand.

The early years of the twentieth century saw prosperous Cuban
exiles in Key West living in two worlds, traveling as often as they
wished to their country of birth to take in Havana's renowned en-
tertainments, shop in world class stores, or frequent highly regarded
doctors. (Pan American Airways launched its maiden flight from
Key West to Havana in 1927.)

MY OWN FAMILY'S move to Key West sixteen years ago was pre-
cipitated, at least in part, by the 2001 terrorist attacks of 9/11. Reper-
cussions from this terrible event led to significant losses in
international magazine advertising. *Newsweek, Time, Business Week,* and
the *Economist* were all forced to cut back. In 2003, *Newsweek* offered
early retirement to more than fifty employees in my department alone.

I was hardly devastated. In fact, I could not have been more pleased. I had loved my job for more than two decades, but at age fifty-three I was ready for a change. Returned to New Jersey, I began coaching Little League baseball, basketball, and soccer. A life-long collector of postage stamps, I started a business trading and selling them. Gloria began teaching. But after three New Jersey winters, the time had come: Cayo Hueso finally became our home.

Once settled in Key West I continued my business selling and trading stamps, did some consulting in magazine marketing, and began volunteering at the San Carlos Institute. For many years now I have opened its doors four days a week to welcome the many visitors who have come to learn of Cuba's culture, beauty, and history. Once again I have a dream job.

I'M GUESSING that today some six thousand people of Cuban heritage live in Key West, divided roughly into three groups: descendants of those who fled Cuba during the war against Spain in the late 1800s, those who came here in the 1960s and '70s following Castro's seizure of power (including those who left by way of 1980's Mariel Boatlift, and those who arrived in the last twenty years as travel restrictions eased somewhat.

Descendants of the first group are very Americanized, and though many speak a bit of Spanish, they have largely assimilated into the general population as professionals or business managers. Though there are exceptions, members of this group rarely travel to Cuba. Many have married outside their culture. Even so, rice and beans, pulled pork, fried plantains, cafecito (called *buchi* in Key West), and cafe con leche remain mainstays of their diet.

The second group, which includes Gloria and me, came to the U.S. in the early days of the revolution. This group maintains, or tries to, traditional Cuban values, customs, and cuisine. But we are also Americans who love our adopted country and have benefited from its opportunities. We are proud of our achievements, particularly in education. (My three children are all multilingual college graduates.)

Most of us in this group do not visit Cuba; we're all too aware that the money we would spend there will find its way into the pockets of the twenty-one families who rule the island like a feudal society. Though we send money to relatives who need it desperately, we de-

Since retiring from his "dream job," Pascual has been encouraging visitors to the San Carlos Institute (above) to appreciate Cuba's culture and history.

spair over where too much of it ends up. Neither my wife nor I plan even to visit our beloved birthplace until there is regime change there.

The third group is comprised of more recent arrivals who coped with restrictions and hardships for so many years. Now they pour their energy into the pursuit of the American dream. Many have found jobs with the city, some are fisherman, and others work at hotels and in restaurants. And some have opened small businesses. Their children are graduating from high school and college. They travel to Cuba and send money to relatives. Some maintain properties in Cuba to which they someday hope to return. Their diet is almost exclusively Cuban.

Gatherings of all three groups are rare. The last such event I remember was in July 2021 after Cuban citizens took to Havana's streets to protest food and medicine shortages and the government's tepid response to the Covid pandemic. Scores of Key West's Cubans turned out in front of the San Carlos Institute to express their solidarity with Havana's protestors.

NO MATTER WHEN they came to the United States, Cubans love music. The old-timers' taste runs to the rich Cuban melodies they learned in their youth while younger exiles prefer reggaeton, a reggae hip-hop mix. (Many of the oldsters still play double nine dominoes.) But young or old, Cubans tend to be family oriented. That's certainly the case in our house where my youngest son's Sunday night visits for his weekly fix of rice and black beans constitute a major portion of our social life. Gloria and I are devoutly stay-at-home creatures and always have been. (As a boy, my mom called me "el hermitano," the hermit.)

On the rare occasions when we do entertain friends, we do so at home, offering mojitos or frozen daiquiris (Hemingway's favorite, especially those at Havana's Floridita bar), followed by dinners of Cuban cuisine topped off by cafecito and, for the men (and some women), a good Dominican cigar.

At home of an evening, we spend a lot of time listening to music: bossa nova, boleros, and flamenco in particular. We also watch foreign movies from the '60s and '70s. (Our guilty pleasure: Brazilian and Turkish soap operas.)

In 1921, Cuba's Jose Raul Capablanca became the first world chess champion from a non-European country— and a national hero.

Gloria often brings work home and when that's taken care of reads for pleasure, mostly biographies and historical fiction. My all-time favorite book is Hermann Hesse's *Siddhartha*. The man who became the Buddha spent his declining years taking travelers from one side of a river to the other. Mine are spent greeting travelers who come to the San Carlos to learn Cuba's vaunted history.

Happy as we are in Key West, I firmly believe—and fervently hope—that the most important chapter in the Cuba–Key West romance is yet ahead of us. I'm sure the day will come when Cuba will again be free and I will breathe Varadero's salty air and walk its silken sands once more.

Be Careful What You Wish For

JUDY BLUME

—————

I KNOW PEOPLE who have always wanted to own a bookstore. Some say it was their childhood fantasy, others say it's their fantasy for retirement, and some have never stopped dreaming the dream. I was *not* one of them. It never occurred to me, though I always loved books and reading. My childhood fantasies were more about being a cowgirl, a detective, or a movie star. Becoming a writer was never on my list either. That I've been writing for more than fifty years is still a surprise to me.

I was always a reader. My mother took me to the public library in Elizabeth, New Jersey, every week from the time I was four. At home I played librarian, wishing I had a pencil with a rubber stamp attached like the real librarians had. The first bookstore I visited was the Ritz Bookshop on North Broad Street in Elizabeth, just around the corner from my father's dental office and across the street from the Ritz movie theater. Where the books at the public library smelled warm and ripe, like a well-loved blankie or stuffed animal, connecting me to all the other children who had read them, the books at the Ritz Bookshop smelled new. I always opened them and sniffed before turning the pages. They had a wonderful scent. Printer's ink, I've learned, though I couldn't identify the smell then.

When my husband George and I first got to Key West in 1994, it was a thrill to find a thriving community of artists and writers, multiple bookstores, and a public library painted pink. We fell in love with the town and the people. One of the used bookstores reeked of cat urine, but that didn't stop book lovers from browsing and buying. I got lost (literally) in the stacks the first few times I tried to find my way to the room in back that served as a gym where

I worked out with Bill Yankee. When Bill moved to a better location, I missed chatting with the regulars who hung out inside the entrance to the store.

A few years later, a charming indie bookstore opened, Blue Heron Books on Duval Street, and for the next couple of years our group of writer friends held all our book signings there. You might find Ann Beatty, Phyllis Rose, Robert Stone, Alison Lurie, David Kaufelt, Bill Wright, and more at a pub party. We all supported one another and came out to celebrate. Two of my publishers, then retired and living in Key West—the elegant Ross Claiborne and the feisty Bill Grose—also joined us. If this town wasn't heaven, I didn't know what was.

But too quickly and sadly, Blue Heron closed. The rent was high, not enough walk-in traffic—the owner also had a day job selling real estate. There was a Waldenbooks on the Boulevard. I shopped there once; the salesperson didn't seem to know anything about books. Then, happy day, a new indie, Voltaire Books, opened at the corner of Eaton and Simonton Streets. Voltaire was small and they didn't have a lot of stock, but they'd order any title you wanted. Plus they sold a cool eyeglass cloth with a map of Key West on it so you'd never get lost.

We started having book signings there. I enjoyed chatting with the owner, a very nice guy who had *always* wanted a bookstore. He spent most of his time in Washington, D.C., working at his real job but was at the store whenever he got to Key West. In the meantime the onsite bookseller liked to dish, and I liked stopping by to hear his stories. He could be snarky. Some people I knew wouldn't go in because they didn't like his attitude. But after a few years, Voltaire closed, too. The usual problems: high rent and not enough street traffic. I was crushed when I heard the news. Where once we had an array of bookstores, this small city with a long history of writers, from Hemingway to Meg Cabot, now had just one, and it specialized in used and remaindered books.

I started to feel the need for a full-service bookstore in town.

WE MET Mitchell Kaplan, founder of Books & Books, and one of the country's preeminent booksellers, when we stopped for lunch at his bookstore café in one of his Miami stores. Before long we were

After writing bestsellers—90 million copies sold!—Judy Blume and her law professor husband, George Cooper, founded a bookstore at the Studios of Key West.

talking about the possibility of Mitch opening a store in Key West. He liked the idea, but there were several problems. Rents in Old Town were exorbitant. The distance from Miami—150 miles— meant staff would have to live in Key West where affordable housing was limited. Finally Mitch said, "This is going to work only if you and George find a space and figure out how to pay for it. Then I'll affiliate with you and be your mentor."

George crunched the numbers. The for-profit store calculations were grim.

The Studios of Key West is a nonprofit thriving arts center— visual arts, theater, music— that had just relocated to the old Masonic Temple in Old Town. As they completed a multimillion-dollar renovation, one question remained: what to do with the storefront space at the corner of Eaton and Simonton Streets.

George, who was on the Studios board brought up the idea at a meeting—how about a bookstore? A bookstore—really? Remember what happened to Voltaire when it occupied the same space? We remembered. George crunched again. He doesn't give up easily. With a favorable rent, creative use of volunteers, and a little help from its friends, he had turned the Tropic Cinema into a showcase four-screen movie theater just two blocks from the Studios. He thought he could do the same with a bookstore.

A few weeks later, at the end of October 2015, half a dozen fans of the bookstore idea coalesced while on a Studios-sponsored arts trip to Tulsa, Oklahoma. On a two-hour bus ride we confronted the essential questions: Was this a pipe dream? What would it take to get off the ground? By the time we arrived, we had pledges of half the money we'd need. And when we got back home and word got out, we had the rest.

BACK TO MITCH, who stepped up very quickly. He had most of the shelving and fixtures in storage from a renovated branch store, which were ours for the taking, along with an experienced store designer/builder who could fill in the missing pieces at a reasonable price. We'd use the name Books & Books @ the Studios. We could draw upon the expertise of his book buyer to stock our shelves and to train our own staff. But we would belong to the Studios and seek to generate a modest profit to compensate for use of the space. We were really going to do this!

The adventure began. The floor was covered with moldy carpet. That had to go, as did the ratty tile under it, leaving an oddly patterned concrete floor with splotches of gray cement to fill in the holes. Could we poly over it and call it a historic artifact, saving $20,000? George convinced me. (I can't tell you how many people called in the beginning asking who did our floor and how to get in touch. Deep breath—our floor, at least, was a success.)

The cash wrap, the hub of the store, where I would—at last— have a cash register, was designed and built by Mitchell's team. My *thing* for cash registers went way back to the toy one I had as a child and where I played butcher shop, carefully crafting hot dogs, hamburgers, and steaks from green, yellow, red, and brown clay. I would argue with my pretend customers when they questioned my prices or the quality of my meats. During the early days of the Key West Film Society (later, the Tropic Cinema),

I would sell tickets out of a cigar box and was known as the slowest change maker ever.

Before we had time to think about what we were taking on, we were up and running. How much did we know about running a bookshop? More than we knew about running a butcher shop, but not that much more.

We hired a manager and an assistant manager. Neither had any experience running a bookstore, but they were local and had housing, almost as important in Key West as having experience. One had worked in retail; the other struck me as someone who could do anything.

Mitchell sent down a crew to install the shelves and Super Bookseller Vivian to train us. I still remember everything Viv said. Keep it fresh. Keep it beautiful. Never stop dusting. She taught us about displays. How to deal with customers. How to keep paperback book covers from curling. Before the books were unpacked, we had customers knocking on the door, sometimes coming in pulling books out of the cartons. *Wait! We're not open for business yet.* The excitement and enthusiasm affected all of us. Apparently we were open for business, if not officially. People were eager to sign up as volunteers.

OPENING NIGHT, February 4, 2016: The store was crowded with customers and well-wishers. It was one of the most exciting nights of my life. (I had no idea then how much there was to learn, how hard the work would be.) Suddenly we had a bookstore, a real bookstore, with the newest titles in most genres and the classic titles no bookstore should be without—more than four thousand of them.

Our first Sunday we opened our doors wide to catch the breeze. It took us a while before we realized an iconic Key West chicken had strolled in and made her way to the back of the store where she seemed to be browsing. We didn't want to freak her out and have her start flying around, pooping on books on display tables. So we very quietly urged her to the front of the store and out the door. I don't think being in a bookstore was her thing, but who knows? Lesson learned.

When we opened, we assumed our business would come mostly from locals. We hadn't thought of Key West tourists as readers. We were *so* wrong! Some came from towns without an indie bookstore and sent boxes of books home. I shamelessly posed for pictures with anyone who wanted one as long as they purchased a book, any book. And how exciting to introduce readers to books I've loved.

I GET ANXIOUS every time we schedule an author appearance, sure no one will show up. Key West is a busy town with multiple events going on every night. It's like giving a dinner party with no RSVPs and a guest of honor you don't want to disappoint. I'm so grateful when people come through the door.

Tayari Jones was scheduled to come to town during her book tour for *An American Marriage*. But a snowstorm in the Northeast prevented Tayari from traveling. We'd billed this as a big event. What to do? We had a large poster of her thanks to her publisher. Now we set it up on a table in front of the audience. Then we got Tayari on the phone, and because Tayari can charm an audience from a thousand miles away, the evening was a hit.

One of my favorite events was the night we hosted Kay Redfield Jamison, perhaps the world's leading expert on bipolar disorder. Her latest book was a biography of Robert Lowell, who suffered from the illness. I'd promised the publisher we could bring in a good audience. George got on the phone and called every mental health professional in the Lower Keys, and we had our biggest audience to date.

And this is how it goes every time. You promise the publicist that you'll do your very best to bring in an audience for their author. If you come through, you'll find it easier the next time. The good news is it's Key West. Writers want to see it for themselves, or they remember the good times they've already had here and want to come back.

Simply, I love it! I get out of bed every morning eager to get to the store. I pet the books. Every bookseller has a word to describe this ritual of walking around, greeting the books, laying hands on them. I haven't met one yet who doesn't do this.

My life as a writer has been better and more adventurous than any fantasy I might have had. But after fifty-plus years of staring at blank sheets of paper, I was ready for something new. I never dreamed the change would be running a bookstore, nor how it would

"George crunched the numbers," says Blume. "The for-profit store calculations were grim. . . . George crunched again. He doesn't give up easily."

affect my life. There's a Yiddish expression I like: *Basherdt*. Something that's meant to be. This was meant to be.

ON MARCH 14, 2020, our grown children—Lawrence, Randy, and Amanda—called to say they were concerned. We really shouldn't be working at the store. Tourists could bring us the new corona virus, and because of our age and the cancer treatments both of us have had, we were vulnerable. We both knew they were right. Even though I'd been giving elbow bumps instead of hugs since the bookstore opened (great advice from our local doctor, Bob Olson), there was no way for me to social distance at the store.

The day we stopped working in the store was a sad day. But Emily, Gia, Robin, and Lori kept the store going. Once we closed for browsing in person, we moved to shopping online and by phone. We even delivered locally—order your book by noon, receive it by 4:00 p.m. A masked and gloved Emily or Gia would bring your book to your door. Emily dropped off boxes of books for me to sign.

But, oh, how I missed my Books & Books family. I was used to spending four days a week at the store. There was always more to do. I'd have worked six days if certain people (*ahem*) gave their blessing. And lunch—I missed lunch in the "cafeteria," a drop-down shelf George attached to one of the two desks in our tiny office. This is the room where we receive and return books, where gifts are wrapped, where Emily and Gia work when they're not on the floor, arranging events, or doing all the business that goes on behind the scenes.

Our volunteers are part of our community, our extended family. I missed admiring Anna's latest necklace, missed hearing Shelli welcoming customers to the store, missed talking books and authors with Michael, our local library director who volunteers on Sundays. I wonder how we ever managed without Gianelle who came to the store one day and asked if we were hiring. She became our assistant manager but had to leave when her husband was transferred. Robin has been there from the beginning. First as a volunteer, now as our director of social media. She started our virtual book club and keeps it going. She knows every YA and middle-grade series and every science fiction title. She has what may be the world's best laugh. She loves every dog who comes to the store and keeps a special treat behind the cash wrap for each one of them. Happy day that Lori, who was a manager at the Tropic Cinema and beloved by all who knew her, came to work for us after her "retirement." She reads more books in a week than I read in a month. Customers call before coming in to make sure Lori will be there to help them find a good book. She is the queen of hand selling.

And then there is Emily, the manager I thought could do anything? Well, it turns out she can. She is the heart of our store.

Recently George installed a Key West Literary Pantheon that wraps around the store above the shelves. When you come in and look up you'll see more than forty names of nationally known writers, from Robert Frost to Robert Richardson, all of whom lived and worked in Key West. In keeping with tradition and avoiding hurt feelings, the pantheon honors only the deceased. The rest of us have to wait.

"Save some room," I tell George.

"Don't worry," he says.

Two Houses

JOY WILLIAMS

KEY WEST WRITERS have done well. Many of them have won the Pulitzer Prize, including Ernest Hemingway, Philip Caputo, Elizabeth Bishop, John Hersey, Wallace Stevens, Joseph Lash, James Merrill, Richard Wilbur, Tennessee Williams, Alison Lurie, and Annie Dillard. (Robert Frost won several Pulitzers as well but came here for the climate rather than the camaraderie, and Key West is rather reluctant to claim responsibility for him.) It almost seems as though with the Pulitzer comes an irresistible urge to move here. Writers like Key West—there may now be more writers in town than bars—but many of them are faithless creatures and they come and go. One of them, Hart Crane, often mentioned as a Key West writer, was in fact never here at all. The nearest he came was the Isle of Pines in Cuba, although a grouping of his poems was entitled *Key West Sheaf*. Tom McGuane, Jim Harrison, Thomas Sanchez—all are associated with this strange Rock, "Mile Zero." Through the decades they pass. Macho, gay, hip, the intellectual elite, the formidable ladies, their reigns overlap. Their houses of Pepto-Bismol pink and lime green and proper white could be duly noted and located. But I prefer to focus on the former homes of two of Key West's fixed and illustrious dead: Ernest Hemingway and Tennessee Williams.

In 1851, Asa Tift, a "brainy, cultured, suave" gentleman from Groton, Connecticut, a merchant and builder of Confederate ships, built a limestone mansion from native coral rock at 907 Whitehead Street. With its mansard roof and iron-flanged pillars of vaguely Second Empire or Spanish Colonial design, the Hemingway house is unlike any other house in town.

Ernest Hemingway and his wife Pauline bought the house in 1931 for $8,000, paid for with a gift from Pauline's wealthy Uncle Gus. The house was in a gross state of ill repair, with a grassless yard dotted with a few scraggly trees. It was a "miserable wreck," according to

The Hemingway house dates to 1851, when Asa Tift, a Connecticut merchant and Confederate shipbuilder, built a mansion out of native coral rock.

Pauline, who also referred to it as a "damned haunted house" after a piece of plaster fell from the ceiling and lodged in her eye. Nonetheless, just before Christmas, the Hemingways, with their two small sons, nurses, and cooks, moved into rooms still jammed with carpenters, plumbers, plasterers, and crates of furniture shipped from France.

Hemingway worked here winters in a small room over what had once been a carriage house until his divorce from Pauline in 1940. At that time, he crated all his belongings—papers, books, guns, and hunting trophies—and stored them in a back room at Sloppy Joe's bar and restaurant on Duval Street. (When Mary Hemingway, his fourth and last wife, went into the room and opened the boxes untouched for decades in 1962, she found original manuscripts blackened with mildew and eaten by rats, uncashed royalty checks, and rotted animal skins.) He then went off to Cuba for a new, if brief, marriage to journalist Martha Gelhorn and a new house, the Finca Vigia or "Lookout Farm," nine miles outside of Havana. It was at the Finca where Hemingway's ghastly collection of inbred, six-toed cats roamed and not in Key West, where the pet population, which numbered several peacocks, included only two cats, one of which the children once dyed a dark green.

THE TENNESSEE WILLIAMS house at 1431 Duncan Street is noted for the large, highly asymmetrical traveler's palm in the front yard. A writer of genius in his early years and considered by many to be the greatest playwright since Eugene O'Neill, Williams continued to write prolifically even though his later plays were poorly received, one critic referring to them as "mere mystic mazes of mumbo-jumbo concerning human despair."

Bought in 1950, this little house with its tomato-colored shutters is almost a miniature house, reminiscent perhaps of one of the small torrid symbols of *The Glass Menagerie*. On the lot he added a gazebo, in honor, he said, of his friend Jane Bowles; a pool; and a studio where he produced some of his best-known work, including *The Night of the Iguana* and *The Rose Tattoo*. The movie version of *The Rose Tattoo*, with Burt Lancaster and Anna Magnani, was filmed in Key West, at this house and on the Casa Marina hotel grounds, in 1955. Williams loved his studio, pointing out its "complete bath-shower and female sockets for electric grills."

Tennessee Williams bought his modest house in 1950. He wrote some of his best-known plays, including The Rose Tattoo, *in the studio he added to it.*

Second Thoughts

PICO IYER

JUST AFTER we'd left college, eager to become writers, the most brilliant reader I'd met—not averse to the more knockabout side of American letters—suggested we go down with his "moll" (now his wife of thirty-three years) to the "Conch Republic." It seemed an important port of call for anyone hoping to enter the House of Literature. We rendezvoused at Miami Airport, drove down a long, thin highway, passing what looked suspiciously like pink flamingoes, and, very soon, were being treated to jumbo-sized ironies: fine cuisine on the sly, leathery ne'er-do'wells, and a magic round of miniature golf lit up by an electrical lightning storm (while the Doors yelled, "This is the end/ Beau-ti-ful friend . . .").

How could I resist? When I fell in love once, I stopped off in Key West on my way back from Havana, to extend the spell. And when the Key West Literary Seminar invited me to revisit, for a session on travel, I was looking into flights before I'd even finished reading the invitation. Months later, a door to another Key West was opening as flip-flopping Pulitzer Prize–winners invited me to Ping-Pong in the backyard, existential novelists in shorts discussed shrimp fishing—as well as those books of the Bible only in the Ethiopian language of Ge'ez—and transcendentalists sashayed through the sun, past the magically welcoming Love Lane home of the Quaker Zen rabbi Miles Frieden, to ask if I'd come out to the beach to play.

How could I not return? Again and again, in fact—stealing across town on a hot winter morning to find an outdoor Ping-Pong table at a bar where my games against archrival Geoff Dyer were annotated by inebriates who assured us they were writers; walking all the way down to the beach to hear novelists I'd adored for years speak about the power of Joni Mitchell; cherishing the sultriness and the warmth of the one place where Cuba meets the U.S. to the tune of mutual delight.

The annual Hemingway look-alike contest attracts "Papas" from near and far. The four-day event raises scholarship money for Keys students.

On my third trip down, six years into the new millennium, I wrote a flip and speedy outsider's piece to try to induce the pinstriped bankers who peruse London's *Financial Times* to throw off their cares and come to Key West. I'm not sure if any of it holds water, but it does show, if nothing else, how the town of eccentric Sirens can waylay the most hardened Odysseus, make him think that he's a writer, and leave him in love with the first rough beast he runs into.

THE AIR, sultry, pulsing, hot even along the pitch-black streets, is redolent of Cuba. The two-story gingerbread white houses, their leafy verandahs looking out on swampy gardens, hammocks swaying under Gothic extravagances, make you think you've landed in Haiti. On one car on sleepy Fleming Street, defiant outlaw legends painted all over it, one of the more prominent declares, "We Seceded where Others Failed." Your passport tells you that you haven't left the United States, but your instincts suggest otherwise: you're in the Conch Republic now, the afterthought of an island off the tip of Florida's nose that seems closer to Fidel Castro's maverick island (only ninety miles away) than to Joseph Biden's nation.

Nothing is quite straight in this offshore home of renegades. You call for a taxi, and a young nurse sidles up in a flamingo-pink sedan with an ad for a strip club around its sides. Down near said "Fetish and Fantasy Role-Playing" shack, an old woman is offering a sanctuary for clawed creatures ("Chicken Are Safe Here"), and a psychic delivers futures next to a gay bar. In the *Key West Citizen*, headlines announce, "Syrup-covered woman arrested after head found," "300-pound man kept smashing his head," and "Man named Noel arrested for urinating on church." The strangest fish of all may well be us pale-faced visitors from colder climes padding up and down the main drag and inspecting the human zoo from behind the safety of our whispers.

The idea of disorder in Key West, to invert the line from Wallace Stevens, is its very livelihood; the little settlement at the southeastern edge of the not-so-United States plays curious games with the idea of law and order, not to mention the norm. Originally a base for chasing pirates, it has set itself up as "The End of the Republic / The End of the Road: Tropical Vacationland," in the words of one large sign, the ideal place for fugitives, or those who just wish to steal away from America without acquiring a visa. There are more writers per capita along its leafy side streets than anywhere this side of Greenwich Village: Tennessee Williams wrote here, Robert Frost, Elizabeth Bishop, Ralph Ellison; these days you can see Annie Dillard sashaying off to a one-house writers' colony, Joy Williams, Ann Beattie. Along Margaret and Amelia and Carolina and Elizabeth, as the pretty lanes are called, rainbow flags announce "gay-friendly" inns, while tanned couples dine by candlelight on second-floor terraces and residents place "Chat Lunatique" plaques outside their ferny bungalows. The idea is to do as little as possible — no industry, little heavy lifting — and make a lifestyle and even an art-form out of it, in the manner of sometime local (and laureate of the carefree cruise), Jimmy Buffett.

Yet even quirkiness can be a commodity for the tourist industry, and so this raffish place for castaways, home to the first American international air flight (when Pan Am flew from here to Havana on October 28, 1927), is a magnet, increasingly, for the rest of us, eager to inspect the outlandish, even to partake of it, before returning to the rat race. Modern Key West is therefore a thoughtful, poetic, largely silent American Alice Springs with a crazy all-night disco at its heart.

Chesty college boys walk the length of Duval Street, drinking a ritual beer at every bar. Shops selling "Deep Sea Drinking" t-shirts

Spring break brings college students to Key West, where the Duval Street Pub Crawl—down a beer in every bar—is a not-for-credit elective.

alternate with embarrassedly chic boutiques that also sell signs saying, "Sorry, We're Open." Key West has become one of those places where real oddity meets its theme-parked shadow—All-You-Can-Eat Oddity—with the curious result that it is sunlit and shady all at once. Fast Buck Freddie's sits very close to the Banana Republic outlet, and head shops peddling "National Pimp Association" stickers stand next to Starbucks.

You can almost see the war between the blue states and the red play out on opposite sides of Duval Street. Step away from it and in two minutes you're in gracious streets where a laundromat doubles as a gas station and moonlights as an Indian restaurant and hidden lanes lead to little cottages where the fans turn slowly, slowly. Elegant restaurants sit among the bungalows, and muscular men in shorts, holding hands, disappear off into the dark. The pace is Bahamian, and the volume is a private whisper. Then you return to the main street and the obligatory carnival is at full blast, as if Johnny Depp had moved, in less than a minute, from *Fear and Loathing in Las Vegas* to *Pirates of the Caribbean*. The house where Hemingway wrote *A Farewell to Arms* is home now to the Pelican Poop Shoppe.

For a small, small world—everyone seems to know everyone else's business — Key West has a lavish history. A center of operations during the Spanish-American War, it was, for fifty years in the nineteenth century, the richest town per capita in the U.S. (in part because it had only two thousand heads), as well as the world's largest source of cigars, its 166 factories churning out 100 million smokes a year. By 1933, however, it was bankrupt, unable even to pay the salaries of city employees, and its status as a place outside the law, and all but outside the country, began to grow. Its aromatic cemetery boasts one section for Jewish people, another for Catholics, a whole area consecrated to those who died on the USS *Maine* in 1900, and another for those who perished during the War of Cuban Independence. One Tom L. Sawyer is there, too, but he's listed as a "community leader."

José Martí, the fiery poet who is a hero of revolutionary independence for both Castro's Cuba and the fervent anti-Castroites in Miami, fomented his Janus-headed rebellion in Key West. Thomas Edison lived here, too, in a house later turned into a "Little White House" by Harry Truman, who made it a perfect neutral spot for American presidents to hold meetings or retreats. In a nice flourish of New Floridian history, the presidential home was purchased by an affluent immigrant from India, who turned the abandoned wooden bungalow over to the state, oversaw its restoration, and opened it as an upstanding tourist spot, somewhat more sonorous than the Ripley's Believe It or Not outlet not many blocks away.

An iguana slinks along a wall outside a beer garden, and next to it slithers a caged snake, while a rooster struts and pecks all about. An elegant African American gentleman, sporting a woolen cap above his suit, is playing a violin for bronzed couples from France savoring *les tristes tropiques*. At sunset, much of the town's wildlife, not excluding most of its visitors, congregate at Mallory Square, down by the water, where a florid man gets three cats to jump through hoops of flame and another who looks like an Irish leprechaun makes two very aged dogs walk along a tightrope. Then the self-professed "Fairly Amazing Groovy Guy" himself tiptoes above the heads of bewildered tourists, while the Jamaican man who's diving through hoops of flame was last seen in the darkness, playing "Edelweiss" on an electric piano.

A large cruise ship called *The World* rocks in the harbor, and a shopkeeper has erected a board on which she's impishly scrawled the

Key West is "one of those places where real oddity meets its theme-parked shadow . . . with the curious result that it is sunlit and shady all at once."

day's temperatures—"Rome 43, Berlin 34, Detroit 30, Boston 40, Key West 78." A tall man is offering "Free Hugs"—though the first rule of Key West is that *free* is never what it seems ("It's Hip to Tip," says a sign at his side). Somewhere on the main drag, near a man selling dirty jokes for $1 each, another man is bawling, "Living is easy, nothing is real," and embellishing his rendition of "Strawberry Fields Forever" with something quite distinctive: an utterly tuneless wail.

Not all Key West is just attitude—I went one evening to a fine and funky seafood place, the Rusty Anchor, on nearby Stock Island, where a mayor used to sneak out with his companions for some dog racing, out amongst the beat-up shacks of the rural South. The golf courses and plush hotels whose absence was once an enticement are now drawing closer. Letters to the paper discuss, with straight-faced irony, what it is to be a "Conch" and why the citizenry can be fined more for parking in the wrong place than for walking around in the nude. "At night the taxi drivers are all drunk," an essay winner informed me in a fit of local pride, "and by day they're stoned."

Still, Key West knows what side its bread is buttered on, and so, among the forty-three cats who slink around Hemingway's house, there's one called Zsa Zsa Gabor and one called Elizabeth Taylor.

On the novelist's birthday, half the visitors in sight are white-bearded salts, here for the Hemingway look-alike contest. A ghost tour of the town begins at its central, multistory hotel and tells, impassively, of the fifteen people who've jumped to their deaths from its roof. "Remember you are unique," says the bumper sticker on a car showing off the American flag. "Just Like Everyone Else."

It might all be a bit much were it not for the simple, lyrical fact that it really is 80 degrees here in January, and there are few better places for brushing your loved one's hair while you sit on a verandah and a torn moon pokes through the clouds, portending sudden rain. It's no surprise that the smiling kids who work at the "Southernmost Starbucks in the United States" wear badges saying they're from Hungary, Uzbekistan, Italy, and the nymphs at one of the town's racier clubs, a U.S. poet laureate told me, hail from Czechoslovakia.

Key West might be becoming, in fact—like Santa Fe or Santa Barbara, Maui or Montana or Provincetown—one of those American hideaways so alluring that everyone is trying to hide away there and get away from everyone else. A tiny cottage can't be had in what is now called "Old Town" for less than a million dollars, and after four hurricanes swept through earlier this century, the entrepreneurs flooded in, seeing they could make a killing out of reconstruction. In the age of telecommuting and early retirement, what beachfront property is not owned by the U.S. Navy is fast being snapped up by landlubbing sharks. Soon, local writers informed me, the place will be nothing but gated millionaires and the earringed Cuban boys who dance attention on them.

And yet the evening I arrived in town, twenty-two years after my first visit, I wandered down to the funky Eden House to be greeted by a sign that boasted the hotel's modest breakfast had been awarded five stars (by no less an authority than its owner, one Mike Eden). The tropical skies, above exquisite terraced houses lit up in the warm dark, belonged to a Wallace Stevens quatrain. And on the radio, as twenty-two years before, the Doors were roaring, urging us all to "break on through to the other side." Key West seemed to be turning into one of those grandes dames with a second face, who still knows that there's nothing wrong with nature that a little art can't fix, and make crookedly distinctive.

Invisible Island

ARLO HASKELL

KEY WEST'S official motto is "one human family," and the city has a proud and often progressive history. The Key West whose heritage I most want to claim is the cosmopolitan one of the 1880s and 1890s, when a multilingual and racially diverse population thrilled to Cuban patriot José Martí's revolutionary demands for liberty and equality in his homeland just ninety miles away. Martí's radically progressive vision not only spurred the successful War for Cuban Independence but tipped the electoral scales in this southernmost city in the South as well, bringing Black men to power as county sheriff and county judge and seating Cuban immigrants as Key West's official representatives in the state legislature.

But the fierce backlash to that era is Key West's history as well. It's the darkest part of this heritage that I will examine here: the story of the Ku Klux Klan in Key West during the 1920s; the reign of terror that sabotaged the Black community's efforts toward political activism and social progress; and the insidious, systematic, widespread effort to harass, incarcerate, and disenfranchise the economic progress of an entire generation of the island city's Black citizens.

Because many historical documents from that time have been lost or destroyed, it is impossible to know every detail of what took place in the 1920s. But it is clear beyond doubt that many of Key West's most prominent and powerful men were sworn members of the Klan during the 1920s. Moreover, circumstantial evidence strongly suggests Key West Klansmen in positions of authority— in law enforcement, city management, and the courts—participated *personally* in Klan violence, though none were ever tried, much less convicted, of any crimes. And it seems almost certain that many of those in official positions knew who was responsible for the violence but chose to allow it to go unremarked and unprosecuted.

The code of silence around these actions has, for the most part, successfully hidden them from view.

When I tell people I have been researching the Ku Klux Klan in Key West, I hear two reactions. Some people are horrified that the KKK has a history in Key West at all. Though the Klan's influence has weakened considerably from its peak a hundred years ago, its success as a terrorist organization was so complete that it continues to instill fear today. Its arcane costumes and strange language, together with its penchant for brutal racial violence, have rooted it in the American psyche in a way that doesn't fit with the way most people think about Key West.

On the other side, from individuals who are more familiar with the era's history, I hear questions like, "Wasn't the Klan basically like the chamber of commerce or the Rotary Club in those days?"

Both of these things are true. It's this combination of racism, terrorist violence, and mainstream acceptance that makes the Klan's history so disturbing.

The Klan of the 1920s was one of the largest social organizations in the United States. Estimates of its membership ranged from one million to ten million Americans, drawn largely from the middle class—the same kind of people who constituted the Rotary or chamber of commerce. Most people think of the Klan as a southern and rural phenomenon, but the Klan of the 1920s was actually stronger in the North than in the South and enjoyed widespread support in many American cities. At its peak, the Klan operated nearly 150 newspapers, two colleges, and a motion picture company.

In public, national Klan leaders disapproved of violence, and the "second Klan" of the 1920s was indeed less violent than the "first Klan" that flourished during Reconstruction (1865–1877) and after. But violence and the threat of violence continued to be essential tools in its campaign for white supremacy in the 1920s. And Florida's Klan was particularly brutal.

During the Klan's first heyday, there were more lynchings of Black people in Florida, per capita, than in any other state. Nationwide, the lynching rate fell steadily after that deadly period, but Florida resisted that trend. In the early 1920s, lynchings of Black people actually increased in the so-called Sunshine State.

Violence was a direct expression of Klan ideology. The KKK Constitution, which every initiate was expected to read, states that "true Klansmen . . . are pledged to maintain the principles of white supremacy . . . against any encroachments of any nature by any person or persons."

On the one hand, white supremacy meant believing that white people were genetically superior; on the other, it required its followers to take concrete actions to ensure that whites enjoyed legal, economic, and political advantages. Although white genetic superiority is a lie, this other kind of supremacy was practical, tactical, and very real.

The reaction to civil rights pioneer Marcus Garvey's mass movement was a major factor in the acceptance of the Klan and its leadership in Key West.

By the 1920s, virtually all of the power in official Key West was in the hands of Klan members, including Police Chief Whitmore J. Gardner, County Sheriff Angus McInnis, criminal court judge J. Vining Harris, Fire Chief J. Frank Roberts, tax collector William J. Maloney, property appraiser Howard J. Sawyer, and city engineer Curry Mareno. Arguably the most prominent person in Key West at that time was Joseph Yates Porter, Key West's first native-born physician and Florida's first public health officer; as its founding leader, his name is at the top of the charter of the Klan of the Keys.

How did this happen? Why did Key West transform itself from the cosmopolitan, open-minded city of the late nineteenth century to one led by white supremacists endorsing a reign of terror?

Part of it was because they were scared of Marcus Garvey.

Born in Jamaica in the West Indies in 1887, Garvey lived in Costa Rica, Panama, and England before returning to Jamaica in his twenties. There, in 1914, he founded the Universal Negro Improvement Association (UNIA) to strengthen ties between Africa and the African diaspora. In 1916, he moved to New York, established UNIA's headquarters in Harlem, and started a newspaper, *The Negro World*.

Garvey argued that Black people were equal to white people in every respect. He preached the need for Black self-respect and self-determination. He coined the phrase "Black is beautiful." Because he had concluded, as a practical matter, that whites in America would never grant full equality to Black people, he proposed that people of African descent from all over the world should establish an independent Black nation in Africa.

Garvey's controversial ideology and mission—pan-Africanist, separatist, and nationalist—drew scorn from many white people of the time, as well as from more conservative Black leaders like W. E. B. Du Bois, who headed the integrationist National Association of Colored People (NAACP). But his impact and influence were enormous.

In addition to the UNIA, Garvey established the Black Cross Nurses, modeled after the Red Cross, to provide health care to Black communities, and the Black Star Line, a Black-owned, Black-operated steamship company that transported passengers and goods to and from Africa. At the peak of Garvey's popularity, his audience measured in the hundreds of thousands. Under his leadership, the UNIA has been called the largest organized mass movement in Black history. Although he failed to realize many of his goals, Garvey's achievements as a civil rights pioneer paved the way for successors such as Martin Luther King Jr., Malcolm X, and Nelson Mandela.

In the summer of 1920, Garvey delivered a "Declaration of Rights of the Negro Peoples of the World," at the UNIA Convention at Madison Square Garden in New York. In a fiery speech, he issued a warning to "the races and the nations that have arrogated to . . . themselves the right to keep down other races. I warn them that the hour is coming when the oppressed will rise in their might, in their majesty, and throw off the yoke of ages."

In the wake of the convention, national membership in UNIA soared, and just two weeks later, a chapter was established in Key

West under the direction of a charismatic Black preacher named T. C. Glashen.

Under Glashen's leadership, the Key West UNIA grew to nearly 700 members in just a few months. (The local NAACP, nearly a decade old, had only 150 members.) Inspired by Garvey's vision for Black economic independence, one of the new chapter's first actions was to establish a cooperative bakery, which sold its goods primarily to the Black community. It made its deliveries in a wagon emblazoned with the red, black, and green flag of the pan-African movement. "One god, one aim, one destiny" was the group's motto, and the painted delivery wagon was a proud advertisement for Garvey's tenets on the streets of Key West.

Just six months after Glashen started the Key West UNIA, Garvey himself came to town for a visit. For three days in February 1921, he stayed with Glashen at his home, delivering well-attended lectures at Samaritan Hall on Whitehead Street.

White residents in Key West didn't like the sound of Garvey's message. On the second day of his visit, Joseph Yates Porter founded the Key West chapter of the Ku Klux Klan, known officially as Florida Klan number 42, the "Klan of the Keys."

A month later, the violence began. Five white men wearing masks stormed a bakery after midnight, where Casimiro Rodriguez, known for baking the coconut bread favored by Bahamian and West Indian immigrants (and probably a member of the UNIA cooperative), was kneading dough for morning. The men fired several rounds into Rodriguez's arms and shoulders before fleeing in a waiting car, leaving their victim bleeding on the floor.

No sooner had Garvey left town than Reverend Glashen was confronted by Chamber of Commerce Chairman Eugene Ashe. "Now I want you to understand that here is the South and the white man's country," Ashe told him, "and I want you to get the hell out of here. Garvey missed it by the skin of his teeth when he was here, but he got out. Now I give you 24 hours to clear out."

Glashen ignored Ashe's warning, as he had ignored others from city officials. In fact, he had already survived an assassination attempt during his brief time in Key West, when unknown assailants fired at him as he walked to a UNIA meeting after sundown. On another occasion Glashen narrowly avoided being lynched when angry white people who had gathered at his home were dispersed by a sudden, torrential downpour. (During a visit to Miami, bomb threats were made against hotels where Glashen had considered staying, and he found a crude image of himself in a noose, hanging in effigy.)

Glashen was undeterred. "White folks," he challenged, "you have a hard time to get me, because death is too small to be afraid of. I take it as I take a drink of cool water; I fear no man." Explaining why he wouldn't leave town, he continued: "If the first man comes and runs, and the second and third run too, there will always be lynchings. But if we always resist . . . there would soon be a stop."

So Glashen stayed. But when, days later, he arrived at the assembly hall, he was forced into a car at gunpoint by Sheriff Roland Curry and taken to City Hall, where an angry white crowd, tipped off to the arrest, was gathering in the courtyard. As Glashen was taken to a secure cell, UNIA members began arriving on the scene. Fears of a riot spread through the city. Not until U.S. Marines were called in did the two opposing crowds disperse.

Glashen was held in jail for three days without being charged. Jailers limited his

The Klan of the Keys Charter was signed in Key West on February 26, 1921, by the KKK's "Imperial Wizard, Emperor of the Invisible Empire."

communication with outsiders and arrested one of his visitors on dubious charges. Finally, Sheriff Curry admitted he could not hold Glashen without charging him. Before Glashen's release Curry warned him that he would be lynched if he did not leave the country immediately. Only after UNIA officials in New York urged Glashen, in a telegram, to take the threats seriously, did he relent, boarding a ship for Havana, never to return to Key West.

THE KLAN often wrapped itself in the banner of patriotism. Klansmen often invoked phrases such as "100 percent American" or "pure American," and racial violence often spiked around the 4th of July. Over that holiday weekend in 1921 Reggie Higgs, a Bahamian minister of Miami's St. James Baptist Church, was abducted by eight men from his home and driven to a field where he was tied to posts hammered into the ground and savagely whipped.

One of the accusations against Higgs was true: he *had* spoken in Key West about equality of the races. But the other allegation against him shows the lengths to which hysterical whites would go to justify their terrorist acts. Higgs, they said, had conspired with Glashen to carry out mass murders of epic proportions in Key West. According to this fanciful scenario, Black cooks working in white households would, on a specified date, add a fatal dose of poison to their employers' evening meal, killing hundreds, if not thousands. The minister's kidnapping caused Black protestors in Miami to take to the streets. Police and American Legion troops with mounted machine guns were called out to control them; several were arrested. Like Glashen, the innocent Higgs was forced to leave Miami—for Nassau.

Until that July, the Klan of the Keys had operated in the shadows. That changed on July 28 when Klansman wearing white hooded robes paraded through the streets of Key West for the first time.

Soon after this intimidating display of strength, letters began arriving in Key West mailboxes, warning recipients they had been targeted by the Klan. "Leave town or suffer the consequences," the letters threatened.

One such letter to O. B. Brown, a white man, said the Klan disapproved of his relationship with a woman of African descent. A frightened Brown prepared to flee, only to be talked out of it by a friend, Manolo Cabeza, a World War I veteran. Days later, masked men abducted Brown from his home and drove him to the eastern edge of the island, where he was tied up and beaten.

One night near midnight weeks later someone pretending to be a Florida East Coast Railway supervisor telephoned a Black railroad employee, Obdalion Higgs, and ordered him to report to work. As Higgs, who reportedly had insulted several white people, walked to the terminal, a man approached him, saying Higgs was under arrest for smuggling liquor. Suddenly, a number of masked men came out of the darkness and forced him into a car. The men drove to a beach where Higgs was stripped naked, tied up, and brutally beaten.

But the most notorious case of Klan violence took place as the bloody year of 1921 drew to a close. Some twenty Klansmen carrying torches and rifles stormed the home of Manolo Cabeza, the same army veteran who had persuaded O. B. Brown to ignore the Klan's warning. Cabeza was beaten, bound with ropes, dragged to a beach, and hanged from a tree.

Miraculously, Cabeza survived. On Christmas Eve he revenged himself by shooting and killing a forty-seven-year-old Klansman named William Decker as Decker sat behind the steering wheel of his car. A shootout ensued, with Klansmen, police, and national guardsmen arrayed against Cabeza, who surrendered. U.S. Marines were summoned to guard him in jail, but early Christmas morning they were dismissed by Sheriff Deputy Angus McInnis, a founding member of the Klan of the Keys.

"Some twenty Klansmen . . . stormed the home of Manolo Cabeza," a World War I army veteran who was beaten, . . . dragged to a beach, and hanged from a tree."

Alerted to the departure of the Marine guard, most likely by McInnis, his fellow Klansmen drove to the jail and beat Cabeza senseless in his cell. They then tied him to the bumper of a car and dragged him across town. On Flagler Avenue, the men hung Cabeza, probably already dead, from a pole and fired dozens of bullets into his body. That same afternoon, as reports of the killing reached the *New York Times* and papers in Ohio, Connecticut, Georgia, and Missouri, the men who murdered Cabeza attended a mass at St. Paul's Cathedral for their fellow Klansman William Decker.

Cabeza's death was widely believed to have been aided and

abetted by prominent Key West officials, and the scandal that followed it led Florida Governor Cary Hardee to order a grand jury investigation. Unfortunately, the grand jury was convened in Key West; in a farce of justice, the all-white jury exonerated Sheriff Curry and Deputy McInnis, saying "the same thing would have happened" under the watch of "any sheriff in the state." The jury further concluded that Cabeza's murder had been carried out "by no organized society, but by individuals unknown to us." Of the fifteen to twenty men who participated in the killing, not one was identified, let alone brought to justice. The message was clear: the Klan of the Keys could get away with murder.

BY 1922 or 1923, Charles Ketchum, a Key West businessman, Washington lobbyist for the city, and founding member of the Klan of the Keys, had risen through the ranks to become Grand Dragon for the state of Florida. It was during Ketchum's tenure that Florida regained its position as the most murderous state in the nation (by number of lynchings per capita). It was also under his direction that the Klan and its odious ideology gained broad acceptance in Key West. Like mainstream organizations, the Klan donated money to various charities, including the Key West Women's Club and the island chapter of the American Red Cross. At least once a year, robed and hooded Klansmen paraded through city streets, some on horseback, carrying the large burning crosses that were their most recognizable emblem. As Ketchum neared the end of his term as Grand Dragon, he boasted of doubling the Florida Klan's membership.

And then things got surreal: the circus came to town.

For six days in January 1926, the Ku Klux Klan teamed up with the Bob Morton Circus to put on what the *Key West Citizen* promised would be "the biggest civic event ever undertaken in this part of Florida." Held at a city park, the circus featured veteran Barnum and Bailey performers, a famous group of touring acrobats, trapeze artists, tightrope walkers, contortionists, "freaks," and clowns. Wearing their pointy hoods and baggy white robes, a Klan band accompanied the acts and, when the circus was not in session, paraded through town. There were even public initiation ceremonies for budding adult Klansmen and for children pledged to join the Junior Order of the Klan.

As many as a thousand people a day were said to have attended the circus, which was billed as a fundraiser for a new Klan of the Keys headquarters. The Klan took out full-page ads in the *Key West Citizen*, which gave the event front-page coverage day after day. The Klan of the Keys had never been more successful or more fully accepted by mainstream Key West.

NATIONALLY the Klan had begun to fall out of favor following the 1925 conviction of D. C. Stephenson, the Indiana Grand Dragon, for the brutal abduction, rape, and murder of a woman named Madge Oberholtzer, a state education official.

Coverage of the case helped expose the hypocrisy of the Klan, whose leaders claimed to be protectors of traditional values, though in many cases they exhibited deep disregard for human life.

But even as the national Klan fell apart, the Florida Klan remained strong through the late 1930s, when lynchings of Blacks continued to outpace every state except Texas. Shifting attitudes toward the KKK seem to have led local Klansmen to operate more secretly than they had during the 1920s, but I've found evidence suggesting the Klan of the Keys remained active as late as 1933.

And whether or not the Klan returned to the sort of violence that marked the bloody year of 1921, the machinery of white supremacy continued. Help wanted ads in the *Citizen* often specified that only whites need apply. Business groups and social clubs adopted whites-only provisions. Deeds to plots of land—even entire neighborhoods—prohibited nonwhites from purchasing them.

That's Key West's history, too. And the consequences of Black disenfranchisement under the Klan years are, unfortunately, part of Key West's present. It would take a long time to right those wrongs, if there was a collective will to do so. But documenting them—bringing them to light—is a start toward a more equitable future.

Serving in Florida

BARBARA EHRENREICH

MOSTLY OUT OF LAZINESS, I decide to start my low-wage life in the town nearest to where I actually live, Key West, Florida, which with a population of about twenty-five thousand is elbowing its way up to the status of a genuine city. The downside of familiarity, I soon realize, is that it's not easy to go from being a consumer, thoughtlessly throwing money around in exchange for groceries and movies and gas, to being a worker in the very same place. I am terrified, especially at the beginning, of being recognized by some friendly business owner or erstwhile neighbor and having to stammer out some explanation of my project. Happily, though, my fears turn out to be entirely unwarranted: during a month of poverty and toil, no one recognizes my face or my name, which goes unnoticed and for the most part unuttered. In this parallel universe where my father never got out of the mines and I never got through college, I am "baby," "honey," "blondie," and, most commonly, "girl."

My first task is to find a place to live. I figure that if I can earn $7 an hour—which from the want ads seems doable—I can afford to spend $500 on rent or maybe, with severe economies, $600 and still have $400 or $500 left over for food and gas. In the Key West area, this pretty much confines me to flophouses and trailer homes—like the one, a pleasing fifteen-minute drive from town, that has no air-conditioning, no screens, no fans, and by way of diversion, only the challenge of evading the landlord's Doberman pinscher. The big problem with this place, though, is the rent, which at $675 dollars a month is well beyond my reach. All right, Key West is expensive. So is New York City, or the Bay Area, or Jackson, Wyoming, or Telluride, or Boston, or any other place where tourists and the wealthy compete for living space with the people who clean their toilets and fry their hash browns. Still, it is a shock to realize that "trailer trash" has become, for me, a demographic category to aspire to.

So I decide to make the common trade-off between affordability and convenience and go for a $500-a-month "efficiency" thirty miles up a two-lane highway from the employment opportunities of Key West, meaning forty-five minutes if there's no road construction and I don't get caught behind some sun-dazed Canadian tourists. I hate the drive, along a roadside studded with white crosses commemorating the more effective head-on collisions, but it's a sweet little place — a cabin, more or less, set in the swampy backyard of the converted mobile home where my landlord, an affable TV repairman, lives with his bartender girlfriend. Anthropologically speaking, the trailer park would be preferable, but here I have a gleaming white floor and a firm mattress, and the few resident bugs are easily vanquished.

The next piece of business is to comb through the want ads and find a job. I rule out various occupations for one reason or another: hotel front desk clerk, for example, which to my surprise is regarded as unskilled and pays only $6 or $7 an hour, gets eliminated because it involves standing in one spot for eight hours a day. Waitressing is also something I'd like to avoid, because I remember it leaving me bone tired when I was eighteen, and I am decades of varicosities and back pain beyond that now. Telemarketing, one of the first refuges of the suddenly indigent can be dismissed on grounds of personality. This leaves certain supermarket jobs, such as deli clerk or housekeeping in the hotels and guesthouses, which pays about $7 and, I imagine, is not too different from what I've been doing part-time in my own home all my life.

So I put on what I take to be a responsible-looking outfit of ironed Bermuda shorts and a scooped-neck t-shirt and set out for a tour of the local hotels and supermarkets. Best Western, Econo Lodge, and HoJo's all let me fill out application forms, and these are, to my relief, mostly interested in whether I am a legal resident of the United States and have committed any felonies. My next stop is Winn-Dixie, the supermarket, which turns out to have a particularly onerous application process, featuring a twenty-minute "interview" by computer since, apparently, no human on the premises is deemed capable of representing the corporate point of view. I am conducted to a large room decorated with posters illustrating how to look "professional" (it helps to be white and, if female, permed) and warning of the slick promises that union organizers might try to tempt me with. The interview is multiple

Waking up in a cold sweat, the author thought of the kiddie meal that didn't come "until the rest of the family had moved on to their key lime pies."

choice: Do I have anything, such as childcare problems, that might make it hard for me to get to work on time? Do I think safety on the job is the responsibility of management? Then, popping up cunningly out of the blue: How many dollars worth of stolen goods have I purchased in the last year? Would I turn in a fellow employee if I caught him stealing? Finally, "Are you an honest person?"

Apparently I ace the interview because I am told that all I have to do is show up in some doctor's office tomorrow to take a urine test. This seems to be a fairly general rule: if you want to stack Cheerios boxes or vacuum hotel rooms in chemically fascist America, you have to be willing to squat down and pee in front of a health worker (who has no doubt had to do the same thing herself). The wages Winn-Dixie is offering—$6 and a couple of dimes to start with—are not enough, I decide, to compensate for this indignity.

I lunch at Wendy's, where $4.99 gets you unlimited refills at the Mexican part of the (now defunct) SuperBar buffet, a comforting surfeit of refried beans and cheese sauce. A teenage employee, seeing me studying the want ads, kindly offers me an application form, which I fill out, though here, too, the pay is just $6 and change an hour. Then it's off for a round of the locally owned inns and guesthouses in Key West's Old Town, which is where all the serious sight-seeing and guzzling goes on, a couple of miles removed from the functional end of the island, where the discount hotels make their homes. At The Palms, let's call it, a bouncy manager actually takes me around to see the rooms and meet the current housekeepers, who, I note with satisfaction, look pretty much like me—faded ex-hippie types in shorts with long hair pulled back in braids. Mostly, though, no one speaks to me or even looks at me except to proffer an application form. At my last stop, a palatial B & B, I wait twenty minutes to meet "Max," only to be told that there are no jobs now but there should be one soon, since "nobody lasts more than a couple weeks."

Three days go by like this and, to my chagrin, no one from the approximately twenty places at which I've applied calls me for an interview. I had been vain enough to worry about coming across as too educated for the jobs I sought, but no one even seems interested in finding out how overqualified I am. Only later will I realize that the want ads are not a reliable measure of the actual jobs available at any particular time. They are, as I should have guessed from Max's comment, the employers' insurance policy against the relentless turnover of the low-wage workforce. Most of the big hotels run ads almost continually, if only to build a supply of applicants to replace the current workers as they drift away or are fired, so finding a job is just a matter of being in the right place at the right time and flexible enough to take whatever is being offered that day. This finally happens to me at one of the big discount chain hotels where I go, as usual, for housekeeping and am sent instead to try out as a waitress at the attached "family restaurant," a dismal-looking spot looking out on a parking garage, which is featuring "Polish sausage and BBQ sauce" on this 95-degree day. Phillip, the dapper young West Indian who introduces himself as the manager, interviews me with about as much enthusiasm as if he were a stock clerk processing me for Medicare, the principle question being what shifts I can work and when I can start. I mutter about being woefully out of practice as a waitress, but he's already on to the uniform: I'm to show up tomorrow wearing black slacks and black shoes; he'll provide the rust-colored polo shirt with "Hearthside," as we'll call the place, embroidered on it, though I might want to wear my own shirt to get to work, *ha ha*. At the word *tomorrow*, something between fear and indignation rises in my chest. I want to say, "Thank you for your time, sir, but this is just an experiment, you know, not my actual life."

So begins my career at the Hearthside, where for two weeks I work from 2:00 till 10:00 p.m. for $2.43 an hour plus tips. Employees are barred from using the front door, so I enter the first day through the kitchen, where a red-faced man with shoulder-length blond hair is throwing frozen steaks against the wall and yelling, "Fuck this shit!"

"That's just Billy," explains Gail, the wiry middle-aged waitress who is assigned to train me. "He's on the rag again"—a condition occasioned in this instance by the fact that the cook on the morning shift had forgotten to thaw out the steaks. For the next eight hours, I run after the agile Gail, absorbing bits of instruction along with fragments of personal tragedy. All food must be trayed, and the reason she's so tired today is that she woke up in a cold sweat thinking of her boyfriend, who was killed a few months ago in a scuffle in an upstate prison. No refills on lemonade. And the reason he was in prison is that a few DUIs caught up with him, that's all, could have happened to anyone. Carry the creamers to the table in a "monkey bowl." Never in your hand. And after he was gone, she spent several months living in her truck, peeing in a plastic pee bottle and reading by candlelight at night, but you can't live in a truck in the summer since you need to have the windows down, which means anything can get in, from mosquitoes on up.

At least Gail puts to rest any fears I had of appearing overqualified. From the first day on, I find that of all the things that I have left behind, such as home and identity, what I miss the most is competence. Not that I have ever felt 100 percent competent in the writing business, where one day's success augurs nothing at all for the next. But in my writing life, I at least have some notion of *procedure*: do the research, make the outline, rough out a draft, etc. As a server, though, I am beset by requests as if by bees: more iced tea here, catsup over there, a to-go box for Table 14, and where are the high chairs, anyway? Of the twenty-seven tables, up to six are usually mine at any time, though on slow afternoons or if Gail is off, I sometimes have the whole place to myself. There is the touch-screen computer-ordering system to master, which I suppose is meant to minimize server-cook contacts but in practice requires constant verbal fine-tuning. "That's gravy on the mashed, OK? None on the meatloaf," and so forth. Plus, something I had forgotten in the years since I was eighteen: about a third of a server's job is "side work," invisible to customers—sweeping, scrubbing, slicing, refilling, and restocking. If it isn't all done, every little bit of it, you're going to face the 6:00 p.m. dinner rush defenseless and probably go down in flames. I screw up dozens of times at the beginning, sustained in my shame entirely by Gail's support—"It's OK, baby, everyone does that sometime"—because, to my total surprise and despite the scientific detachment, I am doing my best to maintain, I *care*.

The whole thing would be a lot easier if I could just skate through it like Lily Tomlin in one of her waitress skits, but I was raised by the absurd Booker T. Washingtonian precept that says: If you're going to do something, do it well. In fact, "well" isn't good enough by half. Do it better than anyone has ever done it before. Or so said my father, who must have known what he was talking about because he managed to pull himself, and us with him, from the mile-deep copper mines of Butte to the leafy suburbs of the Northeast, ascending from boilermakers to martinis before booze beat out ambition. As in most endeavors I have encountered in my life, "doing it better than anyone" is not a realistic goal. Still, when I wake up at 4:00 a.m. in my own cold sweat, I am not thinking about the writing deadlines I'm neglecting; I'm thinking of the table where I screwed up the order and one of the kids didn't get his kiddie meal until the rest of the family had moved on to their key lime pies. That's the other powerful motivation—the customers, or "patients," as I can't help thinking of them on account of the mysterious vulnerability that seems to have left them temporarily unable to feed themselves.

After a few days at Hearthside, I feel the service ethic kick in like a shot of oxytocin, the nurturance hormone. The plurality of my customers are hardworking locals—truck drivers, construction workers, even housekeepers from the attached hotel—and I want them to have the closest to a "fine dining" experience that the grubby circumstances will allow. No "you guys" for me; everyone over twelve is "sir" or "ma'am." I ply them with iced tea and coffee refills; I return, midmeal, to inquire how everything is; I doll up their salads with chopped raw mushrooms, summer squash slices, or whatever bits of produce I can find that have survived their sojourn in the cold storage room mold-free.

There is Benny, for example, a short, tight-muscled sewer repairman who cannot even think of eating until he has absorbed a half-hour of air-conditioning and ice water. We chat about hypothermia and electrolytes until he is ready to order some finicky combination like soup of the day, garden salad, and a side of grits. There are the German tourists who are so touched by pidgin "Wilkommen" and "Ist alles gut?" that they actually tip. (Europeans no doubt spoiled by their trade union–ridden, high-wage welfare states, generally do not know that they are supposed to tip. Some restaurants, the Hearthside included, allow servers to "grat" their foreign customers, or add a tip to the bill. Since this amount is added before the customers have a chance to tip or not tip, the practice amounts to an automatic penalty for imperfect English.)

There are the two dirt-smudged lesbians, just off from their shift, who are impressed enough by my suave handling of the fly in the pina colada that they take the time to praise me to Stu, the assistant manager. There's Sam, the kindly retired cop who has to plug up his tracheotomy hole with one finger in order to force the cigarette smoke into his lungs.

Sometimes I play with the fantasy that I am a princess who, in penance for some tiny transgression, has undertaken to feed each of her subjects by hand. But the nonprincesses working with me are just as indulgent, even when this means flouting management rules — as to, for example, the number of croutons that can go on a salad (six). "Put on all you want," Gail whispers, "as long as Stu isn't looking." She dips into her own tip money to buy biscuits and gravy for an out-of-work mechanic who's used up all his money on dental surgery, inspiring me to pick up the tab for his pie and milk. Maybe the same high levels of agape can be found throughout the "hospitality industry." I remember the poster decorating one of the apartments I looked at, which said, "If you seek happiness for yourself, you will never find it. Only when you seek happiness for others will it come to you," or words to that effect.

At Hearthside, we utilize whatever bits of autonomy we have to ply our customers with the illicit calories that signal our love. It is our job as servers to assemble the salads and desserts, pour the dressings, and squirt the whipped cream. We also control the number of butter pats our customers get and the amount of sour cream on their baked potatoes. So if you wonder why Americans are so obese, consider the fact that waitresses both express their humanity and earn their tips through the covert distribution of fats.

Ten days into it, this is beginning to look like a livable lifestyle. I like Gail, who is "looking at fifty" but moves so fast she can alight in one place and then another without apparently being anywhere between. I clown around with Lionel, the teenage Haitian busboy, though we don't have much vocabulary in common, and loiter near the main sink to listen to the old Haitian dishwashers' musical Creole, which sounds, in their rich bass voices like French on testosterone. I bond with Timmy, the fourteen-year-old white kid who busses at night, by telling him I don't like people putting their baby seats on the tables; it makes the baby look too much like a side dish. He snickers delightedly and in return, on a slow night, starts telling me the plots of all the *Jaws* movies (which are perennial favorites in the shark-ridden Keys): "She looks around, and the water-skier isn't there anymore, then *SNAP*! The whole boat goes . . ."

I especially like Joan, the svelte fortyish hostess, who turns out to be a militant feminist, pulling me aside one day to explain that "men run everything—we don't have a chance unless we stick together." Accordingly, she backs me up when I get overpowered on the floor, and in return I give her a chunk of my tips or stand guard while she sneaks off for an unauthorized cigarette break. We all admire her for standing up to Billy and telling him, after some of his usual nastiness about the female server class, to "shut the fuck up." I even warm up to Billy when, on a slow night and to make up for a particularly unwarranted attack on my abilities, or so I imagine, he tells me about his glory days as a young man at "coronary school" in Brooklyn, where he dated a knockout Puerto Rican chick—or do you say "culinary"?

I finish up every night at 10:00 or 10:30, depending on how much side work I've been able to get done during the shift, and cruise home to the tapes I snatched at random when I left my real home—Marianne Faithful, Tracy Chapman, Enigma, King Sunny Ade, Violent Femmes—just drained enough for the music to set my cranium resonating, but hardly dead. Midnight snack is Wheat Thins and Monterey Jack accompanied by cheap white wine on ice and whatever AMC has to offer on TV. To bed by 1:30 or 2:00, up at 9:00 or 10:00, read for an hour while my uniform whirls around in the landlord's washing machine, and then it's another eight hours spent following Mao's central instruction, as laid out in the Little Red Book, which was: Serve the people.

Paradise Lost

PHILIP CAPUTO

NOT LONG AGO, the Florida Keys had the power to quicken the blood and stir the soul. It was a place like no other on this continent, a tropical wilderness where mangrove islands shimmered in silver seas so clear you could drop a dime ten feet down and tell if it landed heads or tails.

It was magic, and what made it so was its wildness—the dangers lurking in its beauty. It might have been advertised as "paradise" in the tourist brochures, but it could bite, sting, scratch, and sometimes kill you. Sharks as long as spongers' skiffs cruised the placid, sunlit waters. A careless boatman could get lost in the mangrove mazes and be driven mad by the skeeters or die of thirst and exposure, if a croc, gator, rattler, or coral snake didn't get him first.

The weather, touted by the chamber of commerce, was unpre-

Caputo says that greed is killing the Keys: "Watching a beloved place die evokes the same emotions as watching a loved one die: grief as well as rage."

dictable, subject to sudden storms, the worst being the one the ancient Taino Indians called *hurukan*.

When one of those roared ashore, the low, flat islands offered no
refuge from the smashing winds, from frothing tidal surges twenty
feet high. The Russells could have told you about that: the pioneer
Keys clan numbered seventy-seven souls at dawn on Sept. 2, 1935;
at sundown, after the great Labor Day hurricane blasted through
the Upper Keys, eleven were left.

The Keys could do that to you, but they could also enchant you
with the emerald silences of their hardwood hammocks or the sight
of roseate spoonbills lofting out of an island rookery. They could daz-
zle you with their crown jewel—a barrier reef running along the Atlantic side for two hundred miles, ablaze with coral colonies that
were home to nations of fish, from palm-size damsel fish to giant
hammerheads.

Above all, the islands offered solitude and sanctuary from the jan-
gling, overcrowded twentieth century. As recently as the late 1940s,
the Keys outside Key West were still so wild and sparsely inhabited
that the federal government considered incorporating them into
Everglades National Park. Even fifteen years ago, a fisherman could
pole the back-country flats all day and seldom see another boat or
hear anything except the squawk of herons or the splash of pelicans
diving on a school of pilchards. I know, because I used to do it.

The Keys were my home for twelve years before I left them in
1988, in sadness and disgust. It was there I raised my two children
and made some of the closest friends of my life. I wasn't a seasonal
"snowbird" who stayed only for the balmy winters, but a year-round
resident, enduring the long, broiling summers when, during hurricane season, each dawn brought with its glory the chance of catas-
trophe. I fished the islands' waters, dived for lobster, and brought
my catches to the table. I explored the out-islands' meandering channels and hidden lagoons and the drowned canyons of the reef. I
learned to read the subtle signs that herald the change of season in
the tropics, which have more wonder in them than the explicitness
of turning leaves and falling snows. I studied the circuits of the
winds, so I didn't need the Coast Guard weather channel to tell me
when a norther was getting set to blow. I have been all over this
country and in most parts of the world and have never loved any

place more than those islands that hang like a broken jade necklace from the marshy tip of Florida.

I loved them not just for their beauty, but for their uniqueness. They are the only tropical environment in the continental United States, home to some of the rarest plants and animals in the world. And the coral reef is one of the few between the Tropic of Cancer and the Arctic Circle. If it is ever lost—and it is being lost—it will be lost forever.

Which is why I hate what is happening to the Keys. Greed and stupidity are killing them.

Watching a beloved place die evokes the same emotions as watching a loved one die: grief as well as rage. Driving down U.S. 1 from Miami one warm afternoon earlier this year, I would feel like tossing firebombs one moment and weeping the next. When I first drove it in 1976, the fabled Overseas Highway possessed a certain ramshackle charm: two narrow lanes passing over forty-two aging but picturesque bridges. A weather-beaten marina here, a funky clapboard cafe there; salty bars frequented by fishermen and lobstermen and warm-water riffraff; ma-and-pa motels; palm and mangrove wilds in between; uncluttered views of a sea that glinted like pewter in its reach for the lighthouses marking the reef. Beyond the reef, where the sea turned to cobalt, a northing freighter might be seen, catching the Gulf Stream to save fuel.

All that began to vanish in 1983, when the Florida Department of Transportation finished a multimillion-dollar reconstruction of the highway. It was widened for most of its 105-mile length—linking the mainland to Key West—to four lanes in some places. New bridges, soaring concrete arches that resemble freeway overpasses, replaced the ones completed in 1912 for Henry Flagler's Overseas Railroad, the highway's forerunner.

To paraphrase something the naturalist Joseph Wood Krutch once said: if you want to preserve a place, don't build a road into it, and if you do, make sure it's a bad one. The old highway used to daunt most modern travelers, who can't seem to go anywhere without an interstate and conveniently spaced exits for food, fuel, and lodging. U.S. 1's new, improved version, I saw last winter, drew traffic as dense as rush hour on the Connecticut Turnpike—a sluggish, fuming river of rental cars, vans, tour buses, pickup trucks towing sailboats and motorboats, gas-greedy Winnebagos driven by self-indulgent senior citizens whose bumper stickers boasted that they were, har-har-har, spending their grandchildren's inheritance.

The cavalcade passed through a wasteland that looked like Coney Island or the Jersey Shore, with Sun Belt glitz thrown in. Acres of mahogany and Jamaican dogwood and gumbo limbo trees had been cleared for blocks of time-share condos, complete with phony British or French spellings (Harbour View, Ocean Pointe) to give them an air of class their architecture belied. Fast-food franchises and chain motels, like some aggressive new species, killed off most of the funky cafes and ma-and-pa motels. Sea views were rare except from the bridges; otherwise, my eye was blocked or distracted by such gimmicks as a mechanical gorilla waving its arms to beckon motorists into a shop, huge fiberglass models of marlin tempting would-be Hemingways to sign up for a charter, and plywood great whites that invited me to "pet a shark!"

Such grotesques, I thought, were more than eyesores. They were acts of vandalism against the beauty of sea, sky, and island. The Keys, once a place like no other, had become like any other place in America: noisy, congested, ugly.

So much frenzied development struck me as more than the result of shoddy zoning laws. It seemed an attempt by people utterly lacking in humility before nature to assure themselves that they were the masters of their environment, to control it with a grip as firm and lasting as the concrete they spread so lavishly. If that was true, then all those highway signs flashing familiar logos—Exxon, Burger King, Holiday Inn—were false beacons of safety, rather like the deceitful lights the old-time wreckers planted on the reef to lure ships to their destruction and the wreckers' profit. Only now the lights were lights of self-deception, for to live in the Keys is to live at sea, and the sea always has dominion. To prove that, all it had to do was shrug its broad, blue shoulders, as it had in 1935.

Key West Is Ruined

NANCY KLINGENER

I HAVE SOME bad news: Key West is ruined.

And I have it on excellent authority, from a journalist of national standing who spent enough time here to know the island well.

"Key West was one of the few remaining American cities that had preserved its cultural autonomy," he wrote. "In an age when the life of this republic has become so standardized that Great Falls, Montana, looks almost exactly like Pittsfield, Massachusetts, Key West remained different and distinctive, with a peculiar outward aspect that was the natural flowering of its peculiar history and culture. Now it is already beginning to be ironed flat, and in that process it will lose half its charm."

That essay appeared in *Harper's* magazine — in 1929.

The writer was Elmer Davis, whose name has all but disappeared from popular memory but was once up there with Edward R. Murrow and Walter Lippman. He worked for the *New York Times* and CBS, won three Peabody Awards, led the National Office of War Information during World War II, and was an outspoken critic of McCarthyism and anti-Communist witch hunts.

But before all that, he liked to hang out in Key West, because it was so different from the mainland. He did not like the idea of masses of people reaching the Keys by car. His essay was provoked by the approval of plans for building the Overseas Highway.

"Key West today is so different from Miami that one can enjoy them both; but Key West developed will turn into something like a little Miami," he wrote. And he had a pretty good idea what big-time tourism would mean for the island: "Once tourists come in numbers, land will be worth more, rents will be higher, the overhead on everything will go up. That narrow gap which separates the possible enjoyment of the poorest man in Key West from those of the richest man will broaden and broaden and broaden."

He wasn't wrong. Except . . . he kind of was. Because the ruination of Key West, or the Keys as a whole, is like the plant life here—ever renewing and springing up in new forms, to the frequent despair of locals who just want things to stay the same for a little longer and look like they did when they first came to love the place, whether that was in childhood, retirement, or points in between.

Ten months after I moved here, in 1991, as I was in the process of falling in love with the place myself, Philip Caputo wrote an essay for the *New York Times Magazine* titled "Lost Keys." "Not long ago, the Florida Keys had the power to quicken the blood and stir the soul. It was a place like no other on this continent, a tropical wilderness where mangrove islands shimmered in silver seas so clear you could drop a dime ten feet down and tell if it landed heads or tails. It was magic, and what made it so was its wildness—the dangers lurking in its beauty," he wrote. But no longer. He'd left the Keys a couple years earlier, "in sadness and disgust. . . . Watching a beloved place die evokes the same emotions as watching a loved one die: grief as well as rage. Driving down U.S. 1 from Miami one warm afternoon earlier this year, I would feel like tossing firebombs one moment and weeping the next."

During the twelve years Caputo lived here, the Keys pivoted from a low-key fishing destination and military town to full-on tourism, at a level Elmer Davis could not have imagined. The old, narrow, scary-to-drive-across bridges of the first Overseas Highway were replaced with wider ones with a pipeline carrying fresh water underneath. The newly created Tourist Development Council used taxes on hotel stays to bring more tourism and promote events. Real estate values and higher taxes drove Conchs to the mainland. Demand pushed up big buildings on the waterfront and seeded subdivisions throughout the island chain.

Even Jimmy Buffett, who named the place Margaritaville and inspired untold masses to aspire to a laid-back, subtropical, mostly mythical lifestyle, threw in the beach towel. Because the town had gotten too commercialized.

But as Caputo was full of rage and disgust at the state of the Keys, I was seeing them for the first time. I didn't come on vacation and stay or dream of retiring here someday. I was twenty-three years old, and I came for a job with the *Miami Herald*. I fully expected to stay

"It didn't take long for me to love a place where . . . the bartenders . . . had my preferred beer out before my body had fully crossed the threshold."

a couple years before moving on to the greater glories of the paper's Broward bureau. Or maybe grad school.

But it didn't take long for me to love a place where I could ride my bike to work, where I could find just about everyone's number in the phone book — or just show up at their office, where my best tips came from the bocce courts, and the bartenders at the Green Parrot bar had my preferred beer out before my body had fully crossed the threshold — these were not things to give up lightly. So I didn't.

Three years after Caputo's *New York Times* lament, the Fort Lauderdale paper ran a story headlined "Tourist Trapped," in which the head of the Hotel–Motel Association wondered how much more visitation the island could take. "This town's success has always been giving people a certain charm, quaintness, quirkiness. Did you see our conch-blowing contest on CNN the other night?" he asked. "How can we sell our unique laid-back attitude when there is a mass of cruise ship visitors moving down Duval like it's Main Street Disney every day?"

You don't even need to live here to declare its ruination. Gore Vidal hung out here with Tennessee Williams in the 1950s. When he returned for the Key West Literary Seminar in 2009, he was interviewed by filmmaker Tim Long for his documentary *Bohemia in the Tropics* (itself a full-on exploration of Key West's lost luster). In that film, Vidal declares, in his upper-class drawl, "There are no birds on the island. There was a period in which we'd always talk about, 'This is when the birds will come back.' They don't come back now. One of the hurricanes blew them out to sea. So it's pre-birds, post-birds. Symbolically interesting."

As someone married to the executive director of the Florida Keys Audubon Society, not to mention having eyes and ears, I call bullshit. Gore, you may have been one of the great American writers and iconoclasts of the twentieth century, but that is not how birds, or hurricanes, work. Symbolically, however, it is interesting. "The bird" was Vidal's nickname for Tennessee Williams. Gore's and Tennessee's Key West, a rare place in the mid–twentieth century where boundary-breaking gay writers could admire sailors on the beach, is gone. (But we still have birds.)

Now you don't have to wait for a high-profile writer who loves the place to declare its ruination in a national magazine or a documentary. You can read or write about it yourself in way too many Facebook groups. Not that I recommend it, because the endless, repetitive arguments in the comment strings don't add much insight, much less resolve anything. But they do display the range of perspectives on when the Keys were ruined, and who is responsible. If there's a consensus, it's the fault of greedy people who got here at some point after you did, and also the people from the mainland who don't spend enough money while they're here.

In those endless, angry comment threads you can hear the anguish of betrayal. Sometimes I feel for those folks. A lot of them worked really hard to get here, or to stay here. Some of them bought into the idea that this really is paradise—the place where you will be happy and get to do what you want. Unfortunately, real life rarely cooperates and we have more than our share of ugly realities—rising seas, increasingly dangerous hurricanes, a cost of living that makes everything from staffing schools to finding health care a challenge. When it turns out this isn't paradise after all, it hurts. Especially when the overwhelming economic impetus is to keep selling that paradise myth to others. Before the pandemic, the Keys were setting all-time records on every front, from tax collection on lodging to traffic on the Overseas Highway, and the number of people flying in and out of the Key West Airport. The latest count was five million people a year. That's flying to a town with a population of a bit more than twenty-six thousand residents at the 2020 census.

I'm a contrarian by nature and against nostalgia in most of its forms. The "good old days" were not so good for lots of people. I've been here twenty-nine years, so I've seen some changes. I've watched my neighborhood convert around me from idiosyncratic Conchs with lots of junk in their yards to upscale-but-sterile second home splendor. I've seen the cool emporium Fast Buck Freddie's replaced by a CVS. I worry about how regular wage-earning locals are supposed to survive here, much less buy a house, when that little Conch cottage is worth thousands more a month as a vacation rental, or serves as a second, third, or fourth home for snowbirds.

But I have faith, despite the allure and expense and very limited supply of land. Like the vegetation that annoys us with its irrepressible growth, whether we want it or not, the island always manages to come up with some weird but interesting thing that's new, or that I just never noticed before. The climate helps, too, adding the seedy patina of decay to everything that's not relentlessly scrubbed, painted, and maintained.

During my first couple years as a reporter here, I felt like I had a special beat—obituaries for beloved watering holes. One was the Full Moon Saloon, a bar and restaurant famous for its fish sandwiches and for a giant marlin, caught by Phil Caputo, hanging on the wall. I went there a few times before the end, appreciating the late-night sustenance and ice-cold AC, both refreshing after a night at the un-air-conditioned Green Parrot. But it closed not too long after I got here.

The Parrot, meanwhile, has adapted and evolved. It's not the same two local acts playing there every weekend, but a different band just about every night now. It's packed with tourists alongside the locals. Some of the bartenders were probably born after I first set foot in the place. But it has somehow retained its essential identity, and I will always return there, after visiting newer, trendier spots that come and go.

If anything ever happens to the Parrot, then I'll know: this place is ruined.

This Beautiful Place

―――

DANIEL MENAKER

There's this beautiful place called Key West
Where no one is ever depressed.
It could be the climate
Or the Key Lime. (It
Is prob'ly the guess that is best.)

Key West

―――

HARVEY SHAPIRO

At the corner of Simonton and Amelia
there is a small junkyard that is
as beautiful to me as the deep
blue sea stretching from here to Cuba.
It has an arching tree over it
and its shards of old cars, tractors,
boating gear shine in the tropic sun
but with an American splendor
like rolling waves of grain. How odd
to have been taught to respond to
junk by my culture, and with
a patriotic fervor, so that the colors
red, white, and blue blaze through the rust.

The Forever Cycle

BY THOMAS McGUANE

WHEN I MOVED to Key West in the late '60s, I met quite a few people who were fed up with all the changes they'd experienced in the years they'd lived there: they were leaving.

I was astonished: I'd never been anyplace so wonderful; and so I felt until the end of the '70s when I thought Key West had changed beyond recognition, and I left.

As I did, I met many people who had also never been anyplace so wonderful and could not imagine why people like me would ever leave.

I expect this cycle to go on forever.

"I'd never been anyplace so wonderful," says McGuane (in 1984 with wife, Laurie, and daughter, Anne), "and so I felt until the end of the '70s."

Absent Friends

John Hersey
1914-1993

Hemingway's Key West

JOY WILLIAMS

ERNEST HEMINGWAY, as every schoolchild knows, fished, drank, and wrote in Key West. There he wrote *Death in the Afternoon*, *The Green Hills of Africa*, and *To Have and Have Not*, as well as a play, *The Fifth Column*, and a considerable number of short stories, including "The Short Happy Life of Francis Macomber" and "The Snows of Kilimanjaro."

A Farewell to Arms was completed in 1929 in a house he and Pauline had rented on South Street, the same house where his mother had sent a chocolate cake and the Smith & Wesson revolver his father had used to commit suicide.

"Christ, this is a fine country!" Hemingway wrote to a friend, enthusiastic about Key West. Between trips to Arkansas to shoot grouse, pheasant, ducks, and geese; to Wyoming to shoot bear, elk, mountain rams, and eagles; and to Africa to shoot elephant, lion, rhino, buffalo, and kudu, Hemingway fished the Gulf Stream. As the biographer Carlos Baker remarks, in somewhat of an understatement, he "enjoyed life immensely without being sensitive to it." Once, when the poet Archibald MacLeish visited him and they went fishing, they found the fish weren't running, so Hemingway "took to shooting terns, taking one with one barrel and the grieving mate with the other." Besides shotguns, he also carried on board a harpoon and a machine gun for sharks and the stray pod of whales.

Hemingway liked marlin fishing best, for marlin were "fast as light, strong as bucks, with mouths like iron." Tuna, perhaps, were not so exciting, even though it could take just as long to catch them. It took him seven hours to land one 11.5-foot, 540-pound tuna, and after getting drunk, he strung it up and used it as a punching bag. Hemingway also once used the poet Wallace Stevens as a punching bag in Key West. He blackened Stevens's eyes and fractured his jaw after the older man had apparently remarked that Hemingway's writ-

On Pilar, *Hemingway (with wife Pauline) loved fishing for marlin, which he said, are "fast as light, strong as bucks, with mouths like iron."*

ing was not his "cup of tea." One mystified biographer wrote, "For reasons that remain obscure, the poet seems to have baited the novelist into some kind of fight." Stevens, a portly insurance executive, was twenty years older than Hemingway and certainly no boxer. When he threw a punch at Hemingway's jaw, he broke his hand in two places.

During his first years in Key West, Hemingway chartered the boats of Eddie "Bra" Saunders, Charles Thompson, and "Sloppy Joe" Russell. In 1934, at the height of the Depression and the same year the town declared bankruptcy, Hemingway bought his own boat—a forty-two-foot black cruiser with mahogany trim built to his specifications in a New York shipyard. "A really sturdy boat," he described her, "sweet in any kind of sea, and she has a very low-cut stern with a large wooden roller to bring big fish over." He called her the *Pilar*, one of his early names for Pauline, as well as the name of a Catholic bullfight shrine in Zaragoza, Spain. He docked her at the navy station, in the submarine pen where he and his friends, "the Mob," liked to swim. She rode out the 1935 hurricane there.

Hemingway did a lot of fishing on the *Pilar*. In 1942 he employed her in a daffy manner as a submarine hunter in the Caribbean, having convinced the navy to equip her as a Q-boat with a supply of bazookas, grenades, and short-fuse bombs. The *Pilar* was seized by the Cuban government in 1960, a year before Hemingway's death, and is still docked in front of the swimming pool at the Finca in Cuba.

Hemingway thought his house on Whitehead Street resembled "Joan Miro's 'The Farm,' as it might have been painted by Utrillo." If that does not exactly crystallize the vision for you, imagine it being, in the 1930s, the finest house in town, a mansion with tall French windows, staffed with servants on an acre of land and possessing the only basement, bathroom, and swimming pool on the island. The pool is sixty feet long and was dug by pick and shovel for $20,000, an amount which, the guides like to point out, would be equivalent to spending more than $225,000 today. Hemingway lived very well here. In 1936, he was putting the finishing touches on his Key West book, *To Have and Have Not*, a novel that showed the poverty-stricken plight of islanders during the Depression as well as Hemingway's considerable disdain for fellow writers, literary hangers-on, Gulf Stream yachtsmen, and tourists. *To Have and Have Not* is a not very successful attempt to fashion a novel by taking three previously published stories—the most excellent one being "After the Storm," about a fisherman and smuggler named Henry Morgan (based on Sloppy Joe Russell) and attaching them to subplots of love triangles and capitalistic boorishness. But it's Hemingway's Key West book, and it captures the jarring rhythms of a town on the skids.

Hemingway became Key West's most famous citizen and immediately fell prey to his fans. "Have been driven nuts by visitors this last ten days," he wrote to the editor Maxwell Perkins. "Everything from movie stars up and down and they have cost me a week's work except for one good day. The people all come at once and always in the cool season when I have to get my work done."

"Christ, this is a fine country!" Hemingway (with pal "Sloppy Joe" Russell) wrote to a friend. The writer became the town's best-known citizen.

In 1937 Toby Bruce, a driver, friend, and general handyman for the Hemingways, built a privacy wall around the property from bricks salvaged from Duval Street, dug up when the town laid down its first sewer system. By 1940 Hemingway was gone. "Those who live by the sword, die by the sword," he said rather uninspiredly, explaining Pauline's replacement by journalist Martha Gellhorn. After all, Pauline had replaced Hadley. And Mary Welsh was to supplant Martha. Pauline, who had provided him with the wealth he so enjoyed and despised, died suddenly in Los Angeles in 1951. When asked by Tennessee Williams, who had met him in Key West, how she had died, Hemingway replied, "She died like everybody else and after that she was dead."

Farther Out

PAUL HENDRICKSON

IT'S MID-JULY 1934, and Ernest Hemingway has had his boat, *Pilar*, for two months. A few days from now he will take her across to Cuba for the remainder of the summer and the fall's marlin season. He intends to be in place for the first quarter of the new moon, by which time the striped marlin will have commenced their yearly run down from Bimini. No one knows why the big fish always appear off Bimini, on the western edge of the Bahamas, a couple of months before they decide to run in Cuba. But they do. As Hemingway put it in a recently published story, "One Trip Across," "They aren't here until they come. But when they come there's plenty of them. And they've always come. If they don't come now they're never coming."

Every part of his fishing machine still has a kind of factory gleam. He's been keeping her at the sleepy Key West Navy Yard. This means she's at anchor not even ten minutes by foot from the front gate of his house on Whitehead Street, ten minutes from the second-floor room behind the main house where pages of his new and experimental Africa book are filling up almost daily.

Like the sentences that made him famous, the beauty of his boat is of the spare, clean, serviceable kind. She's been written, you could say, in the deceptively plain American idiom. She is long, low-slung, sexy, a black hull, a green and canvas-cladding topside, and butternut-colored decks and side panels. Her heat-reflecting green—which is mainly what you would see if you were looking at her from the air—is not quite turquoise, not quite jade, not quite emerald, but something blending all three. As for her mahogany brightwork—on the decks and cabin sides and transom—well, it's almost as if you're gazing at the insides of a lit jack-o'-lantern.

Tied up at the dock, nodding in the wash like a thoroughbred aching to go, she is apt to put you in mind of one of those classic open-cockpit racing cars at Indy, whose drivers climb in wearing skintight aviator caps and outsize goggles. A large part of the sleekness is owed to the way her curved and raked stern has been cut so low — a whole foot lower than usual, the better for bringing over the thousand-pounders of her master's deep-sea imagination.

When she's out on the water, starting to move at a good clip, slicing through whitecaps, with both engines hooked up — the big seventy-five horsepower Chrysler, the little four-cylinder Lycoming — she will appear a little less submariney. Three years from now, when her flying bridge is constructed over the top of the cockpit, she'll look more upright. But even then, her lines will still be quite aesthetic. Like her owner's prose, there will always be something linear about her.

If she'll never be a speedboat on the high seas, the lady's got some surprising wheels. She can do sixteen knots at top speed and do it almost without breaking a sweat. It's true you get a pretty strong vibration at that level. When he cuts off the little engine, the ride goes much smoother, mainly because the big Chrysler beneath the floorboard is rubber mounted. Typically, he keeps her at about ten knots an hour. This saves on gas. He can troll her all day on ten gallons, and at low speeds *Pilar* runs quiet as a watch, or at least this is how the captain brags about her.

She's got a twelve-foot beam, and a three-and-a-half-foot draft. Her cockpit is both an open air and enclosed sedan-like structure on the back third of the boat. Seven or eight people can fit into this space without feeling suffocated. It's the vessel's nerve center and the place where you'll most often see him, portside, at the helm, unless he's taking a nap or fighting a fish astern from his high-rigged, slat-back swivel fishing chair. Several of the cockpit windows are screened, and others have roll-down canvas curtains, providing a tent-like, house-like feeling. The ventilation throughout is generally superb, even on the fiercest Gulf Stream days, when "the sun gives you something to remember him by," which is how the owner put it in his latest *Esquire* dispatch.

There's a bell in the cockpit, and he loves to clang it loudly with a loop of cord.

Her name, *Pilar*, his favorite Spanish feminine name (and his wife Pauline's nickname), is painted in handsome lettering at the center

Many of Pilar's *parts would be replaced but not her wheel, Hendrickson writes.*
Hemingway liked to stand behind it and wave to folks on shore.

of her stern, along with "Key West," her home port. The name appears again below the cockpit window, out of which her master,
standing at the wheel, can often be seen leaning and waving to folks
onshore as he's easing off.

She's got no ship-to-shore radio. The throttles for the two engines
look like handlebars on a bicycle. There's a dashboard with gauges
and switches for monitoring such things as oil levels and engine temperatures and for turning on the bilge pumps and running lights.
But, really, this whole cockpit lash-up seems almost as elementary
as what you'd encounter on the dash of a Ford tractor. And yet everything's here to navigate in and around and through the shoals of
surprise, if you just keep your nautical wits about you.

Many parts of *Pilar* will get replaced over the next three decades,
but never her wheel. It's made of wood, with six tapered knobs built
on three shafts, each shaft running to a hub. Set into the wood, flush
with it, is a circular plate bearing the manufacturer's name in raised
brass lettering: "Wheeler Shipyard, Brooklyn, New York."

Like Hemingway's early sentences, "his boat is of the spare, clean, serviceable kind," says Hendrickson, "...written, you could say, in the deceptively plain American idiom."

Inside the cockpit, on either side, are two long, cushioned bunks, for general lounging, as well as for seating at meals. At the factory, they've custom built the starboard side bunk to be a foot wider than the one on the other side, the better to accommodate the bulk of *Pilar's* master when he's taking a siesta or using it as his nighttime bed. At mealtime, a table gets put in place and secured on two outer legs from its stowed position a few feet behind the wheel. *Presto!* — a stable space for four diners, maybe more if they're willing to get elbow to elbow. *Presto!* — a cockpit becomes an open-air dining salon with two banquettes, with the food and the wine brought up from the galley below. When Mrs. Hemingway's aboard, tablecloths get spread, and real dishes and silverware will get put out — well, not always. Sometimes things go grungy.

Forward of the cockpit is the main sleeping compartment. You step into it through a varnished half door. There are upper and lower berths down here, a tight toilet, a cubbyhole galley. Also down here, forward of the main sleeping compartment, is a smaller compartment, which gets used for storage as well as bunking. On a boat you never have enough storage room. Belowdecks is its own little universe.

On the topside, in the middle of *Pilar's* long snout, a hinged hatch cover serves as an air scoop for the main sleeping compartment. At the bow another hinged hatch and a small sliding doorway provides access to the two interior compartments and also helps with air flow. Everything about her design feels artful, tidy, crafted, efficient, thought out.

The forward cockpit—really just a small, triangular, walk-around and open-air space at the bow—is where the anchors and winches and ropes and throw-off lines and "fenders" get stowed. Fenders are those cushioned pads—sometimes old tires are employed—that protect the side of the boat when she's settling in at the dock. When the boat is underway, the fenders get hauled up and stowed with the ropes and anchors. A boat with her fenders showing is a damn sloppy boat.

Pilar's captain has been so devoted to learning her quirks and tics that he's been more or less willing to leave the actual fishing of late to his guests. The fact is, on this side of the Gulf Stream, the Florida side, the fish aren't big enough. He needs marlin, and they're over there, across the Straits of Florida, off Cuba's north coast. Meantime, on this side, waiting to go, he's been practicing his swivel maneuver. With one engine pushing forward, the other in reverse, Pilar can turn in her own literal length. The swivel maneuver is both tricky and crucial when it comes to chasing a large fish. The enraged, terrified animal wants to dive beneath you, tangle your line in the other fishing lines, drag you and your thirty-eight-foot machine around the sea as if she were a toy.

You're adjusting the throttles and listening for the pulse of the engines as they start to synchronize. You're eyeing the tachometers. This swivel skill is about your ear as much as your eye, and you learn in roughly the same way that a student pilot learns to shoot approaches on a runway: by putting aside the manuals and strapping on a chute and going up with the instructor and then just practicing over and over. *Pilar's* master has been serving as his own instructor, learning by the seat of his pants, not that he's yet got her turning on a nickel and returning him some change. But soon.

Hilariously, Hemingway ordered custom-made sailor suits for his "crew." They're in both navy blue and summer-dress white. They have his boat's name stitched across the breast. He's sent them on ahead to Cuba. You'll forgive him this bombast. In a year or so, the monogrammed uniforms will get ditched.

Pilar, as I said, snoozes at night less than ten minutes by foot from where her master's been toiling on his new book from about 8:30 in the morning until 1:30 in the afternoon. In April he'd begun this work not really knowing where it was taking him, on rustle-free onionskin sheets, and the slanted sentences were then getting written in a small, concentrated hand: it was as if you could sense the torture of the start just by the size of the words. At page 91, in early June, he'd switched to newsprint, cheaper even than onionskin, the kind on which he used to pound out his newspaper copy in Kansas City and Toronto and Paris. On page 201 he'd evoked a shady little hotel porch in Africa, and his wife dancing with the manager to a scratchy gramophone, and the emetine they'd shot him through for his amoebic dysentery, and the wind that blew like a gale, and, not least, the smoking-hot teal and fresh vegetables that the waiters had brought to the table on that cold night. You render something like that on the page, and it's as if you've earned your afternoon on the boat, rid of everything mental, just the blessed life of action once more.

So picture him getting up from his desk, going down the stairs, grabbing a few things from the main house, saying good-bye to Pauline, calling to the kids to behave themselves, and promising to be home by supper. It's in the vicinity of two o'clock. He walks west-by-northwest, cutting through the old Afro-Bahamian raw-board houses, the roosters roaming with the freedom of sacred cows, the curbside food stalls, the hair-straightening parlors, the female cyclists pedaling lazily along with their dresses provocatively hiked up. He moves through the white glare of a Key West afternoon in the curious, rolling, cantilevered, ball-of-the-foot, and just-off-kilter gait that suggests a kind of subtle menace. He's on dense and narrow and aromatic streets bearing people's first names—Olivia, Petronia, Thomas, Emma, Angela, Geraldine. He's Tom Sawyer on a Saturday in Hannibal, tooting like a steamboat, rid now of Aunt Polly's clutches, left to his own devices, not to show back home until the sun is slanting in long bars. He's Jake

Barnes on a spring morning in Paris, when the horse chestnut trees are in bloom.

Jake's creator has been to cockfights in this quarter. He knows where the second-floor bordellos are here. He has refereed boxing matches in one-bulb arenas on dirt flooring scuffed smooth as talc. (The local fighters, a few of whom he sparred with, have wonderful monikers: Shine Forbes, Iron Baby Roberts, Black Pie Colebrooks. Even the venue for a lot of the weekend fights has a wonderful name: the Blue Goose. They set up a ring beneath a huge Spanish lime tree.) And now, having angled and shortcutted and cantilevered his way to the waterfront, Jake's creator is heaving into the yard, through the main gate, across the corduroy planking, and he sees her, the first goosebumping glimpse, right ahead, bobbing in the sparkle of a deep body of water known by the locals as the submarine pens. He spies her registration number painted on a wooden plaque toward the tip of her angled nose: K26761.

Hemingway completed his only novel set in Key West, To Have and Have Not, *in 1936. It traced the plight of the islanders during the Depression.*

For the last several books and years, Ernest Hemingway's world-famous prose style has been discernibly if subtly altering, but no more so than just now, on the eve of crossing over. What explains this evolving artistic change, which the critics have begun to take notice of but don't especially like and can't quite seem to reconcile with the writer whom they've fixed in their parsimonious imaginations? This is the modernist who wrote all of those not-quite-duplicable Dick-and-Jane-go-up-the-hill-seeming sentences, so evocatively free of the subordinate clause, yoking his strange declarative music with the simple conjunctive and. Sentences such as: "I saw the faces of the first two. They were ruddy and healthy-looking. Their helmets came low down over their foreheads and the side of their faces. Their carbines were clipped to the frame of the bicycles. Stick bombs hung handle down from their belts."

That's from *A Farewell to Arms*, in the extended and magnificent account of the retreat from Caporetto. But now, as a prose innovator seeks to marry the morning landscapes of Africa to the afternoon pleasures of the Gulf Stream, something new and exhilarating is occurring. Ernest Hemingway's prose line is filling up, is growing much more expansive, and there are many subordinate clauses. The pattern has been in evidence for the last several years but never more freeingly than just now. The critics aren't privy.

Could the artistic change have something to do with getting out of those tight, damp streets of Europe, away from those repressive, four-square enclosures of Oak Park so bulwarked against nature and the cold? Could his fuller prose line, his more complex sentence structure, have to do with a kind of literal and metaphorical thawing out, a throwing open of all the windows and doors? In the decades to come, there will be any number of scholarly explanations and interpretations and theories and analyses of this loosening, a word the artist himself employed in a late spring, 1934 letter. "Have gotten to like writing again," he'd said. "Was about through with it for a while but am getting the old 4th dimension back in the landscape again and loosening up in the rest of it and believe I'll make a writer yet."

I believe *Pilar* was a key part of the change, allowing him to go farther out, where you don't see shoreline.

A Poet's House

LYNN MITSUKO KAUFELT

WHEN I LIVED in the vicinity, I used to go out of my way to bike by the house at 624 White Street and wonder who lived there. Certainly *someone* had lived there. On the outer fringe of Key West's Old Town, it is a house that broadcasts character and charm. The porch and first floor were obscured by plants, making it appear to be a house with a deep but benevolent secret. The grounds were overgrown with palms and tropical shrubs and one of the largest pandani on the island.

It is a nineteenth-century house, built in the eyebrow style, unique, it is said, to Key West. There are thirty such houses on the island. The eyebrow is an extension of the roof, providing shade to the second-story windows and to the pillared porch below. It is a modest house, facing a military cemetery that, a marker reads, "originally held the remains of Civil War soldiers who died from yellow fever."

When I was biking past the house, I would fantasize about the current occupants. I'd catch glimpses of two elderly women fanning themselves on the porch in metal and vinyl folding chairs and wonder what they were talking about. Yet it was the house I was fascinated by. There are so many surprises in Key West's Old Town—hidden mansions and undiscovered lanes—but that house on White Street trapped me in a way no other did. With a rare prescience, I felt it was a poetic house. I had never heard, I'm sorry to say, of Elizabeth Bishop. That is, until I took responsibility for the author's room at the East Martello Museum, and John Malcolm Brinnin—poet, author, a genuine gentleman of letters—told me he would consider it the greatest honor if his books were placed next to Elizabeth Bishop's. So I began reading Elizabeth Bishop's poetry and prose and fell under her considerable spell in much the same way I had become enchanted by her house.

"It is a nineteenth-century house, built in the eyebrow style, unique, it is said, to Key West," Kaufelt writes. "There are thirty such houses on the island."

When I finally learned that the hidden, poetic house on White Street had belonged to Elizabeth Bishop, I felt as if I had been vouch-safed a rare and lovely secret. The house was so clearly *her* house.

She was born in Nova Scotia in a town called Great Village. Her father died shortly after she was born. Her mother wore black for the next five years until she was committed to a sanatorium. It was the last time Elizabeth was to see her. She was taken in by her father's family, rich and well-connected New Englanders. Eventually she went to live with her mother's sister in a South Boston tenement and then to Vassar where she discovered the poet Marianne Moore. The Vassar librarian arranged an introduction. It was Marianne Moore who insisted that Elizabeth go to Europe, that she pursue writing rather than medicine. Elizabeth Bishop became, of course, a great poet, but she was also a great traveler, sometimes staying on in a new place for years, settling in, and then moving on.

She liked to fish, and in 1938, while fishing off Florida's west coast, she decided she'd investigate the reputedly first-rate fishing in Key West. She found she liked the town. She arranged to return the following winter. The scale of the place was right. Key West was suited to her size.

When she arrived during the Depression, Key Westers were living off the WPA and grunts (a fish) and conch meat. Hemingway was preparing to leave, but a number of literary types—Mob members and otherwise—still found their way to the island, though there's no record of Bishop having much truck with them.

She had met Tennessee Williams at a dinner party, but that event went unrecorded. I wonder if she and Hemingway ever met, or what they made of each other if they had. If Hemingway was our lion, forging his own legend, Elizabeth Bishop was our lamb, retreating from hers.

Elizabeth Bishop bought her house on White Street and proceeded to plant her garden, to bike over to the Electric Company to pay her bills, to mind her cats, to swim, to work on her writing, and to indulge in a new interest: painting. She once said in an interview that "Key West didn't offer any special advantages for a writer. But I liked living there. The light and the blaze of colors made a good impression on me."

Elizabeth Bishop made many friends, some of them artists, during the half-dozen years she lived there. She believed herself "more visual than most poets. Many years ago, around 1942 or '43, somebody mentioned something to me that Meyer Shapiro, the art critic, said about me: 'She writes poetry with a painter's eye.' I was very flattered."

And in Key West, she painted. Many of her watercolors are of houses, and some have appeared on her book jackets. She painted, also, of course, in words, and the riotous colors of Key West give meaning and a wry sort of grace to her prose and poetry and most especially to her depiction of houses.

JAMES MERRILL has written of her: "She disliked being photographed and usually hated the result. The whitening hair grew thick above a face each year somehow rounder and softer, like a bemused, blue-lidded planet, a touch too large, in any case, for a body that seemed never quite to have reached maturity. . . . A 1941 snapshot . . . shows her at Key West, with bicycle, in black French beach togs, beaming straight at the camera: a living doll." She had, he goes on, the "gift to be simple under whatever circumstances . . . another of her own instinctive, modest, life-long impersonations of an ordinary woman."

Eventually, at the end of summer in 1946, Elizabeth Bishop sold her house, but on one condition: no structural change would ever be made to it.

One enters the house directly into the living room through a shuttered front door. The walls, painted white, are made of pine. To the left, stairs ride to the second floor where there are two tiny bedrooms and a bath. At the back of the house is the dining room and off the dining room — this is a wonderfully typical eccentric Key West layout — is the largest bedroom. On the other side of the dining room is a little kitchen. A shuttered room known here as a Florida room looks out on the back and side yards.

The backyard, also planted by Elizabeth Bishop, is a place where she used to like to sit to listen to the sounds of the neighbor's roosters, which she wrote about in *North & South*. Descendants of those roosters can still be heard from the neighboring yard.

Elizabeth Bishop stopped coming to Key West altogether around 1955. It was a conscious decision. She wrote, then, to her friend, Key West watercolorist Martha Sauer, that "I could not come back to a place that I loved." Her house, so imbued with her spirit, would seem to argue that she never left.

In the late afternoon, when the light is just right, one can imagine Miss Bishop, still in her house, getting ready to come out, to sit down and discuss not literary matters, but the events of the day. Her writing is as fresh and incisive as if it were just completed. Her spirit, not even a little dimmed, lives on in that house she left so many years ago. And I still find myself detouring by it, even more enchanted by its secret now that I've read Elizabeth Bishop's poetry and prose and seen her paintings.

Where Greatness Lived

Today in the upstairs bedroom
I stood where greatness lived
Where greatness laid her head
I wondered if the spot I stood on
Was where she placed her bed

Finally, a woman poet
On this island of bones
She lived right down the street from me
Greatness lived here
Greatness lives in me
Greatness *is* me

E.B. molested by a relative — that's me
She liked alcohol — that's me
Loved the island of Key West — that's me

So I've been walking around greatness
That I didn't know was even here
And I've been talking to greatness
They happen to be my peers

E.B. wrote erotica — that's me
She was a great poet — that's me
Fucked-up childhood — that's me

I can feel greatness
Rising up in me
I can feel greatness
Is something I must be
It's a stirring inside
An opening of third eye

All this time
I've been walking around
Kind of blind
Here at E.B.'s house
Is where I was found

"All this time I've been walking around," the poet writes, "kind of blind. Here at E.B.'s house [above, in 1970] is where I was found."

Ready and Willing

THOMAS TRAVISANO

ELIZABETH BISHOP and Louise Crane, both avid fisherwomen, were first lured to Key West in early 1937 by tales of spectacular fishing. Bishop described the island's surrounding waters as "the most beautiful clear pistachio color," adding that "it is so pretty when you have actually caught one of these monster fish and have him all the way up to the side—to see him all silver and iridescent colors in that blue water." Bishop promptly wrote to her friend, Frani Blough, to say, "I hope [Key West] will be my permanent home someday." For her part, Crane extolled Key West's "row on row of the most fascinating old houses, mostly dilapidated & all in a very particular local style."

Years later, Bishop told an interviewer, "I liked living there. The light and blaze of colors made a good impression on me, and I loved the swimming. The town was absolutely broke then," she continued. "Everybody lived on the W.P.A. I seemed to have a taste for impoverished places in those days." Along with cheap rents, Key West, with its warm and generally agreeable climate, offered Bishop a possible release from the struggle for breath she had experienced since childhood due to chronic asthma.

In January 1938, a year after first coming to Key West with Louise Crane, "Bishop returned alone . . . ready and willing to make the island her home."

Far from Manhattan's madding crowd, Bishop found a quiet setting where she might concentrate productively. Here, too, almost uniquely in America, she found a place where authorship

"Far from Manhattan's madding crowd, Bishop [at right with Crane in 1940] found a setting where she might concentrate productively."

tended to be recognized as a genuine profession. (Ernest Hemingway was then and remains Key West's most famous citizen.) An author's nonwriting hours might be filled with outdoor activities or domestic observations that might lead, in Bishop's case at least, to notable poems. And for writers such as she, who shared a taste for funky night-life, that too might be readily discovered in Key West.

Lynn Mitsuko Kaufelt, author of *Key West Writers and Their Houses*, has observed that the island draws writers who find it "reminiscent of some ideal childhood world where one can wear short pants, polo shirts, and sneakers all of the time and stay home from school." The island also offered attractions for a woman with a preference for other women.

Bishop and Crane soon enlisted the services of the now-legendary Captain Eddie "Bra" Saunders. Bishop fairly gushed to Frani, "By good luck we happened to get the best Captain to take us fishing that there is." She added, "He has been Ernest Hemingway's, my dear, for years and years (Ernest lives here now) and Dos Passos (the BIG MONEY was *written* there)." Bishop went on: "Captain Bra (his rather odd name) told us a story that we recognized as having been taken down verbatim by Ernest in his last book of stories."

In a contemporaneous essay, *Harper's* writer Elmer Davis compared Key West to Greenwich Village or Montparnasse because on adjacent barstools in its most popular nightspots one might find "a duke, an anarchist, and a fan dancer." But Bishop insisted that "Key West is nice, not because of all this sport and these he—men litterateurs, but just because it is so pretty, so inexpensive and full of such nice little old houses."

In January 1938, a year after her first arrival with Crane, Bishop returned alone to Key West ready and willing to make the island her home, thus beginning a period of residence that, while never quite year–round, would keep her coming back, season after season, over the course of the next decade.

Crane, who had been hospitalized in New York for an illness, joined Bishop in Key West once she was well. Upon Crane's arrival, Bishop found a room in a boardinghouse at 528 Whitehead Street that cost her, she boasted to Frani, just four dollars a week. Crane took up residence with Bishop at the boardinghouse, sharing what she described as "nice big rooms in a nice big house."

One of the side benefits of the rooming house, Bishop wrote to Frani, was the amusing view it offered from its upstairs veranda of her elderly landlady's "pink bloomers, which she hangs on the tree every morning." She added, "I am doing absolutely nothing but work, scarcely even read, and the results, for quantity, anyway, have been quite satisfactory so far."

Bishop was using these early days in Key West to prepare a sequence of poems and prose pieces for publication. She worked to such effect that 1938 would prove, along with 1937, a banner year in Bishop's publication history. (Part of the reason might be attributed to the late arrival of Crane, whom Bishop described as "a magnet for all odd people, animals, and incidents.")

One product of Bishop's intensive spate of writing during her early months on the island was "Late Air," Bishop's first Key West poem, which was published by *Partisan Review* in the fall of 1938. "Late Air" reveals the poet musing on the nature of love as she sits on a Key West veranda late on a humid summer night, hearing the intermingled strains of recorded music wafting toward her from the wireless sets through the open windows of her neighbors' houses, as if "from a magician's midnight sleeve," so that the radio singers "distribute all their love–songs / over the dew–wet lawns."

These randomly dispersed and interwoven songs of love touch a raw nerve since "like a fortune–teller's / their marrow–piercing guesses are whatever you believe." Her title, "Late Air," plays on multiple meanings. While "air" could refer to a song, it might also refer to the humidity of the warm night sky, laying a semi-erotic glaze of dampness over neighboring lawns.

Bishop attempted to lure her mentor Marianne Moore to join her in Key West, touting the island's natural beauty, quirky detail, and low cost. But Moore, never one to journey very far beyond the confines of her Brooklyn apartment, demurred.

In a January 31, 1938, letter to Moore, Bishop apologized for submitting a story, "In Prison," to *Partisan Review* before it had received her mentor's vetting. (Bishop had received an urgent request from *Partisan* to send in a short story to meet a February 1 prize deadline, and she had sent the only piece she had on hand.)

Moore greeted Bishop's apology with the tart reply, "If it is returned with a printed slip [of rejection], that will be why." Bishop lamented to Frani that *Partisan Review*, which was becoming a favored venue, had "almost forced a story from me, and now I wish I had it back." Far from being returned with a printed slip, however, Bishop's "In Prison" won *Partisan*'s $100 prize—enough to cover half a year at the boardinghouse.

Perhaps in part due to her growing appreciation of Bishop's maturity as a writer, Moore at last—four years after their first meeting—invited her to address her by her first name. Bishop replied in a July 12, 1938, handwritten missive with the salutation "DEAR MARIANNE" in capital letters surrounded by sparklers, as if illuminated by the lights of a theater marquee.

Not long after Crane joined Bishop on Whitehead Street, the couple began searching for a house together. They ultimately chose a two-story house at 624 White Street on the edge of Old Town, built in the island's signature eyebrow style. Bishop, who all her life had been a guest in other people's houses, now found herself bursting with pride at sharing a home of her own with her romantic partner. She reported to Moore that she and Crane had moved into this dwelling and that "the house seems perfectly beautiful to me, inside and out." Knowing her mentor's passion for flora and fauna, Bishop added, "In the yard we have 1 banana tree, 2 avocados, 1 mango, 1 sour-sop, 1 grapevine (1 bunch of acid-looking grapes) and 2 magnificent lime trees, one loaded with large limes." She added that they had "all sorts of insects and lizards, of course," and reported that she was currently reading "a terrifying tract" titled *The Truth about Termites.*

Crane had noted to her mother Bishop's discovery of "the most wonderful primitive" painter. The day after she was writing to Moore about her new house, Bishop told Frani Blough of her discovery of the work of this same talented primitive artist, one of whose paintings had caught Bishop's eye when she encountered it by chance in the window of a Duval Street cigar store. He was the Cuban-born Gregorio Valdes, whom Bishop described as "our Key West Rousseau." Valdes was "very small, thin and sickly, with a childish face and tired brown eyes—in fact he looked a little like the *Self-Portrait* of El Greco." She and Crane commissioned Valdes to do "a big painting of the house" and were most pleased with the result, in part because it blended a plethora of actual details with appealing additions that went beyond the actual. These elaborations included, as Bishop described it, "a parrot and a monkey, several types of strange palm trees, and the sky 'all pinkee,' as he says." Bishop explained that when Valdes delivered his finished painting, no one was home to receive it, so he had left it facing outward on the porch next to the front door. When Bishop approached her home, she felt she was recognizing multiple images of the house, each inside the other, receding perhaps into infinity "like the Old Dutch Cleanser advertisements."

Not long after her discovery of Valdes, Bishop arranged to have this large painting of her house displayed along with a smaller one at the Museum of Modern Art as featured works in an exhibit, "Unknown Painters." In part because of such recognition, Valdes began enjoying an increasing number of artistic commissions, and as a result he changed from the small palette in front of his studio advertising his skills as a "Sign Painter" to a much larger placard reading, "Artist Painter." Sadly, Valdes fell ill just a few months after his belated discovery as an artist painter, and he died of double pneumonia in May 1939. In a memorial appreciation of Valdes published in *Partisan Review*, Bishop observed that Valdes was at his best painting something "that he knew and liked." In such paintings, he combined a meticulous level of close observation with the capacity "to make just the right changes in perspective and coloring" to give his work "a peculiar and captivating freshness, flatness, and remoteness." This was exactly the direction in which Bishop's own art was moving as she sought to render her experience of Florida into words.

Late Air

ELIZABETH BISHOP

From a magician's midnight sleeve
the radio-singers
distribute all their love-songs
over the dew-wet lawns.
And like a fortune-teller's
their marrow-piercing guesses are whatever you believe.

But on the Navy Yard aerial I find
better witnesses
for love on summer nights.
Five remote red lights
keep their nests there; Phoenixes
burning quietly, where the dew cannot climb.

"Late Air" was the first poem Bishop wrote during her first months on the island. In it she muses on the nature of love on a summer night.

Gregorio Valdes
1879-1939

ELIZABETH BISHOP

THE FIRST PAINTING I saw by Gregorio Valdes was in the window of a barbershop on Duval Street, the main street of Key West. The shop is in a block of cheap liquor stores, shoeshine parlors, and poolrooms, all under a long wooden awning shading the sidewalk. The picture leaned against a cardboard advertisement for Eagle Whiskey, among other window decorations of red and green crepe-paper rosettes and streamers left over from Christmas and the announcement of an operetta at the Cuban school, all covered with dust and fly-spots and littered with termites' wings.

It was a view, a real View, of a straight road diminishing to a point through green fields, and a row of straight Royal Palms, on either side, so carefully painted that one could count seven trees in each row. In the middle of the road was the tiny figure of a man on a donkey, and far away on the right the white speck of a Cuban cabin that seemed to have the same mysterious properties of perspective as the little dog in Rousseau's *The Cariole of M. Juniot*. The sky was blue at the top, then white, then beautiful bluish pink, the pink of a hot mosquito-filled tropical evening. As I went back and forth in front of the barbershop on my way to the restaurant, this picture charmed me, and at last I went in and bought it for three dollars. My landlady had been trained to do "oils" at the Convent—the house was filled with copies of *The Roman Girl at the Wall*, *Horses in a Thunderstorm*, etc.— and she was disgusted and said she would paint the same picture for me, "for fifteen cents."

The barber told me I could see more Valdes pictures in the window of a little cigar factory on Duval Street, one of the last few left in Key West. There were six or seven pictures; an ugly *Last Supper* in blue and yellow, a *Guardian Angel* pushing two children along a path at the edge of a cliff, a study of flowers—all copies, and also copies of local postcards. I liked one picture of a homestead in Cuba in the same green fields, with two of the favorite Royal Palms and a banana tree, a chair on the porch, a woman, a donkey, a big white flower, and a Pan American airplane in the blue sky. A friend bought this one, and then I decided to call on Gregorio.

He lived at 1221 Duval Street, as it said on all his pictures, but he had a "studio" around the corner in a decayed, unrentable little house. There was a palette nailed to one of the posts of the verandah with *G. Valdes, Sign Painter* on it. Inside there were three rooms with holes in the floors and weeds growing up through the holes. Gregorio had covered two sections of the walls with postcards and pictures from the newspapers.

Bishop spotted her first Valdes painting in a barbershop window. Thanks to a gift by editor and professor Alice Quinn, it will hang in Bishop's house again.

One section was animals: baby animals in zoos and wild animals in Africa. The other section was mostly reproductions of Madonnas and other religious subjects from the rotogravures. In one room there was a small plaster Virgin with some half-melted yellow wax roses in a tumbler in front of her. He also had an old cot there, and a row of plants in tin cans. One of these was Sweet Basil, which I was invited to smell every time I came to call.

Gregorio was very small, thin and sickly, with a childish face and tired brown eyes—in fact he looked a little like the *Self Portrait* of El Greco. He spoke very little English but was so polite that if I took someone with me who spoke Spanish he would almost ignore the Spanish and always answer in English, anyway, which made explanations and even compliments very difficult. He had been born in Key West, but his wife was from Cuba, and Spanish was the household language, as it was in most Key West Cuban families.

I commissioned him to paint a large picture of the house I was living in. When I came to take him to see it, he was dressed in new clothes: a new straw hat, a new striped shirt, buttoned up but without a necktie, his old trousers, but a pair of new black and white Cuban shoes, elaborately Gothic in design, and with such pointed toes that they must have been very uncomfortable. I gave him an enlarged photograph of the house to paint from and also asked to have more flowers put in, a monkey that lived next door, a parrot, and a certain type of palm tree, called the Traveler's Palm. There is only one of these in Key West, so Gregorio went and made a careful drawing of it to go by. He showed me the drawing later, with the measurements and colors written in along the side, and apologized because the tree really had seven branches on one side and six on the other, but in the painting, he had given both sides seven to make it more symmetrical. He put in flowers in profusion, and the parrot, on the perch on the verandah, and painted the monkey, larger than life-size, climbing the trunk of the palm tree.

When he delivered this picture, there was no one at home, so he left it on the verandah, leaning against the wall. As I came home that evening, I saw it there from a long way off down the street—a fair-sized copy of the house, in green and white, leaning against its green and white prototype. In the gray twilight they seemed to blur together, and I had the feeling that if I came closer, I would be able to see another miniature copy of the house leaning on the porch of the painted house, and so on—like the Old Dutch Cleanser advertisements. A few days later, when I had hung the picture, I asked Gregorio to a vernissage party, and in spite of language difficulties, we all had a very nice time. We drank sherry, and from time to time Gregorio would announce, "more wine."

He had never seemed very well, but this winter when I returned to Key West he seemed much more delicate than before. After Christmas I found him at work in the studio only once. He had several commissions for pictures and was very happy. He had changed the little palette that said *Sign Painter* for a much larger one saying *Artist Painter*. But the next time I went to see him he was at the house

Valdes painted two pictures of the Bishop house. In the first (whereabouts unknown), he added a parrot and a monkey climbing a palm tree.

at Duval Street, and one of his daughters told me he was sick and in bed. Gregorio came out as she said it, however, pulling on his trousers and apologizing for not having any new pictures to show, but he looked very ill.

His house was a real Cuban house, very bare, very clean, with a bicycle standing in the narrow front hall. The living room had a doorway draped with green chenille Christmas fringe, and six straight chairs around a little table in the middle bearing a bunch of artificial flowers. The bareness of a Cuban house, and the apparent remoteness of every object in it from every other object, gives one the same sensation as the bareness and remoteness of Gregorio's best pictures. The only decorations I remember seeing in the house were the crochet and embroidery work being done by one of the daughters, which was always on the table in the living room, and a few photographs—of Gregorio when he had played the trombone in a band as a young man, a wedding party, etc., and a marriage certificate, hanging on the walls. Also, in the hall there was a wonderful clock. The case was a plaster statue, painted bronze, of President Roosevelt manipulating a ship's wheel. On the face there was a picture of a barkeeper shaking cocktails, and the little tin shaker actually shook up and down with the ticking of the clock. I think this must have been won at one of the Bingo tents that are opened at Key West every winter.

Gregorio grew steadily worse during the spring. His own doctor happened to be in Cuba and he refused to have any other come to see him. His daughters said that when they begged him to have a doctor, he told them that if one came, he would "throw him away."

A friend and I went to see him about the first of May. It was the first time he had failed to get up to see us, and we realized that he was dangerously sick. The family took us to a little room next to the kitchen, about six feet wide, where he lay on a low cot-bed. The room was only large enough to hold the bed, a wardrobe, a little stand and slop jar, and the rented house was in such a bad state of repair that light came up through the big holes in the floor. Gregorio, terribly emaciated, lay in bed wearing a blue shirt; his head was on a flap pillow, and just above him a little holy picture was tacked to the wall. He looked like one of those Mexican retablo paintings of miraculous cures, only in his case we were afraid no miraculous cure was possible.

That day we bought one of the few pictures he had on hand—a still life of Key West fruits such as a coconut, a mango, sapodillas, a watermelon, and a sugar apple, all stiffly arranged against a blue background. In this picture the paint had cracked slightly, and in examining it I discovered one eccentricity of Gregorio's painting. The blue background extended all the way to the tabletop, and where the paint had cracked, the blue showed through the fruit. Apparently he had felt that since the wall was in back of the fruit he should paint it there, before he could go on and paint the fruit in front of it.

The next day we discovered in the Sunday *New York Times* that he had a group of fifteen paintings on exhibition at the Artists' Gallery in New York. We cut out the notice and took it to his house, but he was so sick he could only lie in bed holding out his thin arms and saying, "Excuse, excuse." We were relieved, however, when the family told us that he had at last consented to have another doctor come to see him.

On the evening of the ninth of May we were extremely shocked when a Cuban friend we met on the street told us that "Gregorio died at five o'clock." We drove to the house right away. Several people were standing on the verandah in the dark, talking in low voices. One young man came up and said to us, "The old man die at five o'clock." He did not mean to be disrespectful, but his English was poor and he said "old man" instead of "father."

The funeral took place the next afternoon. Only relatives and close friends attend the service of a Cuban funeral, and only men go to the cemetery, so there were a great many cars drawn up in front of the house filled with the waiting men. Very quickly the coffin was carried out, covered with the pale, loose Rock Roses that the Valdes grow for sale in their backyard. Afterwards we were invited in, "to see the children."

Gregorio was so small and had such a detached manner that it was always surprising to think of him as a patriarch. He had five daughters and two sons: Jennie, Gregorio, Florencio, Anna Louise, Carmela, Adela, and Estella. Two of the daughters are married, and he had three grandchildren, two boys and a girl.

I had been afraid that when I brought him the clipping from the *Times* he had been too sick to understand it, but the youngest daughter told me that he had looked at it a great deal and had kept telling them all that he was "going to get the first prize for painting in New York."

She told me several other anecdotes about her father — how when the battleships came into Key West harbor during the war he had made a large-scale model of one of them, exact in every detail and had used it as an ice-cream cart, to peddle ices through the streets. It attracted the attention of a tourist from the north, and he bought it "for eighty dollars." She said that when the carnivals came to town, he would sit up all night by the light of an oil lamp, making little pinwheels to sell. He used to spend many nights at his studio, too, when he wanted to finish a sign or a picture, getting a little sleep on the cot there.

He had learned to paint when he and his wife were "sweethearts," she said, from an old man they call a name that sounds like "Musi" — no one knows how to spell it or remembers his real name. This old man lived in a house belonging to the Valdeses, but he was too poor to pay rent and so he gave Gregorio painting lessons instead.

Gregorio had worked in the cigar factories, been a sign painter, an ice-cream peddler, and for a short time a photographer, in the effort to support his large family. He made several trips to Cuba and twenty years ago worked for a while in the cigar factories in Tampa, returning to Key West because his wife liked it better. While in Tampa he painted signs as well, and also the sides of delivery wagons. There are some of his signs in Key West—a large one for the Sociedad de Cuba and one for a grocery store, especially, have certain of the qualities of his pictures. Just down the street from his house, opposite the Sociedad de Cuba, there used to be a little café for the workers in a nearby cigar factory, the Forget-Me-Not Café, *Café no me Olvidades*. Ten years ago or so Gregorio painted a picture of it on the wall of the café itself, with the blue sky, the telephone pole and wires, and the name, all very exact. Mr. Raphael Rodriguez, the former owner who showed it to us, seemed to feel rather bad because since the cigar factory and the café have both disappeared, the color of the doors and window frames has been changed from blue to orange, making Gregorio's picture no longer as perfect as it was.

This story is told by Mr. Edwin Denby in his article on Valdes for the Artists' Gallery exhibition: "When he was a young man he lived with an uncle. One day when that uncle was at work, Valdes took down the towel rack that hung next to the wash-basin and put up instead a painting of the rack with the towel on it. When the uncle came back at five, he went to the basin, bent over and washed his face hard; and still bent over he reached up for the towel. But he couldn't get hold. With the water streaming into his eyes, he squinted up at it, saw it, and clawed at it, but the towel wouldn't come off the wall. 'Me laugh plenty, plenty,' Valdes said."

This classical ideal of verisimilitude did not always succeed so well, fortunately. Gregorio was not a great painter at all, and although he certainly belongs to the class of painters we call "primitive," sometimes he was not even a good "primitive." His pictures are of uneven quality. They are almost all copies of photographs or of reproductions of other pictures. Usually when he copied from such reproductions, he succeeded in nothing more than the worst sort of "calendar" painting, and again when he copied, particularly from a photograph of something he knew and liked, such as palm trees, he managed to make just the right changes in perspective and coloring to give it a peculiar and captivating freshness, flatness, and remoteness. But Gregorio himself did not see any difference between what we think of as his good pictures and his poor pictures, and his painting a good one or a bad one seems to have been entirely a matter of luck.

There are some people whom we envy not because they are rich or handsome or successful, although they may be any or all of these, but because everything they are and do seems to be all of a piece, so that even if they wanted to, they could not be or do otherwise. A particular feature of their characters may stand out as more praiseworthy in itself than others—that is almost beside the point. Ancient heroes often do penance for and expiate crimes they have committed all unwittingly, and in the same way it seems that some people receive certain "gifts" merely by remaining unwittingly in an undemocratic state of grace. It is a supposition that leaves painting like Gregorio's a partial mystery. But surely anything that is impossible for others to achieve by effort, that is dangerous to imitate, and yet, like natural virtue, must be both admired and imitated, always remains mysterious.

Anyway, who could fail to enjoy and admire those secretive palm trees in their pink skies, the Traveler's Palm, like "the fan-filamented antenna of a certain gigantic moth," or the picture of the church in Cuba copied from a liquor advertisement and labeled with so literal a translation from the Spanish, "Church of St. Mary' Rosario 300 Years Constructed in Cuba."

This essay was first published in 1939.

Charming Tennessee

LYNN MITSUKO KAUFELT

I HAD BEEN introduced to him once in New York, but the first time I met Tennessee Williams in Key West was at David Wolkowsky's Sands Club, which has since been torn down. My husband and I were having lunch with our friend, literary agent Dick Duane. Williams, wearing a vaguely naval hat of the sort tourists buy in Greek resorts, stopped by our table and said, in the new continental accent he was assuming, "Dickie. I have not seen you in *ages*. You must come to dinner tonight. I insist, Dickie." My husband and I were to be brought along.

Dick warned us that we might arrive at the house on Duncan Street and find no dinner, no Williams, or Williams in a bathrobe, or fifty people drinking champagne. "Fasten your seat belts," he said.

Williams greeted us at the door in perfectly acceptable garb. There were to be only six to dinner, including his new "secretary," a nice young man who was six feet eight inches tall. Williams was charming, he was sensitive, he was extremely gracious. When I told him my idea for a book about Key West writers and their houses, he was immediately supportive and agreed to an interview, insisting it be the next day. "One never knows," he said and laughed that contagious laugh.

Dick said not to be surprised if that didn't happen, but it did. The interview took place the next day, but my book was delayed by motherhood and other phenomena. I saw Williams—Tom, as many people called him—throughout the next couple of years, until his death, at parties and restaurants in Key West, and he was invariably interested in the little progress I was making.

Tennessee Williams was born Thomas Lanier Williams on March 26, 1911, in Columbus, Mississippi, the son of a traveling salesman, Cornelius Coffin Williams, and Edwina Dakin Williams. He told me he adopted the name Tennessee because his father's family helped to create that state. "And, of course, I liked the sound of it." He said that his given name was the sort sported by those who turn out sonnets to spring and so "when I turn out sonnets to spring, I write under that name, Thomas Lanier Williams."

"I was born a writer, my dear." He was talking slowly, watching me scribble because neither he nor I trusted tape recorders. We were in his Key West garden and could hear the sound of Leoncia, his housekeeper, in the living room, vacuuming. "A born writer." He claimed that until he reached the age of eight, he was a bully. "I used to beat up all the kids on the block and steal their marbles. I was especially fond of the black ones. Marbles, that is." Followed by his uproarious laugh.

But after a bout of illness, he became shy, and he agreed that shyness had never left him. "I took to solitary amusements," he said in a southern accent—I think he was playing Blanche for the moment—"and developed a very fine, very deep imaginative life."

By age eleven, he said, he was writing "seriously" with a ten-dollar typewriter given to him by his mother. His first published work consisted of two poems appearing in his junior high school newspaper in 1925. He received his first writing award in 1927 when he was sixteen: It was for a letter in response to the magazine's question, "Can a Good Wife Be a Good Sport?" In 1939, he published his first short story under the name Tennessee Williams, "The Field of Blue Children."

He had put in some time at the University of Missouri, but "I was, my dear, the most ill-prepared college student you could imagine." He traveled, and he took what jobs he could find. "I was a manual laborer. I was a clerical worker. I waited on tables. I was a telephone operator in a hotel, and I liked that because I became addicted to listening in. I have never heard more peculiar conversations since. When I went to California, I worked on a pigeon ranch. Later, I came to Florida to work as a teletype operator in Jacksonville. It wasn't until after the disaster of *Battle of Angels* in Boston in 1941 that I visited Key West."

He was thirty years old, shy and frail. He had been writing plays since he was twenty, working at odd jobs during the day, staying up all night to write. "I have an important sense of visualization. My plays simply materialize. And they get clearer and clearer and clearer the more I work on them until suddenly they are all there. Presto."

He came to Key West, he said, to rewrite *Battle of Angels* and "because I like to swim. And because Key West was the southernmost

In 1949, Williams bought the house he would call home for the rest of his life: "I loved Key West. I work best here. I decided to make my home here."

point in America." And because his great friend Marion Vaccaro had a mother, Cora Black, who ran "a very genteel boarding house" called the Tradewinds in one of the great Key West mansions. "In the late forties," Williams wrote, "it was the center of the action for the pub-crawlers and night people, Navy officers, singers, entertainers, artists and writers and some members of the town's social set."

He described the Tradewinds as a former slave quarters, a little cabin behind an antebellum mansion constructed totally of mahogany. Legend had it that the main house had been built by a sea captain for his New England fiancée. Mrs. Black charged him and a companion five dollars for their first night at the Tradewinds in the bridal suite. Falling under Williams's charm, she let him have the slave quarters for eight dollars a week, which is what he said he had been paying for a room at a New York YMCA.

Williams and his friends spent most of their evenings in the Tradewinds' piano bar: Gore Vidal, Carson Mccullers, Christopher Isherwood, Françoise Sagan, and anyone else whom Williams thought interesting or attractive or merely "sympathetic." Williams stayed on through that winter, reworking *Battle of Angels*.

"The ghost of Williams hovers above Key West," says the author. "I can still see him . . . regaling his guests with hilarious anecdotes."

"I was so happy then," he told me. "I adored Mrs. Black, who knew when to be intrusive, and I adored Key West, which was a small-time place. I don't like living in big-time places, and I'm very sorry to say, my dear, that Key West is becoming a big-time place, in a small way. Holiday Inns and McDonald's."

In the early forties, as now, Key West was home to a great many artists and writers. Arnold Blanch, Doris Lee, and Grant Wood were living there and often met with Williams in the evenings at Sloppy Joe's. Pauline Hemingway liked this group and Williams especially. "She was a lovely, gracious woman," he said, "just a little given to crystal chandeliers."

He traveled constantly, even during the war years, "gathering experiences." He was very fond of his maternal grandfather, whom he called, formally, Grandfather Dakin, and he brought him to Key

West in 1946. "Grandfather Dakin liked hotel life," Williams said, explaining their move from Mrs. Black's slave quarters to the renovated La Concha hotel at the corner of Duval and Fleming Streets.

"I worked on *Summer and Smoke* in a tiny room while Grandfather Dakin gossiped down in the lobby and walked up and down Duval Street, making friends every step of the way. In the evenings we'd go either to Sloppy's or up to Pauline's and eat and drink and gossip some more. We had a fine time."

He finished *Summer and Smoke* in his room on the hotel's sixth floor, looking out across the tin-roofed houses of Key West to the Atlantic Ocean. "Grandfather Dakin read every word and loved it, of course. Grandfather Dakin loved everything I ever wrote." Williams sent the play to his agent, Audrey Wood, who was "appropriately ecstatic," and then he went to Charleston to meet with her and Irene Selznick, who produced it.

In 1949, Tennessee Williams bought the Key West house he was to call home for the rest of his life. "It was one of the few thought-out decisions of my life. I loved Key West. I work best here. I decided to make my home here."

The home at 1431 Duncan Street is an old Bahamian house in what was then a workingman's neighborhood of Key West, equidistant from the smarter Old Town and the Casa Marina sections.

When Williams bought the house, everything north of Duncan Street was mangrove swamp. It was only later that it was filled in and middle-class housing built. "Everyone kept saying 'neighborhood,'" Williams told me. "But I wasn't making an investment. I was purchasing a home, not a house. I kept looking for a home and there was this old house, just a little redone, at the end of my particular world, and I bought it, and I've never been sorry."

Williams's house is modest, even with his improvements. One and a half stories, white clapboard, it has "festive" (his word) bright red awnings and shutters. It has a primary bedroom suite and bath at the rear of the ground floor. The upstairs bedroom was reserved for houseguests: Carson McCullers, Gore Vidal, and Truman Capote often visited. Tallulah Bankhead stayed with James Leo Herlihy in his house on Johnson Street, but she was one of Williams's great favorites. (After her death, Williams took over her suite in the Hotel Elysee on East 54th Street in New York, where he was to die in 1983.)

There was a well-publicized falling-out when Tallulah Bankhead played Blanche in a revival of *Streetcar*, and it was said (sometimes by Williams himself) that at one point Williams went storming out of the theater, shouting, "That woman is ruining my play." For the inevitable reconciliation, he gave her a "grand" party on Duncan Street. "We sat in deck chairs at the pool, stony-faced, until I looked at her and started to laugh and couldn't stop, and then Tallulah emitted that roar and soon we were in each other's arms. She was a lady with balls, my dear. Big balls."

Williams furnished the house with old wicker brought back from Havana, covered the floors with sisal, and had a white picket fence built around the property. Over the years, he collected the works of the local Cuban primitive artist Mario Sanchez and the bright flower and goat paintings by his good friend, Key West eccentric Henry Faulkner.

It was well known that Williams liked to keep his friends compartmentalized. He once attended a party at Bets and Chip Reynolds's house on Peacon Lane, next door to Henry Faulkner's. "What the hell are you doing here, Henry?" an outraged Williams wanted to know when Henry made a somewhat dreamy entrance through the garden door. "I live here, Tom."

"Well, go back where you belong," Williams said, turning to his hostess, ignoring Henry for the rest of the evening.

Before he put in the swimming pool in the early fifties, he and Jamie Herlihy developed a tradition of meeting in the late afternoons at White Street, walking to the White Street beach, reciting their favorite Wallace Stevens poem, "The Idea of Order at Key West," then diving into the sea.

After the swimming pool — "which I never for a moment regretted" — he added a writing studio, a square, one-room shack at the far end of the pool, which he called the "Mad House." "The Mad House is for me and no one else. I'm terribly selfish about it." There was only one key, and the door had no doorknob.

"I work every day," he said. He woke at dawn and sometimes earlier, had coffee, and thought about which of three projects — he always had three "on the boil" — he would work on. Then, wearing a robe and shorts, he would cross the patio to his study, have a glass of wine, and go over what he had written the day before. "After a couple of glasses of wine, I'm inclined to extravagance and excess, and while that is sometimes all to the good, most of the time it's to the bad. I blue pencil a great deal." After the blue penciling of the previous day's work, he would sit at his manual typewriter and begin again.

When he finished his morning's work, he would swim, "allowing my mind to go all blank while I listened to the beguiling song of the Australian pines." He found the sound they made in the wind "restful, like rain on a tin roof."

The Williams compound was completed to his satisfaction when he added a guesthouse next door to the Mad House. It's equally tiny, a ship's cabin with a double-decker bunk bed. "I like living here," he told me. "I like living in a house. I like to travel and stay in hotels and order room service, but after I get the traveling out of my system, I like to come home and cook spaghetti."

Williams's plays and poems are filled with vivid color and sound, both emotional and literal. The colors from his writing spilled over into his paintings. He painted, after his morning's writings, in the afternoon on the patio. "I'm the sloppiest painter that ever lived," he said, pointing out the paint smudges still on the doors he had opened with his paint-covered fingers.

But except for his paintings and the green kitchen, his house was devoid of color. "If anything," he said, "there's too much color in Key West."

Many of Williams's paintings—primitives, interesting because he painted them—are set in Key West and used to be sold in local galleries. "They can't give them away," Williams said, laughing, "but I do." After his death, their value escalated—rumors of ten thousand dollars per painting—understandably irritating Key Westers who failed to buy them when they were fifty dollars at Farrington's.

Few of his plays are set in Key West. *The Gnadiges Fraulein*, which takes place on the front porch of a boarding house on "Cockalooney Key," is an exception. It's a comedy that was produced in New York in 1966 to unkind reviews, though Williams said this was his best work of the '60s.

The Academy Award–winning film version of his play *The Rose Tattoo* was shot in Key West in 1956. "They used the front porch on the house next door," Williams told me. "Anna [Magnani] stood on it, screaming at Burt [Lancaster] and all the roosters came running,

A Key West Literary Seminar advanced the notion that Williams's later plays "may be as good as his early ones, but only time will tell."

which broke us all up, and Anna laughed but she wasn't really amused. We could see that, and so we used to tease her about her roosters."

St. Paul's Episcopal Church and the Casa Marina Hotel were also used as settings, and the cast included a great many local residents. I was walking along Petronia Street one night last fall when *Tattoo* was on television, and I barely missed a line from the soundtrack, every house tuned in. "My Lawd, there's Margaret. Fat as ever," I overheard someone say.

He wrote *Night of the Iguana* in Key West and, although it's set in Mexico, more than one Key Wester professes to recognize the characters in it. When I asked Williams if this were so, he only laughed that laugh, so I assumed it was.

He liked to involve himself in local theater, of which Key West has more than its fair share. The Tennessee Williams Fine Arts Center, on the Florida Keys Community College campus on Stock Island, opened in 1980 with his latest play, *Will Mr. Merriweather Return From Memphis?*—though it was ill-received by the Miami critics. The Key West Players produced several of his one-act plays for the first time. One of them, *The Unsatisfactory Supper*, was the seed for *Baby Doll*. The Green Street Theater opened with the first production of *Suddenly Last Summer*. Williams made last-moment script changes right up until opening night.

Williams liked to have his family around him and brought his sister, Miss Rose, to Key West, buying her a peculiarly situated house. A former barracks, it was moved to where it now sits in the Casa Marina section of town. His cousin, Stell Adams, came to care for Miss Rose in the Casa Marina house for a year before taking her to a nursing home.

The ghost of Williams hovers above Key West, paler than Hemingway's but no less profound. As he said, his house was not so much a setting as a home, and I can still see him in the green kitchen with the stained-glass window making a huge salad for lunch, regaling his guests with hilarious anecdotes.

During the last part of his life, his mood changes give credence to the belief that he was on drugs of one sort or another fairly constantly. Whether his later plays would have been improved had he been sober during those years is one of those speculations people like to engage in. A Key West Literary Seminar devoted to his work advanced the notion that his later plays may be as good as his early ones, but only time will tell. Whatever the critics and scholars have to say, Tennessee Williams believed he did his best writing in Key West.

Tennessee in Extremis

JOY WILLIAMS

TENNESSEE WILLIAMS was born in Mississippi in 1911 and christened Thomas Lanier. His father more than once called him "Miss Nancy." His older sister, Rose, was a little odd and was in and out of sanatoriums until she was given a lobotomy at the age of twenty-eight. The procedure was safe and sure, the physicians assured the family, and they offered to do it for free because Rose would be one of the first persons to undergo it. The operation would not be a complete success. Tennessee was devoted to mad Rose throughout her life, and she visited him in Key West often, along with their grandfather, the Reverend Walter Edwin Dakin. The Reverend, elderly and almost blind, was extremely sanguine about his grandson's lifestyle, considering homosexual bonding an elite and rather stylish manner of living. Rose occupied her time by watering the trees in the garden with glassfuls of water from the kitchen sink. Tennessee, the master of duality, took up painting, as did Elizabeth Bishop. He was tutored by the eccentric Henry Faulkner, who lived on Peacon Lane with his goats, with whom he loved to take showers. Williams said that painting was relaxing and didn't wear him out like writing did.

In 1969 Tennessee's younger brother, Dakin, visited him in Key West and could not help but notice that Tennessee was heavily beholden to drink and drugs. He fell down a lot and could barely complete a coherent sentence. Dakin's solution was to have him convert to Catholicism, which he did at St. Mary's church on Truman Avenue. He was even baptized there, which shocked the faithful. Tennessee later said, "I loved the beauty of the ritual but the tenets of the Church are ridiculous." Later that year Dakin returned to Key West again, this time to take Tennessee back to St. Louis, where he committed him to a psychiatric hospital. Going through total withdrawal of all drugs (he was particularly fond of

"Williams's talent died twenty years before he did," the author says. "Key West [became] just another place where he failed to find inspiration or peace."

Doriden), he suffered three grand mal seizures and two heart attacks. He was cured, more or less, and returned to Key West later
that year, where he had only one drink a day and "limited" drugs —
at least for a while.

One of Williams's more interesting infatuations was with Fidel
Castro. In fact, he had a fantasy of being kidnapped by Castro and
Che Guevara. He visited Havana several times from Key West and
chatted with Castro, whom he found gentlemanly and charming.
Castro referred to Tennessee as "that cat," knowledgeable, at the
very least, of the titles of the playwright's classics.

Tennessee wrote that ordinarily his life was "50 percent work
and worry about it; 35 percent a struggle against madness, and 15
percent devoted to friends and lovers." Williams was happy in Key

West. Early on he felt that it was the most fantastic place he had ever seen in America, more colorful than New Orleans, San Francisco, or Santa Fe. In the pictures taken of him there he is always smiling, happy with his pet bulldogs, his houseguests (who included Carson McCullers and Gore Vidal), his writing (in which the town never figures), and his friends.

By the '70s, however, Key West's huge parties and catty social intrigues were wearing Tennessee out. Donald Spoto, in his book *The Kindness of Strangers*, notes that "Key West, once a quiet retreat where he could work well and live a reasonably ordered life, was now really no longer suitable for him. The crowd around him gave him nothing but a phony admiration and took whatever they could get."

There was an incident in the late '70s where Williams and a friend, Dotson Rader, were roughed up late one night as they walked drunk and singing up Duval Street. They were singing the old gospel hymn "In the Garden."

> Ohhhh He walks with me
> And He talks with me
> And He tells me I am his own
> And the joy we share as we tarry there
> No other has ever known

The lyrics achieved certain implications never dreamed of by their creator. Some young toughs pushed the men down and kicked them, and although the incident was highly publicized and caused considerable concern among gay people in Key West, Tennessee dismissed the misadventure. "Well, I suffered no injury," he said. "Fortunately, an ice-cream shop was being shut right behind us and a man picked up the phone, called the police, and said, 'Some men are attacking Mr. Williams on the street.'" Williams later mused that his attackers might not have been punks at all, but New York theater critics.

Three weeks prior to the incident, the caretaker of his house on Duncan Street had been shot and killed. While going through his effects, the police found that he had pilfered many of the original copies of Williams's manuscripts. "Well," Tennessee said dryly, "I guess he thought he was going to die after I did."

"Near the end of his life, Williams was living on wine, Seconal, and coffee, writing every day, all of the work hopeless and virtually unperformable."

Tennessee Williams's talent died twenty years before he did, and he knew it. His travels became constant and neurotic and Key West just another place where he failed to find inspiration or peace. Near the end of his life he was living on wine, Seconal, and coffee, writing every day, all of the work hopeless and virtually unperformable. He died alone in New York City at the Hotel Elysee at the age of seventy-two. His wish to be "buried at sea between Key West and Cuba, dropped overboard in a clean white sack" was not granted. His brother arranged that his body be buried in the city he loathed, St. Louis.

Not long ago in New Orleans, someone moved into the tiny apartment in the French Quarter where Williams wrote *A Streetcar Named Desire* in 1946. The new tenant set off six roach bombs in the eight-by-ten kitchen, and the place blew up. This should have happened in Key West, of course.

Killing Me Softly

THOMAS McGUANE

THE HEMINGWAY period had come and gone, but an authentic giant remained: Tennessee Williams. We all knew him, a little or a lot. When you encountered Williams, you would never be quite sure what to expect. On the best days, you found a thoroughly literary person surprisingly alert to the work of other writers. On some days he was decidedly elsewhere. At a meeting in front of Fausto's grocery store, he told me admired one of my books. I thought he was kidding, but he wanted to discuss it with me. While I looked forward to the chance it might happen, I wasn't holding my breath.

It *did* happen: a note tossed over the hedge of my house on Von Phister Street inviting me to dinner. I had a linen coat I was proud of;

McGuane (with Williams) says that when he arrived at the playwright's house for dinner, "Tennessee was already less than on the planet."

I wore that, tried and rejected a tie, made my long hair inconspicuous with rubber bands, and headed for Tennessee's not particularly atmospheric house on Duncan Street. We sat down to dinner right away. Tennessee was already less than on the planet, but we started a pleasant discussion anyway. He wondered if I had always lived in Key West and wanted to discuss the granular things in my book — streets, locations, debris, characters.

Well, he *had* read it, I consoled myself. On a record player right next to the dining room table, he played Roberta Flack's "Killing Me Softly," an all-too-obvious Tennessee Williams tune, over and over — and over — while refilling his drink and gliding steadily toward unconsciousness, which arrived with an indecorous face plant. I slipped away from the table, cast a last glance at the uneaten scraps, and walked home feeling overdressed in the prized linen coat. It wasn't quite dark.

Ebb and Flow

JOHN LESLIE

THEY ARE GONE NOW. But long before coming to Key West, four writers had established friendships in their academic and literary careers. Apart from the Pulitzer Prizes and other literary awards—one of them would even become poet laureate of the United States—three of them had in common a game played from those early years, one that continued into old age, indeed until death. They brought it with them to their winter homes in cloth bags filled with small wooden tiles.

In Key West Tales *John Hersey unveils himself to his fellow players as a "big threat to the others . . . whenever the remotest nautical or pelagic possibilities turn up."*

In John Hersey's *Key West Tales*, published in 1994, a year after his death, "A Game of Anagrams" recounted a fictional version of their recreational pursuit.

Here's Hersey's opening:

Three poets and a novelist play anagrams in Key West every Wednesday afternoon.

You will recognize the poets' names. They are Paladin, Forester, and Drum. . . . The poets are comfortable with each other, because all three have won both the Pulitzer Prize and the National Book Award.

While the names are fictitious, their identities are easily recognized, at least to those of us who knew them. How many Pulitzer-winning writers can Key West claim? Certainly more than three. But coupled with further descriptions, such as the one for Drum, Hersey has offered a rather tender portrait of the poet James Merrill: "By nature mild and ultra-peaceable; a delicate flinch crosses his face when competitive sparks fly across the anagrams table, as they sometimes do in bright blue heat."

Mild and ultra-peaceable, yes, but it's the delicate flinch finely etched on Merrill's face that I remember best.

As for Forester, Hersey paints a vivid picture of the poet laureate Richard Wilbur: "Forester's poems will recall the profusion of fauna in them. . . . The other three players . . . expect Forester to purloin their own little prize wordlets . . . and to rescramble them into the names of very obscure creatures—extant, extinct, mythical."

Although nothing's obscure in Wilbur's poem, "Having Misidentified a Wild-Flower," the fauna does fly forth.

> A thrush, because I'd been wrong,
> Burst rightly into song
> In a world not vague, not lonely,
> Not governed by me only.

Paladin is recognizable by his girth and his love of dictionaries as John Ciardi: "He weighs two hundred eighty pounds and is, with his left hand, so to speak, a lexicographer." (Are we then to presume that Ciardi "poets" with his right hand?)

Among the four original Key West players, Ciardi was the first to die, at sixty-nine, in 1986. Shortly before his death, he managed to scribble his own amusing epitaph:

> Here, time concurring (and it does);
> Lies Ciardi. If no kingdom come,
> A kingdom was. Such as it was
> This one beside it is a slum.

Up last, Hersey unveils himself as Chalker: "A big threat to the others . . . whenever the remotest nautical or pelagic possibilities turn up: THOLE, DIATOM, VANG, MIZZEN."

In his novel *Blues*, published in 1987, Hersey celebrates the bluefish in particular and sea creatures in general in the bay near his summer home on Martha's Vineyard. From his knowledgeable exposition we do indeed find those very same nautical and pelagic references.

"SHALL WE SLAP down some tiles?" marked many a game's opening salvo. During play, customary rituals were observed. For example, halfway through a game, play paused while the host brought out beer—Becks being the preferred brand—along with a bowl of popcorn or potato chips. After a bit of chitchat, the game would resume as now greasy fingers reached for tiles. And although there was no declared limit to how long a player could ponder a move, if an undue amount of time elapsed, someone would tap a tile—often repeatedly—until the laggard took action. Invariably, the impatient tile-tapper had spotted a play of his own and was anxious to get to it before it could be stolen by another player.

AFTER A DEATH, the remaining players were all too aware that a fresh recruit was required to keep the game alive. Poet John Malcolm Brinnin, responsible for introducing Dylan Thomas to America and writing his biography, was also one of the game's original members. There was Wilbur, of course, and Ciardi, after whose death, Hersey, once an alternate, was elevated to full status.

Around this time, *Esquire* fiction editor Rust Hills and his wife, Joy Williams, arrived on a scouting expedition in search of a retreat even warmer than Sarasota's Siesta Key, where they'd long spent winters.

Rust was always up for a game—whether it was pool, poker, or the double acrostic in the *New York Times Magazine*. No sooner had he taken up residence in Key West than he was enlisted as an alternate anagramer. Rust appreciated the game's institutional longevity, as well as the comradery of such acclaimed writers; two hours of banter once a week was likely as much a draw as the game itself. Indeed, in a short essay he wrote for *Esquire* in 1966, he called it "the best game ever. Simple and sweet." As for Scrabble, to which anagrams is often compared, he called it "a silly and superficial game," adding, "After anagrams, you'll never go back to Scrabble."

As a vocal proponent of the game's perpetuation, Rust began his own recruitment efforts. He didn't have far to look. Other literary lights were then brightening the southernmost city.

On New Year's Eve, 1992, Harry Mathews arrived with his

wife, Marie Chaix, a French memoirist and translator. As a well-regarded poet and inventive novelist, Mathews had lived in France most of his adult life and was then the sole American member of Oulipo, the French literary society that dealt in avant-garde fiction and poetry. Mathews came into the game as an alternate soon after his arrival.

With introductions to Merrill, and others, Harry and Marie were soon making the social scene, attending Merrill's and his partner David Jackson's annual Valentine's Day gathering at their Elizabeth Street home near Solares Hill (at sixteen feet above sea level, Key West's highest point). A higher high than Solares Hill was provided by the impish David Jackson, who served homemade brownies laced with pot. It was also Jackson who'd made the offer on the pair's Elizabeth Street house, while Merrill, ambivalent about giving up their home in Greece, wrote a poem "Clearing the Title," about the painful closing.

> No. No, no, no. We can't just cast
> Three decades' friendships and possessions out.
> Who're our friends here? (In fact I recognize
> Old ones everywhere I turn my eyes—
> Trumpet-vine, cracked pavement, that faint sulphur smell,
> Those see-through lizards, quick as a heartbeat . . .)
> But people? (Well, the Wilburs live downstreet . . .)

As snowbirds, Merrill and Jackson happily took up residence with the trumpet vines and see-through lizards in 1979; and, yes, Richard Wilbur and his wife Charlotte, known as Charlee, were just down the street, as were John and Barbara Hersey, living in the same Windsor Lane compound. Merrill was soon recruited to the game.

Some time before Merrill's untimely death, at sixty-eight, in 1995, Rust Hills had invited me to play two-handed anagrams, which I only later suspected had been an audition. Having bought a home on Pine Street, he and Joy maintained a convivial atmosphere of mixers and dinner parties that brought together Key Westers of all stripes—swains as well as swells. By then Rust and I had become good friends, playing in a weekly poker game, and it was at one of his mixers that, drink in one hand and his ever-

Anagrammers all—top, left to right: Wilbur, Ciardi, Merrill. Bottom, left to right: Hills, Mathews, Brinnin. "Shall we slap down some tiles?"

present cigarette in the other, he extended the invitation.

My rendezvous with Key West had begun in 1974, having reached my own end of the road after more than a decade of living a nomadic life in Europe, Saudi Arabia, Libya, and Iran. Though I had never been to the island before, I immediately felt I'd arrived at a place to call home. Another decade would pass before my own writing career began with the publication of my first novel, a mystery.

Although I'd heard Rust proclaim more than once that he wouldn't walk across the street for a mystery, I'd also heard him mention Dashiell Hammett and Raymond Chandler admiringly, so I took his remark not as a blanket indictment but as an expression of standards.

And so the anagrams audition began—just the two of us. Sitting across from me at his dining room table one evening, Rust removed three Scrabble sets worth of tiles from a cloth bag and spilled them onto the table.

After turning them facedown to hide their letters, we each made a pile in front of us, keeping the center of the table clear to serve as battlefield. Each of us then drew a single tile and turned it faceup to decide the order of play. Whoever drew the tile nearest the letter "*A*" in the alphabet would lead off, and the two letters now exposed would begin a "pool" at the table's center—from which we would make our words, at least three letters each.

After I turned up an "*R*" and Rust a "*T,*" I led off. With the "*A*" Rust had added to the pool, I was able to make *RAT*, which meant it was still my turn—time to draw another tile to add to *RAT*. Turning up another "*A*," however, I saw no way to rattle my rat, so I put my "*A*" faceup in the discard pool, and it was Rust's turn. With a "*W*" held concealed in his hand, he was able to "steal" my *RAT*, making *WART* and earning himself another play.

As may be obvious, two-handed anagrams has its limitations; boredom being one of them. Fewer players means fewer letters in the pool, as well as fewer words in front of each player, thereby reducing the opportunities for manipulation and stealth. But no matter the number of players—two, three, or four—the same rules apply, and the first to corral eight words is the winner. As in most games, luck plays its part, but an arcane vocabulary is invaluable, as is the ability to find words within words and to visually rescramble letters to create entirely new words.

Thus, having lost *RAT* to Rust's *WART*, I added an "*H*" to make *WRATH*, only to watch Rust add my discarded "*A*" and a "*T*" to make *ATHWART*.

Richard Wilbur called these frequent shifts in momentum "the ebb and flow of the initiative." I have no memory of who won that first game, but athwart would always find a way to shift the momentum. Nevertheless, having apparently passed the audition, I joined the group as an alternate. An odd mix you may think: only in Key West could a fledgling mystery writer find himself in such lofty literary company.

One might wonder why women were left out of the mix. An unforgettable moment does not explain the sexist neglect but may be worth recounting: lacking a fourth for a game in John Malcolm Brinnin's Truman Annex apartment, our host asked a female houseguest to sit in. On her first play, she proudly employed a "*T*" to convert John Hersey's *SUM* into *SMUT*.

"*Must* you?" Brinnin asked archly.

In 1992, in his distinctive calligraphy, Brinnin penned a rather campy note to a friend in Key West. He begins by saying: "Miss you, word of you, words with you—on the board, so to speak—as well as tête-à-tête." He closes by quoting a mutual friend's affectionate sign-off: "As anagram obsessed Lenny would sign himself, Chum Vole."

If the reference to anagrams isn't obvious in Brinnin's note, it's affirmed in his sign-off. "Chum Vole" is, of course, an anagram for "much love," and "Lenny" is Leonard Bernstein, a frequent visitor to Key West, whose obsession with the game led to his creating his own rules or, more accurately, abandoning all rules, including the taking of turns. As one might expect from the composer of *West Side Story*, a certain amount of syncopated chaos resulted.

John Malcolm Brinnin's death, at eighty-one, in 1998, left Richard Wilbur the sole survivor of the core group.

CONTINUING INTO the new millennium, the game carried on with Wilbur, Hills, Mathews, and me until Wilbur, then in his mid-eighties, returned to his farm in Covington, Massachusetts, where he would remain until his own death, at ninety-six, in 2017.

Recalls author John Leslie (above): "Rust Hills had invited me to play two-handed anagrams, which I only later suspected had been an audition."

Wilbur's departure left Rust, Harry, and me to push on with three-handed anagrams—Rust bemoaning that he was sure the game would wither and die once he was gone. Soon after his own death, at eighty-three in 2008, his lamentable prediction would come all too true.

Having made feeble attempts to continue the tradition, Harry and I finally agreed that the momentum could no longer be shifted. Two-handed anagrams held insufficient appeal; we'd failed to replace the likes of Merrill, Ciardi, Wilbur, Brinnin, and Hersey in their world of words.

The ebb and flow had run out of initiative.

HARRY MATHEWS died, at eighty-six, in 2017. A year later, his widow Marie placed his ashes in a vault in the Key West Cemetery. A pair of his glasses, a notepad, pen, and a cloth bag filled with his tiles accompanied him, along with a fitting epitaph from his own poetry.

HARRY MATHEWS
1930–2017
Where are we going?
That at last is decided
Thunder and Lightning.

Eleven years after Rust's death, Joy Williams returned to Key West in search of a place to inter her husband's ashes. In talking with the sextant at the cemetery she learned that a vault was available next to Harry's.

L. RUST HILLS
November 9, 1924–August 12, 2008
ATHWART

And there they reside, two of my best friends for so many years. When asked why she'd chosen *athwart*, Joy reminded me that it was Rust's favorite word. Still unable to find a way to steal it with the addition of a single letter, it will continue, for me at least, to stand the test of time.

The bag of tiles passed to me from Rust, bequeathed to him by Richard Wilbur, lies in a drawer at my home in Key West. Who knows when the next wave of wordsmiths might rise up, ready to slap down some tiles?

A Good Omen

JOY WILLIAMS

THERE IS A STORY in Key West, a legend in its time. A couple drive down the Keys over the dozens of bridges, and they go over the last little humpback skirting the mangroves that the unhoused have colonized, and they are finally in Key West, on Truman Avenue headed toward Duval, passing Bayview Park with its bandstand and tennis courts, where they see, unmistakably, the famous, the *beloved* poet Richard Wilbur on his bicycle or dismounted and locking his bicycle or approaching his bicycle. His is a large, handsome presence, radiantly obvious, all in white, tennis whites true, but emitting the clarifying light of the true bard.

Or these awed travelers see Richard Wilbur, poet laureate, winner of two Pulitzer Prizes, celebrity of the theater, lyricist, hymnist, in shorts and bucket hat peddling about, giving crisp hand signals for sweeping turns, headed toward Louie's Back Yard or Fausto's Food Palace or to a casita on the water for a lively game of anagrams, and this sighting is clearly such a good omen, such a sign of the little town's casual embrace of excellence, happiness, and delights that the visitors discard everything less meaningful in their lives and buy a house in Key West.

Bard of Pleasures

PHYLLIS ROSE

Adapted from a 2005 essay by Phyllis Rose in Poetry *magazine*

AS LONG AS HE LIVED — he died at age ninety-six in 2017 — Richard Wilbur maintained a handsome, youthful air. And like his countenance, his poems showed no deterioration over time. Early and late, they are powered by elegant rhyme and beautiful metric patterning. The poems are witty, imaginative, and ultimately reassuring. The later poems are as elegant and intricate, as devoted to musical pleasures, as fully achieved, as the earliest.

Two of the best love poems written in my lifetime are by Richard Wilbur: "A Late Aubade" and "For C." An aubade is a lover's farewell song, usually sung at dawn. This one is "sung" by the poet to a woman with whom he has naughtily spent the morning and who finally insists she must get on with her day. The poem cites things she might have been doing if she had not stayed in bed with the poet. She might be

> planting a raucous bed
> Of salvia, in rubber gloves,
> Or lunching through a screed of someone's loves
> With pitying head,
>
> Or making some unhappy setter
> Heel, or listening to a bleak
> Lecture on Schoenberg's serial technique.
> Isn't this better?

Much better to spend the morning in bed with your husband than on self-improvement. For surely this gardening, lunching, dog-training, Schoenberg-liking woman is Wilbur's wife, Charlee. The whole tone of the poem is domestic, even connubial.

"For C." ran initially in a Valentine's Day issue of the *New Yorker*. I remember thinking, "Why don't I get valentines like that?" This poem is also for "Charlee"—the same dog-training, hard-gardening object of the poet's affections as in the aubade of thirty years before, with the kind of intricate rhyming that Wilbur seems to toss off effortlessly and that his many fans delight in.

> And bittersweet regrets, and cannot share
> The frequent vistas of their large despair,
> Where love and all are swept to nothingness;
> Still, there's a certain scope in that long love
> Which constant spirits are the keepers of,
>
> And which, though taken to be tame and staid,
> Is a wild sostenuto of the heart,
> A passion joined to courtesy and art
> Which has the quality of something made.

How Richard Wilbur and how refreshing, this celebration of long-lasting love, the "wild sostenuto of the heart," emotion shaped and sustained by "courtesy and art."

Wilbur is the poet of the long run. Perhaps that's why he's such a long-running poet. The poem often cited as typical of Wilbur, "Love Calls Us to the Things of This World," was written fifty years ago. It opens with a vision of laundry hung to dry on clotheslines outside an apartment window—laundry bodied out in the breeze, laundry imagined as angels. Wilbur's conceit, his yoking of radically different entities, laundry and angels, rescues the reality of clothes drying on a line and makes it permanent.

I enjoy the imaginative transformation of the laundry into something greater than itself in the same way that, were I a sixteenth-century Venetian, I would have enjoyed a painting of the Madonna for which my niece had sat as a model, the sacred tied to the everyday. But the poem in its conclusion insists that the laundry remain laundry, untransformed.

> Oh, let there be nothing on earth but laundry,
> Nothing but rosy hands in the rising steam
> And clear dances done in the sight of heaven.

Wilbur never harangued or bullied, says Rose, "He always seem[ed] graciously to assume we [would] understand him." Photograph by Rollie McKenna.

For those of us who were educated under the old "Great Books" and "Masterpieces of English Literature" curriculum, Wilbur is our Donne, our Milton.

And as postmodern buildings pay homage to architectural styles of the past, Wilbur's poetry pays homage to the poets of the past, and we, his readers, take a kind of generational pride in seeing how he recalls and measures up to them. He was schooled in their verse and uses poetry to the same ends they did, conceiving his function as a public poet offering language that delights and instructs—not by preaching but by clarification.

Wilbur never harangues or bullies. He always seems graciously to assume we will understand him. He doesn't try to impress or ask us to admire him. The shape of his career is of little interest; he has merely produced a body of work of singular, self-effacing consistency.

Wilbur started writing poetry in college and, later, to calm his nerves as a soldier under fire in World War II, living in foxholes under near-continual bombardment. "When you are living in a hole on a hillside subject to harassing artillery fire," he said in a postwar interview, "you can never quite escape anxiety." But you do the best you can by sleeping, chatting, reading, daydreaming, or writing. It's not hard to see how, for such a man in such a situation, rhyme and meter might impose an anxiety-reducing discipline on chaos.

From his 1947 poem, "Potato," in praise of a tuber that is "beautiful only to hunger," up to recent poems like "Bone Key," in which he praises the mangrove, capable of finding nourishment in salt water, and the screw pine, which attaches itself to bits of rock, Wilbur admires survivors and that which furthers survival. In "Still, Citizen Sparrow," he recommends to the innocuous sparrow the virtues of the vulture, which recycles life and thus helps it continue, even comparing the carrion bird to the biblical Noah, who "carried on" the human race.

Wilbur (left, with John Malcolm Brinnin) "is the poet of the long run," Rose writes. "Perhaps that's why he's such a long-running poet."

In one of his rare autobiographical poems, "Cottage Street, 1953," Wilbur reconstructs meeting over tea with Sylvia Plath and her mother. He has been summoned to exemplify to the suicidal Sylvia "the published poet in his happiness":

How large is her refusal, and how slight
The genteel chat whereby we recommend
Life, of a summer afternoon, despite
The brewing dusk which hints that it may end.

Wilbur is a bard of everyday pleasures. In "C Minor," he thanks his wife for turning off the radio when it plays Beethoven during breakfast. Another wonderful domestic poem, "The Writer," is based—as so many Wilbur poems are—on a yoking of two seemingly unrelated images: his daughter in her room at a typewriter trying to write a short story and that of a bird, accidentally trapped in the same room two years before, battering itself as it tries to find its way out. He wishes his daughter, whom he imagines as the captain of a ship, a "lucky passage." The clattering of the typewriter stops "as if to reject my thought and its easy figure." Then the image of the bird trying to free itself comes to mind, deepening his understanding of his daughter's efforts to write:

It is always a matter, my darling,
Of life or death, as I had forgotten. I wish
What I wished you before, but harder.

This is the music of daily life.

It's hard to overemphasize the importance of verbal play in Wilbur's poetry. I, for one, can spend a long time savoring just one pentameter couplet, like the mention in "The Eye" of "Charlotte Amalie, with its duty-free / Leicas, binoculars, and jewelry."

But Wilbur, however famous, however loved and respected he has been throughout his career, has rarely been fashionable. He was unfashionable when confessional poetry was all the rage. He was unfashionable when difficult, deconstructive poetry was respected. His devotion to a tightly constructed formalist poetry has seemed retro for decades. He has been famous my entire adult life without ever being (in that cursed vulgarism) "hot."

Masses of students turned out by MFA programs must look in wonder at a literary personage who doesn't really care how high his stock rises. Perhaps this smart and self-contained man knew all along that if he lasted long enough, his time would come. What seemed recalcitrance would be recognized as integrity. WASP coolness would turn into vision, moderation, and character. Not that Wilbur chose to be contrarian; rather he had the self-possession to endure it. Imagine the strength of character it takes to stand against the currents of one's time.

Wilbur has made no secret of his devotion to physical activity. He is a dedicated tennis player. In a *Paris Review* interview published more than thirty years ago, Wilbur reported a conversation he'd had with Stanley Kunitz (who lived to be one hundred years old) prompted by John Berryman's suicide. They were talking about how hard it is to live as a poet in a culture never satisfied with what has been done but is always asking *what next?* Publish one book of poetry in this country, Kunitz said, and "you are in the prison of poetry." Wilbur said Berryman lived only for poetry, and while Wilbur thought that admirable, he also thought it wasn't such a good thing. "I think it can break up your health and destroy your joy in life and art," he said. To live a life of freedom in this country, self-determined, outside the "prison of poetry" (or any other prison created by public expectation), requires silence and cunning. And maybe tennis.

I have had the luck to share a community with Richard Wilbur at two points in my life. I didn't know him well, but I have been able to witness some of what I believe to be true about the man. For twenty years he was a professor of English at Wesleyan University in Connecticut, where my own teaching took place. We overlapped for seven years there in the early seventies, when he was at the pinnacle of accomplishment, esteem, and fame. A more dignified, genuinely humble man could not be imagined. Punctilious about fulfilling his university responsibilities, he always attended our interminable department meetings. Once, sitting next to him, I saw that he was holding under the table a volume of Ben Jonson's poetry at which he would now and then discreetly glance. This made me respect him even more.

More recently, I have been spending winters in Key West, where many artists live for at least some of the year. Here, too, Richard Wilbur preceded me, living in a compound that originally included John Ciardi and Ralph Ellison as well as John and Barbara Hersey. Here the Wilburs would entertain, and I recall one eye-opening conversation about driving with dogs between New England and Florida, in which the master of language revealed that "I'd like a ground-floor room" is code for "I have a dog." In Key West Wilbur was friends with Leonard Bernstein, with whom he collaborated on *Candide*, writing the brilliant lyrics. Here the poet, his muse, and I all did leg lifts and pulldowns at the same gym. Or, as he put it,

> We poets at the gym begin in fatness,
> Whereof come in the end resiliency and flatness

Perhaps Wilbur has a side known only to intimates, but from my oblique view he seems to be as clever, courteous, responsible, courtly, witty, generous, and authentic in life as in his art. I've never glimpsed up close a writer in whom there was less of a gap between public and private. I imagine he is as much the poet when he plays tennis as he is a tennis player when he writes poetry. He seems to move easily inside his life and identity, and being a poet needn't be turned on and off.

Once in Key West we both attended a performance by a young actress reading Elizabeth Bishop's poetry. I happened to walk down the street next to Wilbur afterward and asked him, as someone who had known Bishop, whether the actress had gotten her right. "She was better at being Elizabeth Bishop than Elizabeth was," he said. Wilbur, by contrast, has never seemed to play Richard Wilbur. He is the splendid person whose name he bears.

Sensible, elegant Richard Wilbur, with his commitment to sanity and concreteness, his savoring of what endures. How I love him. How I value his Miltonic sense of the poet's role as a service to the community, and how I also value what he has denied himself. What a relief to pick up *Collected Poems* and find nothing long, no *Changing Light at Sandover*, no bid to write a work that might sit on the shelf next to *The Divine Comedy* or *Paradise Lost*, no effort to boost his oeuvre into a higher sphere. In his acceptance of the marginality of poetry, Wilbur may come eventually to seem the wisest and most timely poet of our days.

Oral History

INTERVIEWS BY NANCY KLINGENER
FOR THE *MIAMI HERALD* (1995)

Ellen Welters Sanchez (1902–2007)

Music teacher and songwriter of "The Beautiful Isle of Key West."
Daughter of Frank Welters of the Welters Cornet Band

I WAS BORN IN 1902. That doesn't make me one hundred, but it makes me ninety-three-plus. . . . I was born right down in that lane across from the courthouse. That's where my grandparents lived, years ago.

My grandfather, he worked at the trolley in those years gone by. That's all I could tell you about that. My father was always, from young, a musician. He was a born musician, and he carried a band after he got old enough to have a band. It used to play all over Key West—Welters Cornet Band. His name was Frank Welters, and the band was named after him. He had an orchestra and used to play for orchestras, too. I played the piano for whatever organizations and whatever programs they needed me for.

My daddy's band played for parades and funerals. After they

Ellen Welters Sanchez (at her piano in 1990) wrote the popular song "The Beautiful Isle of Key West. "It came [right] out of my brain," she said.

organized it, they got uniforms—it had stripes in it, I can't remember the color of it—it was blue or green, it wasn't red. Sometimes they would give him some money, tip them for playing whatever the organization was playing for. My daddy's band used to play a lot for nothing. Parades of all kinds. They used to have military organizations, if they'd go out marching, [and] they didn't have a band, then my daddy's band used to be the ones. They played for the military, for the city and organizations that invited them to come out. He was the head musician in those days of Key West. They didn't have a white band then, they had the colored bands.

I used to sing with the band, sure, anytime they needed singing done. . . . I learned my first music listening to my daddy teaching other people. I would be where he was teaching them. That was the beginning of my learning music, but eventually I did go under the Sisters of the Convent playing the piano music. I did increase myself under their instruction. I went to the Sisters' school the Catholic sisters' school for the colored. I graduated from there. It was run by the Catholics, and my teachers were nuns. They were good teachers. . . .

Sanchez's father, Frank Welters, "was a born musician" his daughter said. "After he got old enough to have a band, it used to play all over Key West."

My sister and I used to play duets together. We played together and separate. She played on programs, I played on programs, and then the people would ask us to play duets together. Me and her, we played all over Key West. She was a little more than two years older than me. I loved to play with my sister—the Welters Sisters, Ellen and Romelda, they used to announce us.

I wrote "The Beautiful Isle of Key West." It came out of my brain. I was inspired by playing the music in the band. When I got home,

The Welters Cornet Band "played for parades and funerals," Sanchez said. "After they organized it, they got uniforms — it had stripes in it . . . blue or green."

I'd say, "The beautiful Isle of Key West." Then I wrote it: "Key West — the beautiful Isle of Key West. The tropical moon, where lovers can spoon — where? On the isle of Key West." From that time on the jazz-playing orchestra, they took it, and the bands took it, and it spread the words and the music was all from Ellen Camille Agnes Welters Sanchez. Ellen Welters wrote that song, that's what I was when I wrote it. I could have been anywhere between eighteen and twenty-one.

After I learned what music was in every form, that's when I started teaching it. I must have been anywhere between eighteen and twenty years old, somewhere right in there. I used to teach at home a little bit before I started teaching out. The children kept saying, "We want to play music like Miss Ellen," and that parent would ask me to take the child in music lessons. Some of them would just be around ten years old, starting to learn music. I didn't teach in the school, but I played to help the Catholic music teachers. They used to get me in to play for them in the Catholic schools. I didn't teach the other instruments. I taught music to those that were playing those other instruments, but I didn't teach the instruments they blow.

Kermit "Shine" Forbes (1914–2000)

Jack of all trades — from diver for coins to boxing cornerman — he took a "poke" at referee Ernest Hemingway for not stopping a fight.

I WAS BORN and raised here [in Key West]. My father was a taxi driver, driving horse and carriage. My grandfather, he was a sponger. Then after that he worked for the city a long time until he died. He'd light the lights. Only certain places, certain streets had lights. He'd light them at night, and he'd go back in the morning and he'd out them. They were gas.

When I was a little boy, a dishwasher job was a big deal. It was $7 a week, but if one person quit there would be five men trying to get that job. The La Concha was a big thing. Kress was a big thing. We had the Casa Marina, that was a big job.

They just started calling me Shine. I didn't like it, but they kept on. I was eight or nine. They had nicknames for people around here. A friend of mine, they called him Pork Chop. I dove money when I was about nine years old. The people would throw the money down. Willy Wickers, he used to dive, too. He was a big fat man, and a fellow called Skinner, the bartender at Sloppy Joe's, he dove [for] money. Willie Wickers had children and Skinner had children. It was fun to see Willie Wickers dive. He had what you call a dry dock, something you'd pull boats up on at the foot of Simonton Street. All of us used to hang there in time to go dive money in the morning until the Cuba boats came in. He had a boat they called the *Honey and the Rock*. All of us would go there to dive money. It was about forty feet deep. We'd dive and put it in our mouths. We'd have a jaw full of money sometimes. Willie Wickers used to dive from one side of the boat and come back out the other side. He wouldn't let us do that because it was dangerous. He knew what he was doing, but he wouldn't let the kids do that.

When we were kids, another thing we used to do, fellows used to come from the north. They used to buy curios, the fish. We'd catch them, and a fellow named Copper Lip, he used to sell them to them. It would be pretty fish like angelfish and cockeyed pollies, just tropical pretty fish. You had to catch them and keep them alive and carry

Kermit "Shine" Forbes was born and raised in Key West. His grandfather (not pictured) was one of the few African American spongers.

them to the dock, you know where the A&B lobster house is. In this place a fellow would come and buy the tropical fish, and he shipped them to New York in a tank. We caught them with a hook and line or sometimes we'd put a round net and we'd scoop them up. At the time, I don't know why, you could look to the bottom and see all kinds of tropical fish.

I ran away from home on the train. I was 'round about thirteen or fourteen something like that. I wanted to see what was on the other side. I had never been ever anywhere, never in my life. I went to Charleston, South Carolina. I don't know where I was going, but I got off the train in Charleston. I went to a place called Mount Pleasant four miles out from Charleston. A man said, "Hey boy, do you know how to plow a mule?" I said, "Plow? I don't know what that is," so he showed me what it was, and I stayed on in South Carolina and went to washing dishes and worked on the farms and sawmills and everything to make a living. I put money in a can to come back to Key West. I wanted to see my home back again.

When I got back here, Joe Mills was running the fights at the Blue Heaven. Joe Mills and a fellow named Black Pie were fighting. Ernest Hemingway was refereeing the fight. Joe Mills was beating him so bad I threw the towel in. I was in Black Pie's corner. When you threw a towel in it means to stop the fight. Ernest Hemingway threw the towel back out. I got on the side of the ring and threw the towel back in. When he threw the towel again, he threw it in my face. I don't guess he meant to do it. I jumped in. I didn't know who the man was. I took a poke at him, swung at him. He held me. After that, everybody jumped in the ring and stopped it. Sweeting said, "You know what you did?" I said, "What?" He said, "You know who that man is you took a poke at?" I said, "I guess it's some old bum here refereeing the fight, trying to pick up a nickel so he can get a bottle of wine." He said, "That's Ernest Hemingway." I said, "What, the writer?" He said, "Yeah, he lives right across from your mother."

When I came back here, they were widening out those bridges from the railroad. I went right up there. When I first went there, they put me on the cement crew. After that they put me down on waterproofing the beams that went across. Then we started pouring for the handrails. I worked until they finished the bridges. I came back to Key West, and things got kind of bad, and I started working for the WPA. Then the war started, the Navy Yard opened up again. This job opened up building a hangar. I worked there until they called me for the army. I went in '42, I got back in '46. I heard there was an opening at the naval hospital for cooks. I went down and signed up for that job. I stayed there for thirty-two years, and I retired right from there.

Not of This World

ALISON LURIE

WHEN JAMES MERRILL and I first met in the hot summer of 1950, we didn't take to each other. If someone had told me that day that we would be friends for forty years, I would have thought they were joking.

Jimmy seemed both coolly detached and awkwardly self-conscious. He was thin and pale and shortsighted, with thick, black-rimmed spectacles (later he would wear contact lenses). Though only twenty-four, he was clearly already an intellectual and an aesthete. He appeared to have read everything and, worse, to be surprised at our ignorance.

As his memoir of those years declares in its title, Jimmy was *A Different Person* then, in both senses of the phrase. He was different from most other persons, and he was different from the person he would become. Most of us change as we age, but Jimmy changed more than most. He not only became more confident and better-looking—eventually elegantly handsome—he also became kinder, more generous, and more sympathetic. He never quite became an ordinary person, but his instinctive scorn of fools, once only half concealed by good manners, relaxed and gave way to a detached, affectionate amusement, such as a highly civilized visitor from another planet might feel.

By 1955, Jimmy had also become something of a dandy. Though he wore conventional suits and shirts and neckties to official academic occasions, his everyday clothes were elegant but odd, sometimes slightly comic. He had a subtle, rather Art Nouveau color sense: he liked mauve and purple and apricot and turquoise silk or Egyptian cotton shirts and bright, flowered ties. At home he often cooked breakfast in a Japanese kimono and sandals. I remember especially some red straw and silk sandals and a gray-striped silk kimono with deep sleeves cuffed in black.

At this time Jimmy had not yet achieved the attentive, contained, charming manner of his later years. He fidgeted with things and was sometimes awkward and uneasy with strangers. He misplaced ordinary objects and did not know how to drive. He frequently became panicky when faced with a mechanical or practical problem: a broken window blind, frozen pipes, missing student papers, a canceled plane flight.

This, I felt then, was to be expected. I saw Jimmy as a kind of Martian: supernaturally brilliant, detached, quizzical, apart. Naturally he was someone with whom the invisible energies of this world would not cooperate, whom they would trick and confuse.

But Jimmy was in stunningly perfect control intellectually. His mind worked faster than that of anyone I'd known: he could answer most questions before you finished asking them. Words for him were like brilliant-colored toys, and he could build with them the way gifted children build with LEGO blocks, constructing and deconstructing elaborate, original architectural shapes and fantastic machines.

Jimmy also had a gift for making everything relevant. He shared E. M. Forster's belief that one must connect with other people—perhaps only some other people, in his case. If Jimmy liked someone, he would often try to find a bond between this person and himself, a coincidence: he was delighted, for instance, to discover that he and a new acquaintance had stayed in the same pension in Florence, or that I'd been born on September 3, exactly six months later than he.

But what Jimmy connected best wasn't people but words and ideas. He was keenly alert to ambiguity and multiple meanings, and scathingly and inventively alert to banality. Sometimes when I was with him, I would hear a cliché hop out of my mouth, like the frogs and toads that afflict the bad sister in the fairy tale. Usually he would only wince slightly, but now and then he would repeat the cliché in his characteristic drawl, half eastern upper-class and half southern. He would play with it in a mild, devastating way, scrutinizing the words with a herpetologist's detachment.

In his writing, Jimmy would often casually rescue clichés from banality. In *Sandover*, for instance, he speaks of "this net of loose talk tightening to verse." He was able to give any word or phrase, even the most ordinary, double and triple meanings, connecting it with weather, music, interior decoration, art, literature, myth, history, or

"His mind worked faster than that of anyone I'd known; he could answer most questions before you finished asking them," Lurie wrote of Merrill.

several of these at once. A kind of poetic, meaningfulness was one of his specialties. One famous early example is the double pun in "Three Sketches for Europa." The nymph Europa, kidnapped by Jupiter in the shape of a bull, eventually becomes Europe:

> The god at last indifferent
> And she no longer chaste but continent.

Jimmy could make puns in several languages at once: both he and his partner, David Jackson, were fluent in French, German, Italian, and modern Greek, and Jimmy also knew classical Latin and Greek. Most readers and listeners were awed, but a few were made uneasy by the flow of wordplay. One of these dissenters, when I praised Jimmy's verbal wit and skill, remarked, "Uh-huh. A disconnected man, a man without a job or a family or a permanent home, no wonder he's fascinated by connections."

Merrill at the Gym

BILL YANKEE

I WAS JAMES MERRILL'S TRAINER. He used to come to my gym a couple of times a week, usually with his friend and fellow poet Sandy McClatchy. The two of them talked and talked the whole time they were working out. Half the time I didn't know what they were talking about. Mostly literature, you know what I mean?

They used to hate the music I'd have on, so I said, "Well, who do you like?" And Merrill said, "Jussi Bjorling." A couple of weeks later I got a CD in the mail from Merrill: Jussi Bjorling. I liked it. I listened to it all the time until I moved the gym and lost the CD.

Best thing I ever heard him say, he was giving a reading, and this woman comes up to him afterward and gives him a flowering plant. She's a big admirer. She tells him how much his work has meant to her, and she wants him to have this plant as thanks. It's an anthurium. And he says, right away, "Well it isn't laurel, but it's hardy."

He was saying things like that all the time—you know, rhymes and words that sound like rhymes. What was that thing he said when he was working out? "Sets and reps, lats and pecs." He was always coming up with shit like that. Sometimes he'd say things, I didn't get them for two weeks.

He really hated working out. He was one of those people who'd say, when I told him to do something, "What if I just say no?"

People were afraid of him. They'd stick their head in the gym and see Merrill was there, and they'd kind of freeze and back out. He was so smart, you know, he could crucify you if he wanted to. But I thought he was a great guy.

Key West Aquarium: The Sawfish

JAMES MERRILL

Before our day, what had the sawfish seen —
His own snout's toothy, prehistoric blade?
His own tank's sun and shade? . . .
Flat white lips of a ghost or libertine

Open and shut, as do the strenuous gills
Which even admit light. Bored in mid-swim,
He sees you — and a sunbeam fills
That frightful mouth. Now if I speak for him

A fellow captive, lips that kissed and told
Declare me — well, almost —
Not of this world, transparently a ghost

Into whom still the bright shaft glides. One old
Disproven saw sinks out of mind;
Love's but a dream and only death is kind.

Merrill wrote this dark sonnet in 1989, but it was not published until after his 1995 death, which it anticipates.

A Poet at Heart

PHYLLIS ROSE

EVEN SOME OF US who saw a good deal of John Malcolm Brinnin in his later years forgot he was a poet. He had published six volumes of poetry, but the last had appeared in 1970, and I didn't get to know him until a good twenty years later when he was in his late seventies. He and I and many other writers spent winters in Key West and often found ourselves at the same festivities. John and I had a special bond because we were colder than most—what the French call *frileux*, shiverers. John dealt with it stylishly, wearing light-colored cashmere sweaters or draping them elegantly over his shoulders. He dressed so well that seeing what he'd be wearing was part of the fun of a party.

For outings by boat to David Wolkowsky's Ballast Key hideaway, he carried an Italian leather backpack and he'd read the *New York Times* as close to the water as he could place a chair. He loved the ocean and big ships. He came early to parties at beachfront houses in order to look at the ocean. His own apartment overlooked the shipping channel so he could watch boats come into port. He loved big ships so much he wrote a book about them, and every year he would check onto a cruise ship with a huge pile of books for the sheer pleasure of being at sea. Most of us in Key West look down on cruise ships as little better than floating dumpsters, pumping garbage into the water and tourists into our streets, so I considered it a terrific act of imagination on John's part to see them as sites of solitude and romance. Abroad, you were most likely to find him in Venice, the wettest city.

John was also known to us, his friends, for the high drama of his eyeglasses, massive horn-rimmed affairs that were as much a product of his wit and conscious choice as were his courtesy, his conversation, his skill at anagrams. A lot of his poetic spirit went into his self-presentation. In retrospect I think we were seeing the last gasp of a tradition that expected a poet to look and act like a poet and imagined him as a man of elegance, a Ben Jonson, a Dryden, Donne, or Pope — not the more recent image of a poet as self-destructive madman. Such are the vagaries of fame and identity, however, that it was a poet as self-destructive madman who more or less obliterated John's own literary identity.

In the early 1950s, John was head of the Poetry Center of the 92nd Street Y, and in that capacity arranged for Dylan Thomas to come to the United States. He became Thomas's friend and unofficial lecture agent, accompanied him on his reading tour, and chronicled his alcoholic implosion and eventual death in a vivid and wildly successful book titled *Dylan Thomas in America*. Ever after that John Malcolm Brinnin was the man who brought Dylan Thomas to America. That is what he was to such an extent, even to his friends, that I was surprised, reading his journals after his death, to discover that that was not how he thought about himself — that he was in his own mind a poet.

Though he published six volumes of poetry, John Malcolm Brinnin is better known as the author of Dylan Thomas in America. *Photograph by Rollie McKenna.*

This is the opening of the title poem of John's last book, *Skin Diving in the Virgins*:

> Alfonso was his name: his sad cantina
> leaned against a palm. Over my head,
> he scanned a coastline only he could see
> and took my order in cuneiform.

My water gear, like loose connections
from some mild machine, dripped on the table. What
a good morning! The wreck I'd shimmied through —
a sunken vessel, like Alfonso, some-
what Spanish in the stern — still weighed its gold,

while angelfish and sunfish still made mouths
to tell me nothing. That kind of poetry
one is, in principle, against. But what
sweet swarms of language to be silent in!
I tasted salt, half dreaming back and down.

All of a sudden came the pelicans:
crazy old men in baseball caps, who flew
like jackknives and collapsed like fans . . .

From which I conclude that John Malcolm Brinnin was *essentially*
a poet and that now, when the poetry of his presence isn't available
to me, I can go on enjoying his presence on the page. A good reason
to have poets as friends.

Letter from Key West, for Elizabeth Bishop

JOHN MALCOLM BRINNIN

Elizabeth my dear,
I found your house,
just as you said I would, by turning right
where "weedy" Southard Street falls off to grass
(one pensive little heron—legs as thin
as wire—watched me, but did not take flight)
beside the old building with the cupcake domes.
Even, I think, without your careful postings,
the place would have quivered, as if in quotation marks—
in much the same way, say, that one clean line
of yours will, on a page, dwell by itself,
simple, pretty and mysterious.

"Arrived at the site," as guidebooks say, "we pause
amidst a picturesque profusion of . . ."
Nothing of the sort. It's all there—open.
The house, four-square and delicate, sits snug—
a small white-shuttered castle in a keep
almost, yet not quite, filling up a space
left to a sprawl of cacti and rock roses.
That pyramid roof. Remember how the sun
shoots from its eaves like a Masonic eye?
(My fancy, dear—too gaudy to be yours.)
There's a sign tacked onto one of the slim pillars
—a smutch of black lopsided lettered crayon—
declaring *Alloe for Sale*, but otherwise
you might have closed your front door yesterday.

(What's this bereaved enchantment makes a man
pilgrim to places he has never left?
I see you circa 1936,
seated on that same white step
in a straw hat, your chin on your right hand,
hardly smiling, yet, for all the grain
in that dim photograph, clearly at home.)

I have some doubts: that diamond on the gate,
upright — one of those you see on playing cards —
is it some unexplained motif of yours?
The Gothic frill along the overhand —
carpenter Gothic, I mean. Did that come later?
The green cast-iron railing by the stairs?
Everything else bespeaks you: purity
of line, strict measure, grace in miniature.
(The angle of the shutters I might add,
allows for looking out but not — ha ha —
unless one stands there tip-toe, looking in.)
TOM MESA is the name on the mailbox.
(A Cuban cowboy? A strayed Navajo?)
Whatever he is, he's immaculate,
If not so hot on draughtsmanship, or spelling.

I don't see why you'd leave it, all in all,
unless — but who am I to speculate? —
even so modest a shape of painted wood
will jail the same spirit it might signify?
"Think of the long trip home" I hear you saying.
"Should we have stayed at home and thought of here?"
"Here" meaning, I see, here, there, anywhere.
I'm glad you turned my steps your way.
                          Love, John

P.S. I've just re-read your letter. (Gulp.)
The house *you* lived in is the one next *door*.
It's now invisible behind big trees,
Except for one high window, facing north.

Watching Screwball Comedies with Harry Mathews

ANN BEATTIE

HARRY MATHEWS, who died on January 25, 2017, was born on Valentine's Day. Now his friends (including those in Key West, who, during the winter, often got to see Harry and his beloved wife, Marie) have to be without him. About the time he turned eighty, maybe a bit earlier, he had to stop bicycling. He did this grudgingly, berating some of us for our concern (expressed as he was about to cycle off after certain . . . let's just say wine-centric dinners). His good friend James Merrill was the person who'd urged the Mathewses to leave wintry New York and come enjoy the sun in Key West. (Merrill, on his own bicycle, was always a delightful sight as he sped toward you wearing his shirt, shorts, argyle socks, and sandals.) Not that Harry needed to imitate Merrill or his other close friend, John Ashbery, at all: his sense of style was singular, as was Harry. But how did I become dear friends with a person who had specially sewn compartments in his shirt pockets for his cigars? How did my husband and I appear, year after year, on New Year's Eve to be poured as much champagne as we wished (forget that "wishing upon a star" nonsense; this was excellent champagne) and to watch a screwball comedy that would be midway through at midnight? He shushed us if we so much as whispered to the person sitting next to us. In the background, we'd hear fireworks, screams, the ubiquitous unmuffled motorcycles, more piercing screams, and soon, very soon, the sirens, like the TV volume, were adjusted upward to a near-deafening level. In Key West, certain individuals get the idea that they might, say, blow up a pier to celebrate the New Year. (Or, at the very least, set their neighbor's garbage can on fire.)

But I don't want to suggest that we were strangely dressed, hedonistic, alcohol-dowsing creatures with no more imagination than to mark the end of the old, in with the new by watching Rudy Vallee. Harry was all imagination. Imagination and detail. He swung between those personal polarities like a watch used to hypnotize, and in a way, he did hypnotize you. Let me say right away that he knew a lot. Please just google Oulipo to get a general sense of the society he belonged to, in which, almost until his death, he remained the *only* American member. He knew about everything from poetic form to opera to Byzantine coins—though if you brought up those coins, he'd suspect you were about to turn ironic and would question you: when and how did you become interested in Byzantine coins? He knew the Latin name of the plant you liked in his garden.

He once stunned Rust Hills by instantly answering one of Rust's many questions. As the carful of people was returning from a lower key to Key West, a beautiful sunset spread across the sky. Harry exclaimed, "Oh, it's like coming into Venice!" And my husband said, "More like coming into Mestre." Somehow the word *propaganda* was used—you think I was keenly focusing on this?—and Rust, who loved information and specialized in mumbling questions to himself, asked, "Where does that word *propaganda* come from?" Harry said, "It originates with the Uffici per la Propagazione della Fede, which was set up by the Vatican under the Counter-Reformation to propagate the faith. It still occupies a building in Rome designed by Borromini."

Harry might also have known how to change a tire—he loved process, and when he cooked certain things, he wore an enormous ticking timer on a string around his neck—but I don't know about that. Though, after his mother's death, he drove her truly enormous car through the narrow streets of Key West until the car itself died. There's one stretch of Simonton Street I never pass without thinking of the sight my husband and I saw one night after we'd parted from Harry and his wife and friends: that enormous car, that cruise-ship-size car, coming down the opposite side of the street with the interior light on, the faces of Harry and John Ashbery, a second's bright hologram flash of merriment. And then they were gone.

At this point, Harry might wonder why I've been mentioning vehicles: cars, bicycles, motorcycles. Is this what someone would be thinking about when remembering Harry Mathews? But I mention earth, the vehicles of earth, only as a point of departure to the air. What about

"Harry was all imagination," says Beattie, "Imagination and detail. He swung between those personal polarities like a watch used to hypnotize. "

all those planes—the big airlines, the private jets, the navy test planes that fly over Key West with such bursts of sound that everyone knows to simply stop speaking until they pass (though sometimes the first words of the overeager person who had the floor get garbled in the plane's fading roar)? Harry would simply raise a finger, and everyone would stop speaking. (He studied music at Harvard, so it's probably fine to think of the obvious: Harry as a conductor.) I don't think he originated the raised finger, but he did it better than anyone. And his facial expression was so clear. It didn't involve the conventional eye roll; the obnoxious noise was too usual to surprise anyone. His expression never varied. It said, *Wait, this will pass.* It suggested that he was in control. The ever so slightly raised eyebrows let *you* know that *he* knew the conversation could pick up right where it left off. Being reasonable wasn't always optimal, but in some cases, well, what can you do? His expression sort of metaphorically replaced a period with an exclamation point. Whereas I think his amazing fiction often implied just the opposite.

Happy birthday, Harry, from those of us here on the ground, looking upward.

Dear Harry

ROSALIND BRACKENBURY

In 2016, poet and novelist Rosalind Brackenbury read from her novel The Third
Swimmer *as Harry Mathews and his wife, Marie Chaix, looked on.*

Why do I think first
of your beautiful shirts?
Like Gatsby's, enough to make one cry.
And your voice, with its surprising
gentleness, asking, how am I?
Guessing when things weren't easy.
Your exact and generous prose,
and the way you wrote blurbs, so
carefully, as if they were poems;
poems as if they were puzzles,
stories that were recipes,

novels that were lists. I think
of your vast intelligence,
often held in check: the space
left in our world without it;
of your Olympian grace
—aristocratic, yes, yet thoroughly
and still American, leaving out
small talk, cutting to the chase.
The pink champagne you ordered
for my birthday that year;
that sense you gave of sure festivity.
I think of your brave last battles, your grimace
of pain, half-joking—"This part
of life's not fun." And how,
faced with the end, you remained so much
a gent. I guessed, you'd had
a plenitude of fun: in life,
in literature, in love, the best; and now
I like to imagine you pain-free, alive,
with glass in hand, at ease to chat with old lost
friends upon some Oulipian cloud,
where no unwanted vowels may intrude,
and all the saddest stories end in jest.

The New Tourism

HARRY MATHEWS

Where is it I came from
And where is it I'm stranded?
Part of the maps is black
And the rest's in borrowed language.

I have nothing to wear
And shops won't take my money.
Kids have buckled my knees
And blear has filled my eyelids.

Iron lips are slick
And burning books are sunny
But I can't see the point
Of the busy wizened creatures.

Why think of fear
At placid foreign features?
Strangest are the tears
Of the busy wizened creatures.

Where is it I came from
And where is it I'm stranded?
Part of the maps is black
And the rest's in borrowed language.

Walks in the Wild

HAL CROWTHER

BIOGRAPHERS DEFINE themselves by the subjects they choose. Some compete for the few big fish who attract publishers and enhance a biographer's reputation by association alone. Others, often humble academics, are obliged to angle in shallow water for fish they hope other fishermen will overlook. Sometimes they hook poor things with too little life in them to put up much of a fight, or make much of a story.

The biographer with a true vocation, the one whose books we read and remember, is neither intimidated nor seduced by the big fish. Size alone—a subject's fame and historical consequence—is never what he's after. Invariably he chooses an individual whose story suits him as an adventure—a person whose life, examined at length, promises to shed light on things the biographer needs to know about himself. Biography is self-expression, really, by a writer wearing a mask; a wise choice means everything. The best biographers devote ten years or more to each project, and that's a long walk without congenial, fit, and stimulating company.

These journeys of discovery aren't overburdened with altruism. A commercial biographer who reimagines Marilyn Monroe, with his eye on a beach house at Hilton Head, isn't necessarily more selfish than the scholar who truly needs to spend a decade walking in the footsteps—or in the shoes—of Ralph Waldo Emerson, however that might affect his other relationships and commitments. Readers are generally in the dark about the deeper connections between biographers and their subjects. They sense that Emily Dickinson and John of Gaunt would not have the same biographer, but they haven't thought about it. The books they read don't offer much help, on the surface, because one of the serious biographer's professional imperatives is to keep himself hidden as much as possible.

Robert D. Richardson (Bob, from here on) spent at least thirty years of his life reconstructing the lives of Henry David Thoreau, Ralph Waldo Emerson, and William James—lives which were spent, for the most part, within a few miles of Harvard Yard, during the reign of Queen Victoria. Richardson himself, like all three of his subjects, was once a student at Harvard. A blue-collar critic might interpret this as evidence of a cloistered, parochial Bostonian bias, of the biographer's reluctance to venture far from the privileged classes and the Harvard Alumni Association. This would be a spectacularly inaccurate interpretation of the spirit and intellectual essence of Bob Richardson.

I've read the books, and I've known the man behind them for twenty years. When *Emerson* was published in 1995, I went back and read Richardson's biography of Thoreau. Knowing that William James was next, I allowed myself a grin of recognition at the way the biographer had structured his life's work. There was never a Back Bay, Victorian stereotype that applied to his triumvirate. They were, in their separate ways, the three wild men of Massachusetts; nowhere in nineteenth-century America were there three less conformist, complacent, or predictable intellects. Thoreau was known in his time as the untamed hermit of Concord, a social renegade who preached civil disobedience and earned his living as a day laborer. He roamed the wilds of Maine with genuine Indians, studied civilization to see how much of it he could dispense with, and searched for the truth in the dust at his doorstep.

The Emerson biography is subtitled *The Mind on Fire*. When Emerson's mind ignited, in those sleepy days when James Fenimore Cooper was the giant of American literature, he lit a fire under Boston's Unitarian intelligentsia that still burns centuries later, and surely contributes to the fact that Massachusetts is the most progressive state in the Union. Richardson's Third Man, the polymath James, was the original wild card of late-Victorian Boston, a man whose thirst for experience led him to mescal and ghost-seeking, among other mind-opening extravagances, and whose unflagging tolerance for strange and unwelcome ideas form a large piece of the bedrock beneath modern science, psychology, and philosophy. They were very different temperaments, these Bostonians, but they were all strong swimmers against the current, and what they had in common is what they have in common with their biographer.

I began to get the idea on the first page of *Emerson*, where Emerson, twenty-eight, opens the coffin to look at his deceased wife, fourteen months dead of tuberculosis (25 years and 540 pages later, Emerson opens the coffin of his son Waldo, who had been dead for 15 years). The point for me was that I would not have done this; my flash of insight was that Bob Richardson almost certainly would have. "He had a powerful craving for direct, personal, unmediated experience," Richardson writes of Emerson. "That's what he meant when he insisted that one should strive for an original relation to the universe."

I should explain that before I'd read a word of Richardson's biographies, I had sailed with him in the North Atlantic — once through a fifty-knot gale — and followed him in a kayak through one hundred miles of Idaho whitewater. Richardson is an intellectual's intellectual, a scholar for whom ideas form all the road signs of the world he walks in. But his path through this world is not for the faint of heart. He writes of "the soldierly quality Thoreau admired, the courage to live deeply and suck the marrow out of life." He discovers that Thoreau was an admirer of Sir Walter Raleigh, arguably the most butch of all canonical English writers: "His writing had boldness it could only have gotten from life, Thoreau thought, and from a life that was, above all else, active."

Once you get the picture, confirmation is everywhere in Richardson's work. One of his finest portraits is Emerson's eccentric aunt Mary Moody Emerson — Richardson's books about men never shortchange the women — who slept in a bed shaped like a coffin and wore her burial shroud when she traveled. "Always do what you are afraid to do," she counseled her nephews. Richardson praises "her hunger for personal experience of the strongest, most direct kind" and speculates that Emerson "was pushed onward by her undrownable spirit." William James, a depressive who was often in poor health, personified one of Richardson's dearest themes, the triumph of pure will over fears and infirmities. From James's essay "Is Life Worth Living?" he quotes: "It's only by risking our persons from one hour to another that we live at all."

The essay continues, "If this life be not a real fight, in which something is eternally gained for the universe by success, it is no better than a game of private theatricals from which we may withdraw at will."

Take courage, in short, and take action. When I began to understand what Richardson admired most about his subjects, I remembered that Bob himself experimented with parasailing in his late sixties—I'm a witness—and inadvisedly climbed a mountain in China a few months after heart-valve surgery. But the Richardson I'll always remember was the skipper of a thirty-eight-foot sloop we were trying to anchor off the coast of Cape Breton as night fell and the wind picked up alarmingly. Six, seven, eight times the anchor failed to catch; another failure or two and we'd have been drifting across the Gulf of St. Lawrence in the dark, praying that we could raise the Coast Guard on the radio. Some of us were cursing and considering whiskey, some were fingering their rosaries; Richardson, in charge, was weighing our odds in his calmest voice and smoking a cigar as if he were day-sailing across Cape Cod Bay.

Though Key West waters no longer teem with record-sized grouper and snapper, due to overfishing, they still provide fresh seafood for local restaurants.

The anchor caught, we survived, I was indelibly impressed. Bob Richardson was a walk-the-walk biographer of impetuous, tempestuous, "undrownable" spirits. He saw life as a physical and intellectual adventure with no guarantees, no safe passage or special favors for the wise or the privileged. Sometimes I suspect that his fearless stoicism was formed by spending so much time with the nineteenth century, when life was so uncertain and sturdy spirits seized it with a passion that seems almost neurotic today. (Both Emerson and James were traumatized by the loss of young sons, and Emerson lost his first wife and his dear friend Thoreau to TB; one arresting thing I learned from Richardson is that in 1825 half the adults in Boston were infected with tuberculosis, which was the cause of one-third of all deaths.)

Robert Richardson, who died in 2020, spent three decades reconstructing the lives of Henry David Thoreau, Ralph Waldo Emerson, and William James.

But these books are more than philosophical chest-beating, demonstrating that nineteenth-century males, even writers and intellectuals, were much richer in testosterone than their descendants. Richardson's wild men were as creative as they were brave, and they're blessed with a biographer who navigates the swirling crosscurrents of nineteenth-century thought as deftly as I remember him navigating the currents in the Strait of Canso. Whatever you thought you knew about transcendentalism, pragmatism, German idealism, or radical empiricism, Richardson will expand and clarify it in an unpretentious prose style that sticks to the layman's ribs.

In his book on James he even pauses, endearingly, at a tricky philosophical intersection, and allows, "This is not easy stuff." These are intellectual biographies, which means that Richardson attempted to read everything his subjects read—which also means that he works just as hard as these death-haunted, pressed-for-time nineteenth-century giants who fascinate him. It's a formidable combination. He's a writer who rewards your trust, for the same reasons we learned to trust him on those sailboats far from shore—he knows what he's doing, and because he's restless, curious, and fearless, he can take you where you might never travel on your own.

Key West Cowboy

GLENN FRANKEL

HE'S ALL BUT FORGOTTEN NOW, sad to say. But fifty years ago James Leo Herlihy was probably the second most renowned writer living in Key West, just a notch below Tennessee Williams, his mentor and occasional swimming companion. It was the movies that helped place him on this pedestal—specifically the 1969 production of *Midnight Cowboy*, directed by John Schlesinger, which was based on Herlihy's raw and gritty second novel of the same name. The book, which traced the dubious progress of a young Texan who travels by bus to New York City to seek his fortune as a male hustler, had been largely overlooked when it was first published in 1965. But the movie was a critical and box office hit and was the first (and last) X-rated movie to win the Academy Award for Best Picture. Jamie Herlihy got roughly 3 percent of the net profits.

The success of Midnight Cowboy *"has made me too well known for my comfort and has put some things off balance," Herlihy confided to a friend.*

He was a tall man with dark, beguiling looks, and a deeply resonant voice. The son of a working-class family in Detroit, he'd served briefly in the navy at the end of World War II, used the GI Bill to study writing and art at Black Mountain College, an arts school in North Carolina, then left for California to take acting classes at the Pasadena Playhouse. He came to New York in 1952, took menial jobs while writing plays and fiction, and fell in love with a handsome pop music singer named Dick Duane, who introduced him to a lively circle of gay artists, writers, and performers at a time when New York was the undisputed capital of the arts world. By the late '50s he'd co-written a Broadway play and published his first novel, both of which were made into Hollywood movies. He wrote about lonely, troubled people—"grotesques," he called them—in the mode of Sherwood Anderson, Tennessee Williams, and Carson McCullers. He also did occasional acting gigs for movies, television, and the theater. But New York wore him down—it was too noisy, too dirty, too full of people he didn't care for or trust. It exacerbated the periodic bouts of depression that had haunted him since childhood. At the behest of Duane, he took a Greyhound bus to Key West.

Although both are islands, it'd be hard to imagine a place less like Manhattan than Key West. No building was taller than three stories, most of the houses were wooden cottages, basements didn't exist, and neither did rush hour. There were just thirty thousand people spread over eight square miles. Except for when revelers hit the Old Town bars at sundown, the island's loudest noise was the sound of the ocean breeze whispering through the palm trees. "You got tired of those New York winters, and for $9,500 you could buy a house here," recalls Kirby Congdon, a poet and painter who moved to Key West from New York in 1959, around the same time that Herlihy started buying property there. Both of them ended up owning cottages next-door to each other on Bakers Lane in the heart of Old Town.

Tennessee Williams had arrived in Key West in the early 1940s, fleeing from the disastrous Boston premiere of *Battle of Angels*, one of his earliest plays. Williams loved Key West's loose frontier atmosphere—including the handsome young sailors and Cuban street boys—its heat and isolation and the fact he could swim in the warm, sultry ocean almost every day of the year. He spent his day at the typewriter in a one-room shack, rode a rented bicycle down the flat, sunburned streets, and danced with his landlady in the evenings at Sloppy Joe's, one of Ernest Hemingway's old hangouts.

Williams liked being surrounded by a worshipping crowd, and he quickly attracted a lively group of friends and followers, including

Gore Vidal, Christopher Isherwood, Truman Capote, and McCullers. They would join him in the late afternoons in the front parlor of the Tradewinds hotel for drinks and gossip. Dick Duane quickly slotted in when he first visited Key West. Jamie Herlihy soon followed.

Duane introduced Herlihy to Williams, whose work Jamie had admired with "total awe," he would recall. Soon he and Williams were swimming off the Monroe County pier at the end of White Street at twilight most evenings. "It was inexpressibly comforting to have the daily company of a kindred spirit," Herlihy told author Lynn Mitsuko Kaufelt. "Just knowing we were both engaged in the same sort of lunatic pursuit provided some essential ground that meant everything to me."

Williams generously praised Herlihy's early short stories and novels. But although Jamie never approached Williams's weight class as a playwright, a certain rivalry developed that Dick Duane could feel at the dinner table whenever the two men got together. "There were times when it was loving and times when it wasn't so loving," Duane recalls. "When people started talking about Jamie, and Tennessee was at the table, there was that envy. There can only be one star in a room."

Still, Herlihy came to love Key West, largely for the same reasons that had attracted Williams: the combination of being part of an exclusive unofficial club of gay artistes who supported each other—at least when they weren't engaged in byzantine feuds—and of having an escape route from the grime, pressure, and simmering hostility of New York's hyperbolic scene.

"The town excited me too much," Herlihy said of Key West. "I spent all my time exploring, walking the streets. The place was mysterious, funky, indescribably exotic. It had much of the charm of a foreign country, but you had the post office and the A&P and the phone worked, so life was easy. The town had a kind of beauty that did not know about itself: it just was."

By the mid-sixties, he was living most of the year on Bakers Lane and encouraging friends from New York like producer Walter Starcke and playwright Evan Rhodes to join him. He also made friends with some of the local talent, including Henry Faulkner, an eccentric artist from Kentucky who showed up every winter with a car full of cats and dogs and had a habit of standing on restaurant tables to denounce eating meat or yelling, "Hey girls!" at the cops as he drove by the Key West police station.

The unexpected commercial success of *Midnight Cowboy* was a huge windfall for Jamie. Besides his share of the movie's profits, he also reaped royalties from the reissued Dell paperback, which sold hundreds of thousands of copies. Jamie was cagey about divulging the amounts involved, telling one interviewer he had cleared only two hundred thousand dollars after taxes. His real take was far more than double that amount.

He claimed that his attitude about the money was one of supreme ambivalence, bordering on annoyance. "When they dumped all this money on me it turned me into a bookkeeper," he told a reporter for the *New York Post*. "I would like to do without money altogether. I feel sort of nagged all the time by people to give it away." Still, he insisted *Midnight Cowboy* had had little impact on his life. "I was old and tough, and I had had other successes," Jamie claimed. "I've had enough money since I was thirty, so it didn't change my life at all."

This was, of course, a barefaced fantasy. Jamie Herlihy had never before had and never again would have a success to remotely rival *Midnight Cowboy*, and the money made a huge impact on his life, although not necessarily a positive one. "*Midnight Cowboy* has made me too well known for my comfort and has put some things off balance," he told Mary Caroline Richards, an old friend. "People whose names I don't know call me collect from distant places and tell me of their need for money. There were three such calls today. My mail contains an average of one a day of similar tales and pleas. Certain people I've known for a long time look at me sideways, and laugh hard when I'm not really very funny. I feel called upon to respond to things that I don't want to have to respond to at all."

Still, the money gave him the freedom to do exactly as he pleased. He used some of it to renovate the cottage at 709 Bakers Lane and build a work studio out back of the main house. The handmade peace sign symbols and the mandalas he painted and mounted on the crossbeams below the living room's ceilings are still visible. He also bought his parents a modest, two-bedroom cottage in town, where they lived until their deaths, his father in 1969, his mother seven years later.

Herlihy regarded Tennessee Williams's work with "total awe." The pair took to swimming most evenings off the end of the White Street pier.

Despite his ambivalence over its success, *Midnight Cowboy* became an unavoidable reference point in Jamie's life. "Everybody would knock on the door at Bakers Lane and ask for the guy who wrote *Midnight Cowboy*," says Bob Thixton, an ex-navy man who became Dick Duane's partner after Dick and Jamie parted ways. "His life became so busy in a way that he never wanted."

At first Herlihy welcomed the young hippies, drifters, runaways, and draft dodgers who showed up at the cottage. He offered up his home and yard as a place for love-ins, be-ins, and weddings in the garden. "I suppose what made me so happy with those beautiful creatures was the sense they gave me that the marginal people to whom I'd been drawn all through my life were suddenly having a heyday," he said. Larry Claypool, a frequent guest in those days, remembers a pillar inside the main cottage that people could climb to a platform with a mattress and high-quality stereo speakers. "You could lay tripping on acid for hours digging the stars through an open skylight and listening to music."

The novelist and screenwriter Thomas McGuane, who lived in Key West and partook of the drugs and alcohol that always seemed on offer, recalls Jamie as "a great fellow, much too generous to us hippies and sorta-hippies who hung around his house abusing his patience." Subject to blue moods, Jamie "seemed to use his own amiability as camouflage for an elusive nature and ever-pending disappearance."

But it all quickly soured. "All the dopers would come on the bus," recalls Thixton. "[Jamie] would have notes—'Shut the Drawer,' 'Knives Go in Here,'—because they would disrupt whatever ordered life he had."

When he finally decided he couldn't handle the constant flow of people and gawkers, Jamie bought a farm property in Hops Bottom in a remote part of Susquehanna County in northeastern Pennsylvania. There were thirty-nine acres altogether, including three inhabitable houses, a nine-acre lake called Jeffers Pond, and six acres of virgin hemlock forest. "I have nine canoes," he boasted. But even there he wasn't comfortable. His visits dwindled.

He started winding down his friendships in Key West, including his long rapport with Tennessee Williams. "I had dinner with Tennessee one night," recalled McGuane, "and Jamie's then current blue mood came up. Tennessee said to me, 'Tom, you know why Jamie's depressed? Because his writing is not very good.' I didn't, and still don't, know what to make of this. Maybe a mentor's envy of his student's popular success."

Author Dotson Rader, Williams's longtime friend, had a different view of the playwright's alienation. Rader says Jamie was "running like a flophouse in Key West. He had a lot of hustlers, street boys, and he was really druggy, a lot of booze. He was out of control. You'd go to a party at his place and the backyard would be full of kids. They were sweet and dear, but you knew they were paying to crash in his pad with sex or drugs. And Tennessee at that point was really kind of turned off by him."

Founded in 1852, St. Paul's Episcopal Church on Duval Street has become a center for musical performances as well as religious services.

In the end, Jamie himself was turned off by Key West and all it had come to represent. He sold the house on Bakers Lane in 1973 and took off for Los Angeles. Many friends were surprised. "I would expect that all of us who knew Jamie in Key West in those days are sorry that he went out of our lives," says McGuane. "He was regarded with great affection by anyone who knew him."

When Jamie got to Los Angeles, he went under the name "Jamie Hathaway" so that none of his old acquaintances could find him. It was as if he had created his own personal witness protection program. "I'm trying not to repeat the errors of Key West," he told his friend Lyle Bongé, "where I had finally become such a public entity there wasn't much for me to chew on."

James Leo Herlihy would live another twenty years, but his dream of becoming a great author was over. After leaving Key West he never published another novel or any other writing.

Sunburned Sage

HAL CROWTHER

IT WOULD HAVE BEEN HARD to stage a better setting for the telling of unguarded stories—a campfire, an ample supply of cheap red wine, possibly even some cannabis in the mix, and the background music of the Salmon River, somewhere in a canyon in Idaho. It would have been hard to find a storyteller with more unguarded stories to tell. Robert Stone had been on the psychedelic bus with Ken Kesey and Neal Cassady; he had seen more of the weird and wild side of America, and several other countries, than any of the rest of us, though this was not an inexperienced crew of river rafters. He'd seen a lot more than he could ever work into his fiction, but Stone's classified stories were ideal for a campfire audience old enough to remember most of the players.

In my imperfect memory, there was a tale about a Merry Prankster who injected a soon-to-be-slaughtered pig with hallucinogenic acid and a whole Mexican village that feasted and freaked out along with their American guests. From those stories of Bob's, I stole one of my favorite phrases—"wolf ticket," meaning a threatening, belligerent presentation, as in "Cassady kept giving wolf tickets to the federales." I claimed it and recycled it at least fifty times. Was it a Stone original? I have no idea. The adventures of Kesey and Cassady have taken on a mythical element, sort of like Paul Bunyan and John Henry if they had been on drugs. Stone was already famous, at least among his friends, for this material that he later mined for the memoir *Prime Green: Remembering the Sixties*. But it was on our retreat from the canyons that my wife and I first experienced a Robert Stone who was not exactly on the same bus with the legendary wild men of the '60s, or even with most of his literary peers. We hadn't known him long enough or thoroughly enough to expect Bob's bloody amazing, damn near supernatural erudition. Even through the psychedelic '60s, a blur of distorted consciousness that he survived and described as well as anyone, his own role models, all along, must have been the great polymaths—double-barreled intellectuals like Bertrand Russell or Isaiah Berlin.

We'd rented a car and Bob needed a ride from the river to the airport in Boise, so it was just the three of us for four hours on the road. In some context I can nowhere near remember, I mentioned Thomas Aquinas. From the back seat, from the sunburned, river-weary novelist still nursing an arm he'd broken in Canada, came a burst of enthusiasm and the first of at least a dozen learned disquisitions on the Scholastics and the medieval church.

I knew that Stone had been "with the nuns" as a child, even in a Catholic orphanage, and I knew that whatever religion he sustained as an adult was far from ortho-
dox. I had no idea that his learning, mostly self-acquired, included enough Catholic theology and church history to qualify him for the College of Cardinals. Delighted and intrigued, I egged him on. A fallen Unitarian is a poor spiritual match for a lapsed Catholic, but a couple of courses in comparative religion and a semester of theology had prepared me, just barely, to ask leading questions and drop relevant names.

"Pope Innocent the Third?" I ventured.

"What a prick," said Monsignor Stone, and went on to dramatize, in great detail, that Unholy Father's successful ef-

Stone had been on the Merry Prankster bus with Ken Kesey, says Crowther, "and had seen more of the weird and wild side of America than . . . the rest of us."

forts to sabotage every monarch in Europe and put every heretic to the torch or the sword. The Fourth Crusade, the sacking of Constantinople, the Albigensian Crusade against the Cathars of southern France—Bob had all of this on instant recall, the way some of us remember every World Series or Final Four. The thirteenth century lived again, in a rented Subaru on a two-lane state road in Idaho. Stone was in his element, or one of them—he'd had to wait a while, perhaps, to find someone who really wanted to hear what he had to say about the Albigensians.

I'd recently given a lecture on H. L. Mencken, who graduated from high school at fifteen and a dozen years later, without benefit of any further classrooms, wrote a book on Friedrich Nietzsche that most philosophers applauded. Stone had also avoided college and claimed that most of his early education came from books he read in the navy. That sunburned sage slouched in the back seat was Mencken's rightful heir, I realized—a prodigious autodidact who had never stopped reading until he was sure he knew more, and knew better, than all the college graduates and all their professors as well. Unlike Mencken, Bob didn't go out to pin people to the wall with his erudition—but neither would he pass up an opportunity to let it shine a little.

About a mile from the Boise airport, Stone's spontaneous narrative reached the bitter end of the Albigensian Crusade, the infamous massacre of Béziers in 1209, where Pope Innocent's army of heretic hunters butchered more than seven thousand men, women, and children in cold blood. As the massacre raged out of control, the papal legate in command, the abbot Arnaud Amalric, was asked what to do about the city's many loyal Catholics. History, Bob reminded us, credits the good Abbot with a command that has been often repeated: "Kill them all, and let God sort them out." In his creative curiosity Bob Stone cast a very wide net, one of the widest I ever encountered. But as all of us who knew him know well, he never turned away from the dark parts.

American Dreamer

MICHAEL MEWSHAW

I SPENT A WINTER in Key West in 1973 when I was a healthy stripling and the island looked to be on its last legs. Jimmy Buffett was playing for tips at the Pier House and Tom McGuane, like me, was an unknown novelist with two books to his name. When I came back at the end of the decade, Key West seemed to have swallowed an overdose of Viagra. Everything had perked up—the real estate market, the restaurant scene, the ubiquity of writers. I sublet Ralph Ellison's house in the Windsor Lane compound where a constellation of literary lights—John Ciardi, Richard Wilbur, and John Hersey—maintained a cool distance in their cottages.

I waited until the turn of the century to start nesting in Key West every winter. By then a more remarkable metamorphosis had occurred. Although the island retained a raffish reputation—a hangover from the epoch when Thomas Sanchez and Shel Silverstein, Jim Harrison and Phil Caputo roistered around Duval Street—it had by 2000 settled into sedate middle age. Novelist William Harrison puckishly referred to the place as a "matriarchal society." Alison Lurie, Annie Dillard, Ann Beattie, and Judy Blume now presided over catered cocktail parties, though Robert Stone, bearded, baggy-eyed, habitually high on drugs or alcohol (or both), cut a curious figure at these events. He appeared to be an avatar of old Key West, a shrimper or deep-sea fisherman, a gnarly hell-raiser temporarily ashore squandering his paycheck and his health.

He didn't, however, behave like an island brawler. His bruises and hastily stitched-up scars came from falling down stairs or stumbling into plate glass doors, not from fighting. He seldom raised his voice—which was surprisingly patrician—and was given to uttering autodidactic monologues. Although a college dropout with a GED high school diploma, he possessed arcane knowledge of the world's religions, art, literature, and history. I remember an evening at an

architect's house when the discussion veered improbably to the subject of anathyrosis. Stone didn't blink. At once he described the process of mason construction without mortar. Thereafter I chose my
words carefully around Bob.

Annie Dillard had invited me to her house specifically to meet
Robert Stone without advising me that he had asked for the introduction. He had read an article I had written about Graham Greene
and wanted to let me know that he loathed the English novelist. Not
that he was obstreperous about his opinion. When he shook my
hand, I realized that he had the softest palm and gentlest grip of any
man I'd ever met.

We remained friends for the last fifteen years of his life—he died
in 2015—and frequently got together for NFL games, which he always had money riding on. It
was a shame, I thought, that
we had to dance around the
subject of Graham Greene.
Bob and Greene had much in
common—disorder and early
sorrow, a weakness for drink
and drugs, and an enduring
interest in women, all tidily
packaged in Catholic guilt.

In the biography *Child of
Light*, Madison Smartt Bell
captures every aspect of
Stone's contradictory nature,
especially his work ethic.
Each of Stone's novels—
from *Hall of Mirrors* (1966)
through the National Book
Award–winning *Dog Soldiers*
(1974) to his final book,
Death of the Black-Haired Girl
(2013)—was achieved de-

*"Bearded, baggy-eyed, habitually high on
drugs or alcohol, . . .[Stone] appeared to be
an avatar of old Key West," Mewshaw writes.*

spite the author's crippling depressions, repeated bouts of ill health,
and unwise dependence on self-medication. One of the best sections
of this praiseworthy biography is Bell's account of a trip he took with

Stone to Haiti, along with one of Stone's mistresses, who had to nurse the novelist when it appeared that he might die while traveling to a voodoo ritual.

Yet sympathetic as he is to his subject, Bell never softens his focus or smooths over Stone's less admirable traits. A great deal of the credit for this candor goes to Stone's widow, whom Michael Herr christened "the patron saint of writers' wives." Janice Stone served as her husband's muse, first reader, typist, cook and caretaker, accountant, travel agent, and life coach. Unlike so many literary marriages, theirs lasted fifty-five years, and after Stone's death, Janice remained her husband's helpmate and his biographer's enabler. Where other widows might protect a great man's reputation (and perhaps their own financial interest) by destroying unflattering documents or restricting access to diaries and letters, Janice set nothing off the record. Along with accounts of Stone's medications (recreational and otherwise), his stretches in rehab, and his suicide attempt, Janice provided information about Stone's sexual escapades and her own affairs, which he encouraged. They had married young, before the sexual liberation of the late '60s, and the Stones allowed each other astonishing leeway. Stone fathered a child with another woman, and even that didn't alienate Janice.

By any objective standard, Stone was a successful author whose novels were critically acclaimed, and he received geometrically increasing advances. Paid $1,500 for his first novel, Stone finished his career with a million-dollar multi-book contract. As Bell told the *New Yorker*, "Stone's life could be read as a fulfillment of the American dream of which his work was so critical."

But he never escaped the damage he suffered during his Dickensian childhood. Raised by an unmarried schizophrenic mother in a series of squalid hotel rooms, Stone wasn't told anything about his father beyond his mother's unreliable report that the man was "a Greek, a Jew, or a Lebanese." (A DNA test contained no information to support his mother's claims.) When his mother became unfit to care for him, Stone was consigned for four years to a Catholic orphanage where the faith was literally pounded into him. By the time mother and son were reunited, Stone was essentially a street kid and, by his early teens, a drunk and a drug user. A stint in the U.S. Navy

The three most popular beaches in Key West are Smathers (above), the Clarence S. Higgs Memorial, and the beach at Fort Zachary Taylor.

introduced him to a "life more abundant," although it also reinforced his appetite for intoxicants and women.

Not unreasonably, Bell maintains that Stone's accomplishments more than outweigh his transgressions. And who would argue otherwise when his wife forgave him everything? She was with him, quite literally, till the end. After decades of nasty falls, Robert Stone fell a last time at his Key West home. Even with the help of Alison Lurie and her husband Edward Hower, Bob couldn't bounce back as he had so often in the past. His instructions were to take no dramatic measures to revive him, and he died where he lay. Still, his novels live on, as do my memories of a writer who started with little, achieved much, and was harder on himself than any man should be.

Misnomer

―――

ELENA CASTEDO

I see Robert Stone, the probing sailor,
looking out beyond the horizon and under the deeps,
at sea with his sea-blue eyes
pen at the helm,
fishing message bottles,
uncorking vulnerabilities,
specters of our Achilles heel,
dredging up bêtes noires; sharks; the gashed;
the innocent risk-takers;
the cruelty spawned from distorted cocoons;
the freaking creatures busy creating their snarled lives,
molding their ill fates;
avoiding or eating each other
fishing fresh wind,
catching lightning that spreads wondrous colors,
and from the darkened depths, perceptions of a world beyond
Robert Stone, sailing on a language of musical beauty,
Stone, revealing the rock-hard places of our times,
protecting with a stone his wounded inner child.
Stone, a misnomer for his own soft and warm heart
Bob Stone, conjoined with Janice,
floating in the foam of his mind-boggling erudition,
a quiet ham, a magical raconteur,
a master of foreign accents,
and musical recall
on waves of merry wit.
It tried hard, his brave and brilliant brain
And we thank it.

Remembering Liz

JOY WILLIAMS

LIZ LEAR HAD MANY, many friends, and many of them were writers and artists. We were all together for a long moment that was our moment in Key West. It was the '70s and the '80s and the '90s, and it was a wonderful, improbable, unfettered moment—and Liz was at the very heart of it. She was an unabashed Key West enthusiast. She wanted interesting people to love it and buy houses there and have parties and be happy there. She brought us together and kept us together. When one wandered off—fame, trouble, a partner who hadn't succumbed to the Rock's singular charms—she

"When one wandered off—fame, trouble, a partner who hadn't succumbed to the Rock's singular charms . . . [Liz Lear] tirelessly sought their return," says Williams.

was saddened and tirelessly sought their return. We were her chicks, her dears.

I see her so vividly. I see her in her pretty dresses, her necklace of keys. Those keys! She was a divine hostess and a faithful friend. She bore the tragedy of her daughter Genevieve's death with tremendous grace. Genevieve said she wanted a portion of her ashes scattered on "a friendly reef," a phrase which Liz delighted in. Liz chose to be buried in the rocky earth. Because it harbors Liz, I can think of it as friendly ground.

A Psalm tells us: we are as grass in the morning, it flowers and grows—in the evening it is cut down and withers.

A Psalm tells us: we spend our years as a tale that is told.

If you're not Bible-y, there is the poet Philip Larkin's encapsulation of our dilemma, which is life:

> And so unreal
> A touching dream to which we are all lulled
> But wake from separately.

Goodbye, Liz. You were such a large and essential part of our touching dream here. Miss you. Love you.

One of a Kind

WILLIAM WRIGHT

THE OLDER I GET, the more I value people who are not like anyone else. After four or five decades, the individuals who pass through one's life tend to fit into recognizable categories—charming, sensitive, thoughtful, stimulating, accomplished, brilliant. However exemplary the individuals might be, they tend to bring to the table a dispiriting whiff of predictability. I'm sure I do.

The Key West developer, visionary, and bon vivant David Wolkowsky, on the other hand, never lost his ability to surprise, to puzzle, and to disconcert. A token example: Some years ago, David fell and broke his hip following a dinner out. His houseman was away and David had forgotten his cell phone, so, at the age of ninety, he lay on his front steps for ten hours until a UPS man found him the next morning and called an ambulance. Like all of his friends, I was aghast. I asked if he had called out.

"I did if I heard footsteps," he replied in his laconic way, then added, "provided they sounded like *nice* footsteps."

Of all the questions coursing through me, the character of footsteps had not occurred to me. But I knew David wasn't trying to make a clever remark or avoid saying the obvious. Wolkowsky, I have come to realize after forty years of friendship, sees life as a game, and whenever possible, he has been bent on keeping it an amusing one. His determination to see the fun in even the grimmest situations is not a studied mindset; it's a reflex.

Another example of his singular humor occurred at a lunch party he gave on his private island, Ballast Key, twenty-six ravishing acres of tropical nature eight miles southwest of Key West. Although the island has been the envy of royalty and film stars and is now valued at upwards of $15 million, meals might include fresh lobster or shrimp but invariably center on turkey hot dogs. That day's group included a young woman who had never been on the island.

Invited by Wolkowsky, "Truman Capote . . . abandoned his role as the Bad Boy of American Letters to be the Very Bad Boy of Key West," Wright wrote.

"Oh, Mr. Wolkowsky," she gushed, "this hot dog is so good. What makes it so delicious?"

"You have to have an island to go with it," he replied gravely.

An integral part of Wolkowsky's strategy for playing the life game has been risk-taking. One of his biggest risks was betting on Key West's future in the early 1960s when the island's economy was devastated by the navy's massive departure. Hopes for salvation as a resort were dashed when major hotel operatives arrived in Key West, looked the place over, and declared it ineligible for resort tourism for a simple reason: beaches.

At the time, David was a successful developer in Philadelphia, his chosen home after graduating from the University of Pennsylvania and, to avoid any anti-Semitism, adopting his mother's maiden name of Williams. A number of post-college jobs had not worked out, probably because he is not a team player. Eventually, he found his niche buying distressed houses just beyond gentrified neighborhoods and renovating them. An architectural wannabe, Wolkowsky would refurbish derelict houses with enough high-style flourishes to show prospective buyers the possibilities—a patio here, a sliding door there—but skimping a bit on the fundamentals. (Anyone can fix a roof.)

The houses came to be known as "David Williams houses" and sold briskly, riding a wave of reverse urban flight by well-heeled buyers who had grown bored with the suburbs of Chestnut Hill and the Main Line and were charmed by Mediterranean balconies in Center City.

As his business flourished, the handsome and suave David became popular with Center City's tight knot of wealthy sophisticates. Until the late 1950s, that is, when David's charmed, bachelor-about-town life came crashing down with some financial reverses that all but bankrupted his firm.

His father, Isaac Wolkowsky, had run a haberdashery in Key West, where David was born, then moved his family to Miami where he prospered in the clothing business. Within a year of Isaac's death in 1961, having inherited some meager parcels of Key West land, David, with typical bravado and impulsiveness, gave up his chic Philadelphia life to try to build his fortune in a derelict town. His move to Key West was the perfect match: a town bursting with possibilities and a developer brimming with vision and optimism.

Once in Key West, David set out to improve the properties he'd inherited. A parcel on shabby Front Street, one of Key West's few areas to draw tourists, he turned into a cul-de-sac of shops. Another building, now Captain Tony's Saloon, he fixed up, dubbed it the Oldest Bar, and staged a gala opening to which he invited distinguished notables and press people from all over the country.

As Wolkowsky's ventures began making money, he was moving toward his grand ambition: a hotel on the gulf that would become a tourist destination. Sixty years earlier, Henry Flagler had had the same idea when he built his oceanfront hotel, the Casa Marina, but that noble structure had been shuttered for years, done in by a handful of short-stay motels for travelers who came to the island to see the Southernmost Point, the Hemingway house, maybe Harry Truman's Little White House—then leave, most likely for someplace with beaches.

David believed that Flagler had been right, the smart hotel people of the early 1960s wrong. He saw that while Key West beaches were too patchy to attract many tourists, the town itself boasted a funky charm; picturesque old houses; dense, jungle-like foliage; and, perhaps most of all, a lackadaisical approach to rules and regulations.

Wolkowsky focused his hotel scheme on a vacant, two-and-a-half-acre waterfront lot next to oil tanks that had sat unsold for years at the laughable price of $101,000. In 1963, he bought it and, for $2,500, hired a little-known but talented Miami architect, Yiannis Antonidas, to create the distinguished design that stands today as the Pier House. The original building cost $280,000.

David's idea was to build a hotel that encircled a swimming pool, bring in beach sand, and position the building to screen out its ugly surroundings. The navy was then dredging the channel in front of the hotel site to make it deep enough for submarines. When they offered David a free acre of fill, he had his beach. The hotel opened with a smattering of guests who would often arrive to find Wolkowsky himself behind the front desk. On many nights, he'd even carry their bags to their rooms, saying the bellboy was sick. Skimping on staff and other economics, Wolkowsky still had to wait ten years before seeing a profit from the Pier House.

David's hotel was not exactly overrun by *le beau monde*, but there was an encouraging trickle of the well known—and there was also

"[David] had flair," Wright wrote. "He bought a defunct 1923 Rolls Royce convertible, . . . had it painted a canary yellow, and parked it by the hotel's main entrance."

the local star Tennessee Williams, whom David both venerated and coddled. While genial and welcoming to the occasional visiting film star, his instincts focused on writers. Peter Fonda and Elizabeth Ashley might be offered a free meal, but his heart went out to the likes of Joseph Lash (*Eleanor and Franklin*), John Malcom Brinnin (*Dylan Thomas in America*), and Nancy Friday (*My Mother, Myself*).

Word soon got around that Key West harbored an eccentric hotel owner who was partial to writers, even known to give them a deal. Before long the Pier House dining room began to look like a tropical Academy of Arts and Letters. Today's strong writerly component owes as much to Wolkowsky's literary enthusiasms as to the Hemingway legend.

Among the more celebrated writers who took to the charms of Key West was Truman Capote, who abandoned his role as the Bad Boy of American Letters to be the *Very* Bad Boy of Key West. Capote's appetite for rough trade caused numerous problems. He once chose for living quarters a trailer awaiting future expansion parked on a vacant lot next to the hotel. One night the trailer was robbed clean by one of Truman's gentleman callers.

In building his hotel, Wolkowsky didn't skimp on the structure or in fashioning the beach, pool, and setting. And he had flair. He bought a defunct 1923 Rolls Royce convertible, installed a Ford motor, had it painted a canary yellow, and parked it by the hotel's main entrance. As a tone-setting accessory, the spiffy antique beat Henry Flagler's potted palms and liveried doormen by a mile—and was a lot cheaper. Inside, cost cutting was unabashedly apparent, most notably in the rooms, which he left bare cinder block. In spite of these oddities, in time the Pier House—imbued with David's quirky personality—became the most popular hotel in town.

It was in 1970 with the Pier House starting to show a profit that I re-encountered David, who I hadn't seen since his Philadelphia days as David Williams. Then the editor of *Chicago* magazine, I was sitting at my desk one day gazing out over Lake Michigan when my phone rang.

"Bill?" an unmistakable voice drawled, "This is David Wolkowsky." No mention of the name change that to him was of no importance. "I have done over a bar here in Key West, and I want to invite you to the opening."

I knew I owed the invitation to my position as a magazine editor, but it didn't matter; I couldn't go. I was having a major set-to with then-Chicago-mayor Richard Daley, who, deeply offended by a published jibe about his syntax, was trying to shut down the magazine. When it indeed closed a few months later, I remembered David's invitation. I called him and asked if I could come see him in Key West.

"Well," he said slowly, "I would be delighted if you visited, but you know the invitation was just for the bar opening." I assured him that I understood, that I just wanted to see him, his new hotel, and Key West. When I arrived at the Pier House, there was a note from David asking me to be his guest for dinner that night and to come to his trailer at 7:30 for a drink.

Upon arrival, I told him how splendid my room was. "You know," he said, "the rooms on the water generally go for $55 a night, but since you are an old and dear friend, I will charge you only the rate for facing the parking lot, which is $45 a night."

Wolkowsky was known as "Mr. Key West" for his role in revitalizing the town and bringing in writers. "David Wolkowsky Street" was designated in the mid-'90s.

In the next years, as I began writing biographies, I would often reach a point when I had to stop researching and start writing. David, who had many properties around Key West, would sometimes call me in New York and say, "I've had a cancellation on an apartment. If you come to Key West tomorrow, you can have it for free for two weeks." And off I'd go.

For me, one moment epitomizes the jolly zaniness of those days. David had to move a potted palm to an apartment he had just renovated. (He frequently completed a building one day, then frantically decorated it the next—sofas, lamps, pictures, rugs—for tenants arriving that afternoon.) With Lee, his housekeeper, we piled into the Rolls—David and I in the front, an unsmiling Lee and the twelve-foot palm in the back—and rolled majestically down Duval Street as pedestrians gawked.

Though golf carts were illegal on the streets of Key West, city hall had given David a special dispensation. (Many city officials enjoyed their after-hours drinks in the Chart Room, a small bar off the Pier House's lobby, where David had offered an out-of-work entertainer by the name of Jimmy Buffett the opportunity to sing and play the guitar for tips.)

By the 1980s the Pier House was making David rich. It was also making him a nervous wreck. I was having lunch with him one day when a distraught workman rushed up to the table. "Mr. Wolkowsky," the guy cried, "all the bathrooms are out in the new wing."

David kept calm, but I could see a small vein throbbing on his face. Such catastrophes were constant, and one day in 1995, he announced he was selling the hotel.

This was during a real estate slump, when the oddly business-indifferent David often sold his prime properties, and he sold the entire hotel complex for $4.5 million. A year later the new owners sold a 50 percent stake in the hotel for $5 million. When asked why he had sold for so little, his reply was simple: "I had to get out. The place was driving me crazy. The next best offer was $2.5 million."

"The developer, visionary, and bon vivant . . . never lost his ability to surprise, to puzzle, and to disconcert," says the author. Wolkowsky died at age 99 in 2018.

A few years later, David bought a run-down restaurant on the ocean called the Sands. It did very little business and was about to close. It also sat on a large piece of land and had one of the few natural beaches in Key West. As soon as he took possession, David tore down the existing building and put up a string of three one-story restaurants: a fancy one, a medium-priced one, and a hamburger–hot dog place for bathers, open to the sea.

Key West builders were inevitably trying to sneak around the city's three-story height limitation—a law that had kept the island from becoming another Miami Beach. To build a one-story commercial building on the ocean, the priciest land of all, is absolute folly. But David never played by business-school rules.

For building one of the Sands restaurants too close to the beach's high-tide line, the town put a stop-work order on its construction. Some months later, it was discovered that David had obtained his building permits before the high-tide ordinance was enacted, and the case was dropped. But because it had delayed the opening beyond the winter tourist season, the ordinance contributed to the Sands' failure and forced David to sell at a hefty loss. The new owner promptly erected a five-story hotel on the property.

But David was not one to nurture grievances. Shortly before he sold the property, staffers from the weekly *Solares Hill* newspaper, which had strongly opposed construction of his three restaurants, were celebrating a birthday at a table adjoining David's. I was stunned when he sent over a complimentary bottle of wine.

"What are you doing?" I said. "Those people are one of the reasons you must close this place."

He shrugged. "Key West is too small to bear grudges," he said.

But while he didn't bear grudges, neither did he forget. Years later I was having lunch with him in New York City, and I arrived all steamed about a vicious review theater critic John Simon had just written about the actress Tammy Grimes. Simon not only tore her apart, he focused mainly on her physical appearance. I asked David how anyone could be so cruel.

"Maybe she built too close to the high-tide line," he replied.

William Wright died in 2016; David Wolkowsky in 2018 —Ed.

Full Moon, Key West

ELIZABETH BISHOP

The town is paper-white:
the moonlight is so bright.
Flake on flake
of wood and paint
the buildings faint.
The tin roofs break
into a sweat
of heavy dew
dripping steadily
down the gutters
click click.
Listen!
All over town
from black gaps
in bedroom gables
from little tables
behind the shutters
big alarm clocks
tick tick.
A spider's web
glints blue, glints red,
the mirrors glisten
and the knobs on the bed.

The island starts to hum
like music in a dream.
Paper-white, drunk,
the sailors come
stumbling, fighting,
mumbling threats

in children's voices,
stopping, lighting
cigarettes
with pink dull fires,
in groups like hands
and fingers on
the narrow sidewalks
of cement
that carry sounds
like tampered wires,
—the long strings of
an instrument
laid on the stream,
a zither laid
upon the flood
of the glittering Gulf.

Contributors

Brian Antoni is the author of *South Beach: The Novel*, which draws on his knowledge of the resurgence of Miami Beach in the past two decades. He also writes frequently for magazines.

Ann Beattie is the recipient of an American Academy of Arts and Letters award for excellence in literature and a PEN/Malamud award for "excellence in the art of the short story."

Elizabeth Bishop was a poet, short story writer, and Consultant in Poetry to the Library of Congress from 1949 to 1950. She won the Pulitzer Prize for Poetry in 1956 and, in 1970, a National Book Award for *Elizabeth Bishop / The Complete Poems*. She died in 1979.

Judy Blume is the author of twenty-nine books for children, teens, and adults, which have sold more than ninety million copies in thirty-nine languages. She and her husband, George Cooper, are the founders of Books & Books @ the Studios of Key West, a nonprofit, independent bookstore.

Rosalind Brackenbury is the author of twelve novels, a collection of short stories, and six books of poetry. Her novel *Seas Beyond the Reef* is set partly in Key West. Her most recently published book is *Elena, Leo, Rose*.

John Malcolm Brinnin brought Dylan Thomas to the United States and is the author of *Dylan Thomas in America*. He also published six volumes of his own poetry. Brinnin died in 1998 in Key West.

Meg Cabot is the author of more than eighty novels for both children and adults, including *The Princess Diaries*. Several of her books are set on islands modeled after Key West. A Midwesterner by birth, Meg has lived in Key West for twenty years with her husband and various cats.

Philip Caputo is a journalist and the author of *A Rumor of War*, about his experience as a marine platoon leader in Vietnam during the war. He has written two memoirs, five books of nonfiction, and eight novels.

Jeffrey Cardenas has written books on natural history and the environment. His photographs have been exhibited in the United States and Cuba, including at Havana's Museo Nacional de Bellas Artes.

Elena Castedo was born in Barcelona, Spain. She is an author and educator who writes in both Spanish and English. Her novel *Paradise* was a finalist for the National Book Award for Fiction.

Billy Collins served as U.S. Poet Laureate from 2001 to 2003 and as the New York State Poet Laureate from 2004 to 2006. He is the recipient of the Mark Twain Prize for Humor in Poetry. He is a member of the American Academy of Arts and Letters.

George Cooper is the author of articles in legal journals and books about historic crimes including *Lost Love* (1995) and *Poison Widows* (1999). In 2004 he led the group establishing the nonprofit Tropic Cinema in Key West and in 2016, with his wife Judy Blume, founded the nonprofit Books & Books @ the Studios of Key West.

Hal Crowther is an essayist and critic, a former syndicated columnist and newsmagazine editor, and the author of *An Infuriating American: The Incendiary Arts of H. L. Mencken* (2015) and five collections of essays. The most recent, *Freedom Fighters and Hellraisers: A Gallery of Memorable Southerners* (2018) won the Independent Publisher Book Award (IPPY) gold medal for creative nonfiction.

Frank Deford's byline graced *Sports Illustrated* for more than fifty years. He was a novelist (*Everybody's All American*), screenwriter, correspondent for HBO's *Real Sports with Bryant Gumbel*, and commentator on NPR. His memoir, *Overtime*, was published in 2012. Deford died in 2017 in Key West.

Barbara Ehrenreich was a journalist, novelist, feminist, and social critic. For her 1998 book *Nickel and Dimed*, she worked at several blue-collar jobs, including as a waitress in Key West. She died in 2022.

Peyton Evans was a writer and editor at Conde Nast, Hearst, and Avon Books in New York City for many years. She has been a member of the Key West Literary Seminar board of directors since 2001.

Glenn Frankel won a Pulitzer Prize for International Reporting (in London, Southern Africa, and Jerusalem for the *Washington Post*). He taught journalism at Stanford University and directed the School of Journalism at the University of Texas at Austin. His latest book is *Shooting Midnight Cowboy: Art, Sex, Loneliness, Liberation, and the Making of a Dark Classic*.

Arlo Haskell is executive director of the Key West Literary Seminar, a poet, and the author of *The Jews of Key West: Smugglers, Cigar Makers, and Revolutionaries (1823–1969)*.

Mark Hedden is a photographer, writer, and semiprofessional birdwatcher. He has lived in Key West full-time for more than thirty years and says he is probably no longer employable in the real world. His work has been published in the *Key West Citizen*, the *Miami Herald*, and the *Washington Post*.

Paul Hendrickson is on the faculty of the Creative Writing Program at the University of Pennsylvania. He was a staff writer at the *Washington Post* for two decades.

Pico Iyer is the author of sixteen books of fiction and nonfiction on subjects ranging from the Cuban revolution and the fourteenth Dalai Lama to Islamic mysticism. For thirty-six years he's been a regular essayist for *Time*, the *New York Times*, *Harper's*, and the *New York Review of Books*. His most recent book, *The Half Known Life*, explores the idea of paradise around the world.

Lynn Mitsuko Kaufelt is the author of *Key West Writers and Their Houses*. After her husband, David A. Kaufelt, founded the Key West Literary Seminar in 1983, she became its first executive director. She also served as the Seminar's president and remains a member of its board of directors.

Kathryn Kilgore is the author of the novel *Something for Nothing*. She has a master's degree from Stanford and has worked as a copy editor, journalist, and book reviewer in New York City.

Nancy Klingener was a reporter for Miami's National Public Radio station WLRN and the *Miami Herald* and *Solares Hill* newspapers. She is president of the board of directors of the Key West Literary Seminar and the community affairs manager of the Monroe County Public Library.

John Leslie is the author of the Gideon Lowry mystery series, set in Key West, and seven other novels. He settled in Key West in 1974 after, he says, "a nomadic life of odd jobs and teaching English in Europe, Saudi Arabia, Libya, and Iran."

Alison Lurie wrote eleven novels including *The War Between the Tates*, a collection of short stories, and many nonfiction books. Her 1984 novel *Foreign Affairs* won the Pulitzer Prize. She died in 2020 at age ninety-four.

Thomas McGuane is the author of ten novels as well as collections of short fiction and screenplays. His most recent book, *Cloudburst*, is a collection of short stories.

Daniel Menaker spent two decades as a writer and editor of fiction at *The New Yorker* before becoming senior literary editor and, later, executive editor-in-chief at Random House. The author of six books, including *The Treatment* and *My Mistake*, Menaker died at age seventy-nine in 2020.

James Merrill was one of the foremost poets of his generation. In 1977, he was awarded a Pulitzer Prize for Poetry for his collection, *Divine Comedies*. He died in 1995.

Michael Mewshaw is the author of twenty-three books of both fiction and nonfiction, including his most recent, *My Man in Antibes: Getting to Know Graham Greene*.

Mirta Ojito is the author of two works of nonfiction: *Finding Mañana: A Memoir of a Cuban Exodus* and *Hunting Season: Immigration and Murder in an All-American Town*. She was a member of the *New York Times* team that won a Pulitzer in 2001 for a series of articles about race in America.

Alejandro F. Pascual is the author of *Key West: Passion for Cuba's Liberty*. Born in Cardenas, Cuba, Pascual came to the United States at age fourteen. From 1981 to 2002, he was market development director for Newsweek International (Latin America/Caribbean). He retired to Key West in 2006.

Phyllis Rose is the author of *Parallel Lives: Five Victorian Marriages*, *The Year of Reading Proust: A Memoir in Real Time*, and *The Shelf*. Her most recent book is *Alfred Stieglitz: Taking Pictures, Making Painters*.

Harvey Shapiro published twelve collections of poetry, including *National Cold Storage Company*. He worked for nearly fifty years at the *New York Times*, where he was editor of the book review and deputy editor of the magazine. He died at age eighty-eight in 2013.

Lee Smith has written fifteen novels including *Silver Alert* (2023), set in Key West; four collections of short stories; and a memoir, *Dimestore: A Writer's Life* (2016). Her novel *The Last Girls* was co-winner of the Southern Book Critics Circle Award. A retired professor of English at North Carolina State University, she received an Academy Award in Literature from the American Academy of Arts and Letters.

Thomas Swick is the author of *Unquiet Days: At Home in Poland*, *A Way to See the World*, and *The Joys of Travel: And Stories That Illuminate Them*. He was the longtime travel editor of the *South Florida Sun-Sentinel*. His work has appeared in *The American Scholar*, *Oxford American*, *Wilson Quarterly*, *Ploughshares*, *Smithsonian*, *Literary Hub*, and the *Los Angeles Review of Books*.

Thomas Travisano is the founding president of the Elizabeth Bishop Society and the author of *Love Unknown: The Life and Worlds of Elizabeth Bishop*. He co-edited *Elizabeth Bishop in the 21st Century: Reading the New Editions* and co-edited the three-volume *New Anthology of American Poetry*. He is Emeritus Professor of English at Hartwick College.

Richard Wilbur was a poet and translator, known for his wit, charm, and elegance. He was appointed the second Poet Laureate Consultant in Poetry to the Library of Congress in 1987 and received the Pulitzer Prize for Poetry twice, in 1957 and 1989. He died in 2017.

Joy Williams is the author of four novels, three collections of short stories, and a collection of essays, *Ill Nature: Rants and Reflections on Humanity and Other Animals*. She is a member of the American Academy of Arts and Letters.

Carey Winfrey is a former journalist and magazine editor-in-chief (*Cuisine, Memories, American Health,* and *Smithsonian*). He is the author of a memoir, *Starts and Finishes,* and co-author, with John Leslie, of *Hail to the Chief,* a political thriller.

Arida Wright is the author of *Then Sings My Soul* and *Crossing the Threshold.* She is a traditional Reiki master and a member of the Key West Poetry Guild and the Key West Writers Guild.

William Wright wrote biographies of Lillian Hellman, Marjorie Meriwether Post, and Luciano Pavarotti among his eleven books of nonfiction. His last book was *Harvard's Secret Court.* Wright died in 2016.

Bill Yankee was a personal trainer in Key West for many years. At the time he trained James Merrill, his business, One to One Fitness, was located on Fleming Street.

Mary Kay Zuravleff is the author of four novels including *Man Alive!,* a *Washington Post* Notable Book, and her most recent, *American Ending,* a family saga set in Appalachia. Her work has appeared in *American Short Fiction,* the *Los Angeles Review of Books,* the *Atlantic,* and numerous anthologies.

Acknowledgments

"Vroom, Vroom, Vroom" by Frank Deford was broadcast by National Public Radio as "Letter from Key West: A Different Air," March 10, 2011. Published courtesy of Carole Deford.

"Finding Mañana" by Mirta Ojito, courtesy of the author, was adapted from her talk at the 2018 Key West Literary Seminar.

"Poetry Workshop Held in a Former Cigar Factory in Key West" from HOROSCOPES FOR THE DEAD: POEMS by Billy Collins, copyright © 2011 by Billy Collins. Used by permission of Random House, an imprint and division of Penguin Random House LLC. All rights reserved.

"The Geographical Cure" by Lee Smith was adapted from her nonfiction afterword to her novella, BLUE MARLIN, Blair (2020).

"A Susurration of Palms" was adapted from THE JOYS OF TRAVEL: AND STORIES THAT ILLUMINATE THEM, by Thomas Swick, Skyhorse Publishing (2016).

"Lucky Ducking" by Arlo Haskell was published in JOKER by Arlo Haskell, Sand Paper Press (2009). Published courtesy of the author.

"Otherwhere." Excerpt from GATHER AT THE RIVER: NOTES FROM THE POST-MILLENNIAL SOUTH, by Hal Crowther, Louisiana State University Press (2005), pp. 99–103.

"The Last Resort" by Alison Lurie, was published by Chatto & Windus as the introduction to a 1998 reissue of a British edition of THE LAST RESORT. Copyright by Alison Lurie.

"Two Houses." Excerpt from THE FLORIDA KEYS: A HISTORY & GUIDE 1998 by Joy Williams, 1987, 1988, 1991, 1993, 1994, 1995, 1997, 2000 by Joy Williams; Illustrations copyright © 1988 by Robert Carawan. Used by permission of Random House, an imprint and division of Penguin Random House LLC. All rights reserved.

"Second Thoughts" by Pico Iyer originally appeared in the FINANCIAL TIMES on December 9, 2006. Copyright © by Pico Iyer.

Excerpt from "Serving in Florida" from NICKEL AND DIMED: On (Not) Getting By in America by Barbara Ehrenreich. Copyright © 2001 by Barbara Ehrenreich. Reprinted by permission of Henry Holt and Company. All Rights Reserved.

"Paradise Lost" by Philip Caputo, excerpted from "Lost Keys," NEW YORK TIMES MAGAZINE, December 15, 1991, Section 6, page 55.

"Key West," by Harvey Shapiro, BOMB MAGAZINE, Oct. 1, 2011. Published with permission of the Estate of Harvey Shapiro.

"Hemingway's Key West." Excerpt from THE FLORIDA KEYS: A HISTORY & GUIDE 1998 by Joy Williams, 1987, 1988, 1991, 1993, 1994, 1995, 1997, 2000 by Joy Williams; Illustrations copyright © 1988 by Robert Carawan. Used by permission of Random House, an imprint and division of Penguin Random House LLC. All rights reserved.

"Farther Out." Excerpt from HEMINGWAY'S BOAT: EVERYTHING HE LOVED IN LIFE AND LOST, 1934–1961 by Paul Hendrickson, Copyright © 2011 by Paul Hendrickson. Used by permission of Alfred A. Knopf, an imprint of Knopf Doubleday, a division of Penguin Random House LLC. All rights reserved.

"A Poet's House" by Lynn Mitsuko Kaufelt was adapted from KEY WEST WRITERS AND THEIR HOUSES, a co-publication of Pineapple Press, Inc., of Sarasota, Florida, and Omnigraphics, Inc., of Fort Lauderdale, Florida (1986). Published courtesy of the author.

"Ready and Willing." Excerpt(s) from LOVE UNKNOWN: THE LIFE AND WORLDS OF ELIZABETH BISHOP by Thomas Travisano, Copyright © 2019 by Thomas Travisano. Used by permission of Viking Books, an imprint of Penguin Publishing Group, a division of Penguin Random House LLC. All rights reserved.

"Late Air" from POEMS by Elizabeth Bishop. Copyright © 2011 by The Alice H. Methfessel Trust. Publisher's Note and compilation copyright © 2011 by Farrar, Straus and Giroux. Reprinted by permission of Farrar, Straus and Giroux. All Rights Reserved.

"Gregorio Valdes, 1879–1939" from PROSE by Elizabeth Bishop. Copyright © 2011 by The Alice H. Methfessel Trust. Editor's Note and compilation copyright © 2011 by Lloyd Schwartz. Reprinted by permission of Farrar, Straus and Giroux. All Rights Reserved.

"Charming Tennessee" by Lynn Mitsuko Kaufelt was adapted from KEY WEST WRITERS AND THEIR HOUSES, a co-publication of Pineapple Press, Inc., of Sarasota, Florida, and Omnigraphics, Inc., of Fort Lauderdale, Florida (1986). Published courtesy of the author.

"Tennessee in Extremis." Excerpt from THE FLORIDA KEYS: A HISTORY & GUIDE 1998 by Joy Williams, 1987, 1988, 1991, 1993, 1994, 1995, 1997, 2000 by Joy Williams; illustrations copyright © 1988 by Robert Carawan. Used by permission of Random House, an imprint and division of Penguin Random House LLC. All rights reserved.

"A Good Omen" by Joy Williams, adapted from a tribute delivered by the author at the American Academy of Arts and Letters Dinner Meeting, November 8, 2018, in memory of Richard Wilbur, who died October 14, 2017.

"Bard of Pleasures" was adapted from "Citizen Poet," by Phyllis Rose in POETRY MAGAZINE, October 30, 2005.

"Oral History: Ellen Welters Sanchez," interviewed by Nancy Klingener. Excerpt from "Notes From an Island Composer," January 28, 1996, MIAMI HERALD.

"Oral History: Kermit 'Shine' Forbes," interviewed by Nancy Klingener. Excerpt from "In Pursuit of Adventure in the Keys, He Dove for Coins, Took a Swing at Hemingway," October 22, 1995, MIAMI HERALD.

"Not of This World." Excerpt from FAMILIAR SPIRITS: A MEMOIR OF JAMES MERRILL AND DAVID JACKSON by Alison Lurie, copyright © 2001 by Alison Lurie. Used by permission of Viking Books, an imprint of Penguin Publishing Group, a division of Penguin Random House LLC. All rights reserved.

"Merrill at the Gym." Adapted from "James Merrill at the Gym," by Bill Yankee, POETRY MAGAZINE, July/August 2007.

"Key West Aquarium: The Sawfish" from COLLECTED POEMS by James Merrill, copyright © 2001 by the Literary Estate of James Merrill at Washington University. Used by permission of Alfred A. Knopf, an imprint of the Knopf Doubleday Publishing Group, a division of Penguin Random House LLC. All rights reserved.

"A Poet at Heart," published as "The Wreck He Shimmied Through," by Phyllis Rose in POETRY MAGAZINE, July/August 2007.

"Letter from Key West, For Elizabeth Bishop" by John Malcolm Brinnin, THE KEY WEST READER: THE BEST OF KEY WEST'S WRITERS, 1830–1990, edited by George Murphy, Tortugas Ltd. (1989).

"Watching Screwball Comedies with Harry Mathews" by Ann Beattie, published in THE PARIS REVIEW DAILY, February 14, 2018. Published courtesy of the author.

"Dear Harry" by Rosalind Brackenbury, published in INVISIBLE HORSES, April 2019. Used by permission of Hanging Loose Press.

"The New Tourism" by Harry Mathews, THE NEW TOURISM, Sandpaper Press (2010).

"Walks in the Wild" by Hal Crowther, was published as "Robert Richardson" in NEW VIRGINIA REVIEW.

"Key West Cowboy" as adapted by the author from his book, *SHOOTING MIDNIGHT COWBOY* by Glenn Frankel. Copyright © 2021 by Glenn Frankel. Reprinted by permission of Farrar, Straus and Giroux. All Rights Reserved.

"Sunburned Sage" by Hal Crowther, excerpt, published in "Remembering Robert Stone, In the Words of His Friends," NARRATIVE MAGAZINE, Spring 2015.

"Misnomer" by Elena Castedo, was published as "Remembering Robert Stone," in LITERARY HUB, July 24, 2015.

"Full Moon, Key West" from EDGAR ALLAN POE & THE JUKE-BOX by Elizabeth Bishop, edited and annotated by Alice Quinn. Copyright © 2006 by Alice Helen Methfessel. Reprinted by permission of Farrar, Straus and Giroux. All Rights Reserved.

All other works in this anthology were provided by permission of the authors or their estates.

———

SO MUCH generosity, so little space:

Of course I feel enormous gratitude to each and every writer who donated a poem, essay, or reminiscence to this long-simmering project.

And to Marilyn Shames, whose encouragement, organizational skills, and unfailing good judgment kept me sane (most of the time).

Meg Cabot (see "Welcome Home") persuaded her literary agent, Laura Langlie, to represent the manuscript, which she did with enthusiasm and perseverance.

Lee Smith ("The Geographical Cure") talked the good people at her own publisher, Blair in Durham, North Carolina, into reading the manuscript.

Judy Blume ("Be Careful What You Wish For") offered advice and encouragement and introduced me to Mitchell Kaplan, of South Florida's bookstore chain Books and Books, who assured me he could sell a million copies. *Ha!*

John Leslie ("Ebb and Flow"), my friend and collaborator (on *Hail to the Chief*, a political novel), kept up my spirits with his good humor and sage counsel.

Arlo Haskell ("Invisible Island") shared his vast knowledge of Key West's literary history at the drop of an email. It was Arlo who initiated the purchase by the Key West Literary Seminar—where he is executive director—of the Elizabeth Bishop House. to which the author's proceeds from this collection will flow.

My special thanks to Blair's dynamic duo, publisher Lynn York and senior editor and associate publisher Robin Miura, for their enthusiasm and guidance.

I'm also grateful that photo editor Laurie Shnayerson volunteered to navigate photography copyrights, corral photos, and secure permissions.

And I'm delighted that Brian Noyes, my former *Smithsonian* magazine colleague, hung up his Red Truck Bakery apron long enough to design this book—impeccably, as always.

My sweet wife, Jane, who makes everything possible, supported this project, and me, every step of the way. There would be no *Key West Sketches* (or happy home) without her.   —CAREY WINFREY

Photo Credits

Contents
Hemingway with tarpon: courtesy of the Ernest Hemingway Collection/
JFK Presidential Library and Museum, Boston

"Finding Mañana"
Havana school photograph: courtesy of the author
Mariel Boatlift: photo by Dale McDonald, courtesy State Archives of Florida

"Poetry Workshop Held in a Former Cigar Factory in Key West"
Newspaper reader, Key West cigar factory, March 12, 1930: Getty Images

"The Geographical Cure"
Lee Smith's parents: courtesy of the author
Operation Petticoat poster: MoviePosters.com

"Duck, Boogie"
Charlie Duck's rental house photograph and duck painting by
Andy Thurber: courtesy Mark Hedden

"Squall"
Approaching storm: courtesy Jeffrey Cardenas

"Varadero Dreaming"
Cuba photographs and Capablanca stamp: courtesy Alejandro F. Pascual

"Two Houses"
Both houses: courtesy Monroe County Public Library, Florida Keys
History Center

"Invisible Island"
Marcus Garvey: courtesy Library of Congress
KKK Charter: courtesy Key West Art and Historical Society
Manolo Cabeza: *Key West Weekly*, March 28, 2019

"The Forever Cycle"
McGuane in hammock: photo by Don Kincaid, courtesy Leon Kincaid

"Absent Friends" opening page
John Hersey: courtesy Key West Art and Historical Society

"Hemingway's Key West"
Hemingway with wife Pauline on *Pilar*: courtesy the Ernest Hemingway
Collection/JFK Presidential Library and Museum, Boston
Hemingway and "Sloppy Joe" Russell with marlin: courtesy Key West Art
and Historical Society

"Farther Out"
All three photographs: courtesy the Ernest Hemingway Collection/
JFK Presidential Library and Museum, Boston

"Where Greatness Lived"
Vintage photograph of Bishop house: courtesy Louise Crane and Victoria
Kent Papers, Yale Collection of American Art, Beinecke Rare Book and
Manuscript Library

"Ready and Willing"
Elizabeth Bishop in Key West with bicycle and Bishop with Louise Crane:
courtesy Elizabeth Bishop Papers, Archives and Special Collections,
Vassar College Library

"Late Air"
Elizabeth Bishop on porch: courtesy Louise Crane and Victoria Kent
Papers, Yale Collection of American Art, Beinecke Rare Book and
Manuscript Library

"Gregorio Valdes, 1879–1939"
Valdes painting of Royal Palms: courtesy Alice Quinn
Valdes painting of Bishop house: courtesy David R. Goode

"Charming Tennessee"
Tennessee Williams with bulldogs: courtesy Key West Art and Historical
Society
Tennessee on bicycle: courtesy Key West Literary Seminar
Tennessee on porch: courtesy Key West Art and Historical Society

"Tennessee in Extremis"
Tennessee smoking: © Yousuf Karsh
Tennessee reaching for champagne: Lawson C. Little © 2023

"Killing Me Softly"
Thomas McGuane with Tennessee Williams: courtesy Key West Art and
Historical Society

"Ebb and Flow"
John Hersey: courtesy Jeffrey Cardenas
Richard Wilbur: courtesy Key West Literary Seminar
John Ciardi: Internet Archive
Harry Mathews: Carey Winfrey
John Malcolm Brinnin: courtesy Jeffrey Cardenas
Rust Hills: photo by Doyle Bush, courtesy Key West Literary Seminar

"Bard of Pleasures"
Richard Wilbur in plaid shirt: Rollie McKenna © Rosalie Thorne
McKenna Foundation, Center for Creative Photography, University of
Arizona Board of Regents
Wilbur with John Malcolm Brinnin: photograph by Richard Watherwax

"Oral History"
Ellen Welters Sanchez: photograph by Robert Stone, courtesy Florida Memories, State Archives of Florida
Frank Welters, the Welters Cornet Band, and Key West spongers: courtesy Monroe County Public Library, Florida Keys History Center

"Not of This World"
James Merrill: courtesy Elizabeth Bishop Papers, Archives and Special Collections, Vassar College Library

"A Poet at Heart"
John Malcolm Brinnin: Rollie McKenna, © Rosalie Thorne McKenna Foundation, Center for Creative Photography, University of Arizona Board of Regents

"Key West Cowboy"
James Leo Herlihy: courtesy Monroe County Public Library, Florida Keys History Center
Herlihy with Tennessee Williams: © Bud Lee Picture Maker

"Sunburned Sage"
Robert Stone: Estate of Robert Stone, courtesy Literary Arts, Portland, Oregon

"One of a Kind"
David Wolkowsky with Truman Capote: courtesy Estate of David Wolkowsky

"Full Moon Key West"
Full Moon Rising—Key West: courtesy Bev Tabet Photography, Fine Art America

Except where noted above, color photographs, including cover, are by Carey Winfrey.

Photo Research by:
Cori Convertito, Curator and Historian Key West Art and Historical Society
Breana Sowers, Archivist, Monroe County Public Libraries

Special thanks to:
Laurie Shnayerson, Carousel Research
Arlo Haskell, Executive Director, Key West Literary Seminar
Dean Rogers, Special Collections, Vassar College Library
Maryrose Grossman, Archivist, John F. Kennedy Presidential Library
Sara Lerner, Archivist, Beinecke Rare Book and Manuscript Library